My Harvest Kitchen

My Harvest Kitchen

100+ Recipes to Savor the Seasons

Gesine Bullock-Prado

Photography by

RAYMOND PRADO

Countryman Press

*An Imprint of W. W. Norton & Company
Independent Publishers Since 1923*

My Harvest Kitchen is a book of recipes intended as a general information resource. Commercial products recommended in this book are ones that the author personally likes. You need to do your own research to find the ones that are best for you. Any URLs displayed in this book link or refer to websites that existed as of press time. The publisher is not responsible for, and should not be deemed to endorse or recommend, any website other than its own or any app or content that it did not create. The author, likewise, is not responsible for any third-party material.

Copyright © 2025 by Gesine Bullock-Prado
Photographs copyright © Raymond Prado

iStockPhoto.com / ricochet64 (barn quilt): 3, 5, 19, 41, 83, 133, 185, 235
iStockPhoto.com / NNehring (floral cyanotype): 18, 40, 82, 132, 184, 234, endpapers

All rights reserved
Printed in China
First Edition

For information about permission to reproduce selections from this book,
write to Permissions, Countryman Press, 500 Fifth Avenue, New York, NY 10110

For information about special discounts for bulk purchases, please contact
W. W. Norton Special Sales at specialsales@wwnorton.com or 800-233-4830

Manufacturing through Asia Pacific Offset
Book design by Raphael Geroni
Production manager: Devon Zahn

Library of Congress Cataloging-in-Publication Data is available.

Countryman Press
www.countrymanpress.com

An imprint of W. W. Norton & Company, Inc.
500 Fifth Avenue, New York, NY 10110
www.wwnorton.com

978-1-68268-916-5

1 2 3 4 5 6 7 8 9 0

Previous page: Richardson Farm

For Raymo

CONTENTS

11 INTRODUCTION
13 THINGS I USE AND LOVE

Good Morning

- 20 Cheddar and Chive Biscuits
- 23 Egg Sando
- 27 Savory Breakfast Toast
- 28 Croque Madame
- 30 Zucchini Waffles
- 33 Krapfen
- 34 Scones with Clotted Cream
- 37 Lemon Crepes with Chantilly Cream

Soups, Salads & Sammies

- 42 Creamy Roast Garlic Soup with Kale
- 46 Roasted Red Pepper Soup
- 49 French Onion Soup (Soupe à l'Oignon)
- 56 German Cucumber Salad
- 58 The Wicked Wedge with Buttermilk Dressing
- 61 "Goat Cheese Party" Pasta Salad
- 62 Salmon Panzanella Salad
- 65 Cold Soba Noodle Salad with Peanut Dressing and Soy-Marinated Eggs
- 70 Cheffy Quinoa and Tuna Salad with Preserved Lemon Vinaigrette
- 74 Creamy Mustard Potato Salad with Broad Beans and Peas
- 77 Sorrel, Spinach, and Barley Salad with Warm Bacon Dressing
- 78 Aunt Sis's Tomato Sandwich
- 81 Summer Sandwich

Nibbles & Sides

- 84 Lemony Labneh
- 87 Butter and Wine–Poached White Asparagus
- 88 Stuffed Grape Leaves
- 92 Spring-Dug Parsnip and Cheese Soufflé
- 95 Homemade Ramp-Infused Farmer Cheese
- 96 Creamed Spinach and Ramps
- 99 French Tomato–Goat Cheese Tart
- 102 Ugly Tomato Cheesy Bean Dip
- 105 Käse Spätzle (Mini Dumplings and Cheese)
- 107 Leeks Vinaigrette
- 108 Summer-to-Fall Focaccia
- 111 Upside-Down Leek Tart
- 112 Creamed Savoy Cabbage
- 115 Sour Cream Spätzle
- 116 Eggplant, Squash, Zucchini, and Tomato Casserole (Tian)
- 118 Green Mountain Arancini
- 125 Brined and Twice-Fried Fries
- 126 Poutine
- 128 Potato Pavé
- 130 Cheesy Potatoes (Pommes Aligot)

Feasts

- 137 Tamago Don with Morels
- 138 Spring Risotto
- 140 Green Mountain Pradonara (A Nontraditional Carbonara)
- 143 Sous Vide Lamb Chops
- 147 Stinging Ravioli
- 148 Korean BBQ Ssams (Lettuce Wraps)
- 150 Ray's Bone-in Rib Eye with Scape Chimichurri
- 152 OK OK Burger
- 154 Saturday Night Meatballs
- 156 White Wine–Braised Short Ribs
- 158 Fish Tacos
- 161 Roast Chicken with Ají Amarillo Verde Green Sauce
- 163 Chicken Schnitzel
- 168 Cali (Turkey) Meatballs
- 171 Preserved Lemon and Saffron Chicken Tagine
- 173 Butter Chicken
- 177 Chicken, Leek, and Mushroom Pie
- 179 Schweinebraten (German Pork Roast)
- 181 Potato Gnocchi with Butternut Squash and Sage Bake

Sweets

- 186 Blueberry-Lemon Bundt
- 189 Ellen's Sunshine Cake
- 192 Mandarin-Poppy Tea Cake
- 195 Key Lime Tart
- 198 Key Lime Ice Dream
- 201 Rhubarb–Olive Oil Cake
- 203 Sour Cherry Pie
- 206 Strawberry-Rhubarb Sherbet
- 209 German Strawberry Cake
- 211 Peach Cobbler
- 213 Philadelphia-Style Vanilla and Honey Ice Cream
- 215 Apple Crumble Tart
- 217 Brown Butter Butterscotch Ice Cream
- 218 I Have Too Much Fruit Cake
- 221 Pumpkin-Mandarin Tart
- 225 Caramel Apple Pudding
- 226 Gâteau Concorde
- 229 S'mores Schoko Crossies
- 230 Pfeffernüsse (German Spice Cookies)
- 231 Tante Erika's Creamy Chocolate Oatmeal Squares

Essentials

EGGS

- 236 Perfect Jammy Eggs
- 237 Hard-Boiled Eggs
- 238 Soy-Marinated Eggs

PIE DOUGH, BREADS & TORTILLAS

- 239 G's Zippy, Flaky Pie Dough
- 241 Brioche
- 243 Vollkorn Brot (German Whole Grain Bread)
- 246 Ciabatta Rolls
- 248 Crusty Bread
- 250 Steamed Buns (Bao)
- 254 Corn Tortillas

GRAINS

- 256 Perfect Japanese Short-Grain Rice
- 257 Perfect Quinoa
- 258 Jasmine Rice

SAUCES & CONDIMENTS

- 259 Chermoula
- 260 Choron
- 261 Fresh Tomato Pomodoro Sauce
- 262 Tzatziki
- 263 Tahini Dressing
- 263 Garlic Aioli

PICKLED & PRESERVED

- 264 Quick! Let's Pickle!
- 265 Ida Mae's Red Salsa
- 266 Italian Sweet and Spicy Pickled Pepper Salad
- 267 Giardiniera (Italian Garden Pickles)
- 268 Pickled Peaches
- 269 Preserved Lemons
- 270 Strawberry Jam
- 271 Peony Jelly
- 272 Currant Jam (Red or Black or Champagne)
- 276 Rose Hip Jelly
- 279 Apple Butter

- 281 ACKNOWLEDGMENTS
- 282 INDEX

INTRODUCTION

The Half-Assed Homesteader

I moved from Los Angeles to Vermont 20 years ago. I wanted seasons, land for a homestead, and an excuse to wear plaid unironically.

I would live the dream of eating from the land!

I would grow my own vegetables, raise farm birds, forage all things wild that wouldn't kill me, and I'd keep bees.

Our table would overflow from our bountiful harvest.

I would compost.

We would leave a minimal footprint on this earth, cultivating our acres and our hearts to align with a greater purpose.

As it turns out, I'm a half-assed homesteader. I get distracted. I forget to label crops. My bees abandon me. I don't read the seed packet instructions. My pasture-raised hens get picked off intermittently by predators. I can't manage to make compost actually decompose. And while my kitchen does see its share of homegrown vegetables, I just don't love eating them as much as I should.

I've almost given up many times, dejected by my failures and lack of commitment to that leafy green life. But then, I took a page from baking, a world in which I'm an expert. I always tell my baking students (and myself) to be patient, practice, don't try to do everything all at once (and perfectly), keep learning, and be gentle with yourself when you screw up. The same should go for my homesteading efforts. And yes, in both cases, make (i.e., grow) the things you love.

With this philosophy in mind, I allow for mistakes. I grow the things I've had success with in the past and that I like to eat. I also try a few new things every year, such as a new beet varietal that promises to be *the* one for non–beet eaters (i.e., me).

But I also grow flowers. Loads of them, because they are a thing I love. In fact, I pepper my vegetable garden with blooms (and lace my flower beds with edibles), creating beautiful spaces that invite me to linger; basically, setting traps for my lazy butt. Once I'm lured to the pretty flowers, I notice the weeds that are messing with my curated landscape and I get my hands dirty for a bit. I also learn. Every day in the garden, I learn something new, I see something new. And in the hibernating months, I plan and I study, having spent one winter studying to become a certified master gardener.

I have finally, within the past two years, disciplined myself to keep notes on what vegetables are planted in what raised bed and then rotate crops for optimal soil and plant health. But, sometimes, volunteer tomato plants or potatoes rise up in the wrong bed and I just shrug and let them be. I also got myself an automatic food recycler to eliminate the middleman (time and rats). I've dedicated an entire vegetable bed to a single varietal of heirloom potato (La Ratte) because I can do whatever I want in my own garden and I'm honest about my preferences: starch over leafy greens.

I call my approach "half-assed homesteading." I try my best, but much of what lands on our table is "harvested" from our local co-op and farms.

I'm trying to improve those ratios, because the reward of landing something unbelievably tasty that I've grown, foraged, or grabbed from the chicken coop is immeasurable. On the other hand, sometimes it is just nice to admire what others grow and reap the benefits of their hard work at your table. I have to remember to be kind to myself, that it's okay if I don't do *everything* I imagined I would do.

I wrote this cookbook to reflect the way I eat through the year. There's the time I call Hope, a season when things are just starting to wrestle their way through thawing ground and I'm hankering for anything fresh after a long winter. These recipes reflect both ingredients that are in season (asparagus, ramps, stinging nettle!) and everyday pantry staples that round out the meal. Then, there's Harvest, when everything seems to be ripe and juicy and *abundant*, almost to the point of panic! Those recipes celebrate fruits and vegetables at their very best, and I provide recipes for eating them *now* and then preserving all that bounty so you'll be able to bring a taste of summer to your winter table (I'm looking at you, tomatoes). And then there's Hibernate, when we just naturally take a few months to get cozy and reset. When meals get hearty and rib-sticking and when long-storing ingredients such as root vegetables, onions, and garlic take center stage, but there's still room for breaking out the treasures from the summer that you've taken the time to preserve to bring a bit of sunshine to the darkest weeks of winter. This cookbook is for everyone, from half-assed homesteaders like me who try their darnedest to live off the land but end up in the grocery store most days, to home cooks who can't (or won't) garden but still want to eke out the best of the seasons—which is to say, most of us.

THINGS I USE AND LOVE

Baking

KING ARTHUR BAKING COMPANY FLOURS: When I call for an unbleached flour, I'm using King Arthur, which promises that the specific protein percentage in every bag of its flour—whether cake, all-purpose, or bread—matches what's printed on the packaging. King Arthur also promises that all its flour is unbleached and never bromated. Bottom line: for my money, this is the flour to use.

ANSON MILLS BRAND NI-HACHI SOBAKOH BUCKWHEAT FLOUR AND ABRUZZI HEIRLOOM RYE FLOUR: When I need a specialty flour that I know was grown and milled not just with care but with expertise and knowledge, I look to Anson Mills. This, my friends, is nerd flour. They tailor flour blends to very specific uses, which helps you get great flavor whatever you're making. From homemade soba to homemade bread, Anson Mills will up your grain game.

MAINE GRAINS BRAND SPELT FLOUR: Spelt (also known as dinkle) is a grain often used in German breads and is a flour I always keep on hand. It's an ancient grain that behaves the most like modern wheat flour in recipes, so it's a great swap-out when whole wheat is called for. Maine Grains grows and mills in New England and is just a hop and skip away from me in Vermont.

RED STAR PLATINUM PREMIUM INSTANT YEAST: Platinum is my go-to yeast. It's instant, which means you can add it straight to the dry ingredients, and it's osmotolerant, which means it works beautifully in lean doughs (just water, flour, salt, and yeast) *and* enriched doughs with added fats and sugars.

GUITTARD BRAND CHOCOLATE CHIPS: When I need a high-quality chocolate that I know is available in the baking aisle of just about any grocery store, I use Guittard. It's smooth and creamy, and their bittersweet is the perfect balance of rich chocolate depth and sweetness.

CACAO BARRY EXTRA BRUTE DUTCH-PROCESSED COCOA: This is my go-to cocoa for everything, and I've tested dozens and dozens. It elevates all chocolate recipes that call for cocoa.

CALLEBAUT 60-40 BITTERSWEET CHOCOLATE: When I need a chocolate for a special occasion recipe, this is what I use. You have to plan ahead, because this chocolate is not usually available in the grocery store.

GELITA GOLD GELATIN LEAF: Take a leaf (see what I did there) from my pastry chef book, and when a recipe calls for gelatin, use gelatin leaves, not powder. It's so easy to use and is incredibly consistent. And the resulting texture can't be beat.

Dairy

CABOT CREAMERY CHEESES AND YOGURTS: For all my Cheddars, Monterey Jacks, and yogurt, I go Cabot. It's a New England company that uses dairy from small farms all around me, including from my friends at Richardson Farms, which helps keep them thriving in a time when small dairies are suffering. If I sit down and take stock of my whole life, Cabot's Seriously Sharp Cheddar would be a main character. And don't get me started on their Greek yogurt. I only use their 10% Greek. I have been ruined for any other yogurt.

VERMONT CREAMERY CHÈVRE AND CRÈME FRAÎCHE: For optimal creaminess and tangy freshness (both requirements in chèvre and crème fraîche), Vermont Creamery is hard to beat. I'm so lucky they are in my neck of the woods but are still available all across the country.

PHILADELPHIA BRAND CREAM CHEESE: Philly is the gold standard of cream cheese. As far as I'm concerned, no other brand beats its smooth texture.

JASPER HILL'S BAYLEY HAZEN BLUE: I once met the cheesemaker responsible for Bayley Hazen Blue and couldn't speak because I was starstruck. This cheese is Oscar-worthy. Even if you *think* blue cheese isn't for you, Jasper Hill's blue will convert you.

SACO PANTRY CULTURED BUTTERMILK POWDER: I keep 3 or 4 containers of this buttermilk powder in my pantry to make batches upon batches of my dressings and dips. I eat more salads and veggies because of this product. It makes everything better.

HIGH-FAT, CULTURED BUTTER, SUCH AS VERMONT CREAMERY BRAND: When a "fancy" butter is called for, Vermont Creamery is the butter I use. I once did a blind taste test of butter. Butters from France, Ireland, England, . . . and Vermont. All three baking professionals taking part, people who live and breathe butter, chose Vermont Creamery, hands down.

Pantry Staples

KEWPIE, DUKE'S, AND HELLMAN'S MAYONNAISE: I love mayo. These three are the only ones I use. I (liberally) apply each of them for different culinary applications, but if you only have the space for one, any one of these will do the delicious job.

DIAMOND CRYSTAL KOSHER SALT: Diamond Crystal just hits different. Literally. When seasoning, the flakes coat meats and dishes in a way that really gives you superior control. It sounds silly but it's true. There's a reason high-end chefs reach for this when they need a kosher salt.

FISHWIFE TINNED SEAFOOD CO. TUNA: This is a high-quality tinned tuna with a great label. I'm not going to lie. That's why I first grabbed it. I was bamboozled by marketing, but they followed through with flavor. There are, thankfully, more and more high-end jarred and tinned tunas available in grocery stores that are rungs above the standard canned tuna, so feel free to experiment.

RANCHO GORDO BEANS: These are the creamiest beans I've ever cooked. Bar none. These beans make the meal for me. There are a few markets that stock them here, but most of the time I order straight from Rancho Gordo online to stock my pantry.

DEL DUCA BRAND PROSCIUTTO: I don't think I've ever met a prosciutto I didn't like, but there's just something about knowing that a local brand makes this, and incredibly well, that turns my head. Del Duca has my loyalty.

BARILLA BRAND AL BRONZO PASTA: I was thrilled when I found "Al Bronzo" from Barilla in my local Price Chopper. It sounds like a small thing, but Barilla's method of making the pasta keeps the exterior of the pasta a little rough, unlike the smooth factory-style strands, and that means sauce just clings to the pasta like no other.

BOILED CIDER: This evaporated apple cider syrup is made by Willis Wood in Springfield, Vermont, and is available at King Arthur Baking Company. You can reduce regular ol' apple cider until it's thick and syrupy as well, but if you can find this product, you'll save time and find ways to use it in everything from my recipes to cocktails, cakes, roasts, and caramels.

SURE-JELL BRAND PECTIN: Sure-Jell is dependable for setting all manner of fruit and it's readily available in most grocery stores.

MISTY KNOLL'S CHICKEN: This is a brand local to Vermonters. I call it out because the difference between a Butter Chicken (page 173) made with this chicken and just regular ol' grocery store chicken is mind-blowing. If you can get your hands on locally sourced, high-quality poultry, I highly recommend trying it.

HIGH MOWING SEEDS AND ROW 7 SEED COMPANY: High Mowing Seeds is a local Vermont company that provides high quality organic seeds and guarantees germination rates. Row 7 offers amazing heirloom seeds that are chef-approved and guaranteed delicious.

SKORDO: My favorite source for the freshest spices, from Kashmiri chili to fenugreek seeds.

MY HARVEST KITCHEN

Kitchen Tools

RONDEAU: A rondeau is a large, flat-bottomed pan with high sides. Not as high as a Dutch oven or stockpot but much higher than a frying pan/skillet. It's a great piece of equipment when you need room but you also need access for stirring and tasting.

BRAISER: A braiser, like a rondeau, is wide and taller than a skillet, but its sides are rounded, making it easier to scrape the sides of the pan. One can stand in for the other, but having at least one in your kitchen arsenal is a game changer.

MICROPLANE GRATER: This is a handheld, super-fine grater that can turn a clove of garlic or a knob of ginger into a fine paste and can zest a lemon, but not the bitter pith, in a single stroke.

CAST IRON FLAME TAMER: A flame tamer is a round piece of cast iron that sits over the burner on your gas stovetop, and I can't live without mine. I *always* use it when I make rice on the stovetop or when I caramelize large batches of onions (as for French Onion Soup, page 49) because it keeps the flame from concentrating in one area and scorching your ingredients. This tool has many different names; you may know it as a "simmer plate," "heat tamer," "heat diffuser," "flame guard," or "heat equalizer."

KITCHEN SCALE: When I tell my baking students to use a scale and then I show them the difference between using a standard measuring cup versus a scale, how much *more* flour goes into the recipe when you use a cup, they are converted instantly, and they report back on how much better their baking has become as a result.

CULINARY TWEEZERS: Perfect for arranging artful salads, plucking saffron strands from fall crocus, and extracting bits from tall jars.

DASH SAFE SLICE MANDOLINE: It's like the "slap chop" of mandolines and gives you professional results without the abject fear of a trip to the hospital. For recipes like my Potato Pavé (page 128), this tool will be a life (and finger) saver.

BEE'S WRAP: This beeswax wrap is my favorite reusable bowl cover when making bread and a general plastic wrap replacement.

THINGS I USE AND LOVE

GOOD MORNING

Cheddar and Chive Biscuits

MAKES 9 BISCUITS

My teenage nephew was staying for a visit during spring break, just when the chives in my courtyard herb garden were busting out in patches amid the snow and begging to be eaten, and the thing that I hoped beyond hope would happen . . . happened.

"Gigi, can we bake something?"

I had to keep my cool, pretend like this was no big deal. Of course, I had a few things ready to recommend should this amazing thing come to pass, recipes that I knew would be fast enough that they'd keep him engaged and delicious enough that he might brag to his friends about his biscuit skills (and his awesome aunt). I had those herbs growing just outside the kitchen door, so there was no downtime for him to change his mind.

We made some epic biscuits from start to finish that day, sweet people. And we made some epic memories as well.

- 2½ cups (300 grams) unbleached all-purpose flour, plus more for dusting
- 1 tablespoon granulated sugar
- 2 teaspoons baking powder
- 1 teaspoon fine sea salt
- ½ teaspoon baking soda
- 1 cup (70 grams) shredded aged Cheddar
- 1 tablespoon finely chopped fresh chives
- 8 tablespoons (113 grams) unsalted butter, cold, cut into small cubes
- ½ cup (118 ml) buttermilk
- ½ cup (113 grams) full-fat sour cream

Preheat the oven to 425°F (220°C). Line a sheet pan with parchment. Set aside.

Stir together the flour, sugar, baking powder, salt, and baking soda in a large bowl. Add the butter pieces and toss to coat. Using the tips of your fingers, gently rub the butter into the flour until the mixture resembles coarse cornmeal with pea-size chunks of butter throughout. The mixture should feel dry and cool. Stir in the Cheddar and chives.

Whisk together the buttermilk and sour cream in a small bowl, then add to the flour mixture. Use a rubber spatula to gently combine, using tossing and slicing motions, rather than stirring.

Transfer the mixture to a floured work surface and gently press into a compact disk. Use a rolling pin to roll the dough into an 8-by-12-inch rectangle. Fold the dough into thirds: the top third down, and then the bottom third over those two layers, like a letter. Then, turn the folded dough by 90 degrees and roll again into an 8-by-12-inch rectangle and perform a second letter fold. Roll the folded dough into a 9-by-6-inch rectangle. Using a sharp chef's knife, trim the sides of the dough and then cut the dough in half lengthwise. Next, cut each half into four equal pieces for eight biscuits total. Place the biscuits close together on the

prepared sheet pan, with just a little space between them, so that as they rise, they will do so evenly rather than tipping over. Gently press the trimmed pieces into a round and place on the sheet pan as well (chef's treat!).

Bake for 10 to 15 minutes, until golden brown. Eat warm or cool! They are delicious either way. Split in half to make a breakfast sandwich.

A NOTE FROM MY KITCHEN GARDEN

My Flock

WHEN I FIRST MOVED TO VERMONT, I HAD DREAMED OF KEEPING ALL MANNER of farm animals, from bird to goat to sheep to cow to horse. Or at least a few of the above. But I'd also started my other dream, of opening a pastry shop. Those baking hours, from 3:30 a.m. to 7:00 p.m., put a damper on my farming life. It simply wouldn't have been fair to leave feathered and furry creatures without care all day long. Once we'd sold the shop and moved to our current location, Freegrace Tavern, I started my small orchard and veggie gardens, but I hesitated on bringing animals into the mix. Until my friend Bonnie, who'd run the front of house at our pastry shop, informed me that she and her partner, John, were coming with a housewarming gift and we'd better have a coop ready for it (them). She knew of my farm animal dreams, she and John bred birds, and she was aware that I no longer kept the pastry shop hours I once had. Our first flock of chickens taught me so much about raising farm animals, including heartbreak. And we expanded our brood when much of Vermont was flooded after Hurricane Irene and I fostered a farm's water fowl. From those birds, I hatched out geese and ducks, leading me to add those to my growing brood of feathered and furred friends.

Egg Sando

MAKES 2 SANDWICHES

Our girls take the winter off and start laying again when the days get longer. Some people choose to put "lay lights" in their chicken coops during winter, tricking the hens into thinking that the days are longer and the warming months are upon them, but I don't want that kind of relationship with my hens. If it's in their biology to take a break during the winter, I'm right there with them. Because of that, we observe a distinct "egg season." In cold weather, they barely want to leave the coop; instead, they hunker down in the snug of their heated perches, venturing out onto the path I make in the snow that I cover in hay or wood shavings to protect their little tootsies. It's also very exciting when the first egg of the year comes, coinciding with the coming of spring and the rebirth of everything around us. And once they're all in the swing of the laying thing (they don't all start at once), I make egg salad sandwiches to celebrate the warm days ahead. This sandwich, a riff on the famous Japanese *sando*, is a full celebration of the egg, including both the grated hard-boiled—cooked just like my Perfect Jammy Eggs (page 236), but for 10 minutes instead of 6 minutes 20 seconds—and then a special guest appearance by halved jammy eggs right in the center. Simple and egg-cellent!

6 large Hard-Boiled Eggs (page 237)
¼ cup mayonnaise
1 teaspoon pure maple syrup
1 teaspoon cider vinegar
½ teaspoon fine sea salt
Ground white pepper
Four ½-inch slices Brioche (page 241)
2 tablespoons unsalted butter, softened
2 Perfect Jammy Eggs (page 236), cut in half lengthwise

Peel the hard-boiled eggs and, using the largest holes on a box grater, grate the eggs into a large bowl.

Add the mayonnaise, maple syrup, cider vinegar, and sea salt. Using a large spoon or rubber spatula, gently fold the mixture together. Season with salt and white pepper to taste. Cover and chill for 20 minutes.

Smear a very light coating of butter on one side of each piece of brioche (the butter provides a protective layer for the bread, so it doesn't get soggy). On one slice, place the halved jammy egg pieces lengthwise, yolk side down, on the middle of the buttered side of the bread. Spoon half of the egg salad mixture over and around the egg halves and then top, butter side down, with a second slice of bread. Wrap the sandwich in waxed paper or parchment (wrapping the sandwich before cutting helps keep its shape), then cut in half exactly where the eggs are positioned. Repeat to create the second sandwich. Serve immediately.

Savory Breakfast Toast

MAKES 1 TOAST

When you make homemade brioche, the world of breakfast sandwiches is open to you. Literally. Sure, you can buy a preservative-packed bag of sliced bread at the grocery store and make a perfectly tasty toast, but what if I tell you homemade brioche toast is *so* much better . . . and cleaner. When you slice your homemade bread, you saw off a 2-inch, Texas toast–thick slice. And then you carefully create an opening at the top of the slice, making a pocket inside that you can fill with all manner of goodness. Tasty and practical. That's a good morning to you!

2 tablespoons Ida Mae's Red Salsa (page 265)
1 ounce green cabbage, very thinly sliced
2 tablespoons mayonnaise
One 2-inch slice Brioche (page 241)
4 tablespoons butter
2 large eggs
1 ounce sharp Cheddar, shredded
Salt and freshly ground black pepper
½ avocado, peeled, pitted, and thinly sliced

Combine the salsa, cabbage, and mayonnaise in a small bowl and stir to make a quick slaw. Set aside.

Using a paring knife, cut the top of the brioche slice as if you are going to cut it into two pieces, but stop at about ¼ inch down. Then, slip the paring knife down the middle, stopping just before you slice to the bottom and then continue to slice, side to side, to create a sealed pocket.

Melt 1 tablespoon of the butter in a nonstick or cast-iron pan over medium heat and then add the bread slice, cooking until golden brown and crisp. Wipe down the pan and then melt another tablespoon of the butter. Then brown and crisp the other side of the bread. Set aside on a plate.

Wipe down the pan again and melt the remaining 2 tablespoons of butter over medium heat.

Crack the two eggs into the pan, making sure not to break the yolks. Using a rubber spatula, carefully spread out the egg white, breaking it up so that it cooks completely. Then, break open the yolks and "framble" until the yolks are *just* cooked through. This style of scrambling eggs is my all-time favorite, making sure that the egg white is completely cooked through before you start cooking the yolks. This keeps the scramble from drying out, leaving the eggs supertender.

Remove from the heat, gently stir in the Cheddar, and season with salt and pepper.

Gently open the bread pocket. Line one side with avocado slices, add the slaw on top, and then gently spoon in the egg. Eat immediately!

Croque Madame

MAKES 2 SANDWICHES

When my husband, Ray, and I were still courting, I went away for a week alone to spend quality time with my dying mom. It was a quiet retreat, no TVs and no phones. It coincided with the series finale of the biggest television show of the age, *Seinfeld*. And though Ray and I loved the show and watched it as appointment television, I wasn't really worried about missing it. Spending time with my mom in her last year with us meant everything. Ray, knowing I'd be returning to Los Angeles filled with love and sadness, surprised me at the airport. He picked me up in a stretch limo and in the back, he'd set up a VHS with the series finale waiting to play. On each seat, there was a fancy takeout box and inside, a piping hot croque madame, the fanciest and gooiest of ham and cheese sandwiches, topped with a perfectly fried egg. It was our favorite. He had the driver cruise the Hollywood Hills as long as it took for us to enjoy our meal and watch our show together. I don't think I need to say much more as to why this sandwich means the world to me. May you have someone as stupendous as Ray to share one with.

6 tablespoons unsalted butter
1 tablespoon unbleached all-purpose flour
½ cup whole milk
⅛ teaspoon freshly grated nutmeg
Salt
4 ounces Gruyère, shredded
4 generous ¼-inch slices Brioche (page 241)
4 slices Black Forest ham
Nonstick cooking spray
2 large eggs
Freshly ground black pepper

Preheat the broiler. Line a sheet pan with parchment. Set aside.

Melt 2 tablespoons of the butter in a small saucepan over medium heat and stir in the flour using a wooden spoon. Continue to stir until the mixture browns slightly and smells nutty, 3 to 4 minutes. Add the milk, nutmeg, and a pinch of salt, then continue to stir until the mixture thickens to the consistency of ketchup. Transfer to a small bowl to cool. Once cool, stir in half of the Gruyère, setting the other half aside.

Place two slices of brioche on a cutting board. Top each with two slices of the ham and then spread one-quarter of the béchamel over the ham on each sandwich. Top each with a slice of the remaining brioche.

Melt 2 tablespoons of the butter in a large skillet over medium heat, turning the pan so the butter is evenly distributed. Add the sandwiches and allow to crisp and brown, 3 to 4 minutes.

Carefully remove the sandwiches from the pan, wipe down the pan with a paper towel, and heat the remaining 2 tablespoons of butter. Gently turn the sandwiches to brown on the other side until crisp and browned, 3 to 4 more minutes. Transfer the sandwiches to the prepared sheet pan.

Divide the remaining béchamel between

the two sandwiches, spreading it on top, and then divide the remaining Gruyère in half and sprinkle on top.

Wipe down the skillet and spray with non-stick cooking spray. Carefully crack the eggs into a cup and slip into the pan over medium heat, making sure not to break the yolks. While the eggs cook, transfer the sheet pan to the broiler to melt and brown the béchamel and cheese. Cook the eggs until the whites are fully set and the yolks still runny. Transfer the sandwiches to separate plates. Using a spatula, slip an egg on top of each of the sandwiches and season with salt and pepper. Eat immediately.

Zucchini Waffles

SERVES 4

Zucchini are the punchline to every gardening joke. They grow so prolifically and unrelentingly that Vermonters only keep their car doors locked during zucchini harvest season, to prevent people from dumping their excess on the passenger seat. But these waffles put all that excess to great and delicious use and for breakfast, no less.

1 cup (120 grams) unbleached all-purpose flour*
1 teaspoon baking powder
1 teaspoon dried dill
4 ounces (113 grams) sharp Cheddar, shredded
4 medium zucchini (2½ pounds/1.1 kg)
1 medium red onion, finely chopped
1 teaspoon kosher salt
2 large eggs
Freshly ground black pepper
Nonstick cooking spray

Whisk together the flour, baking powder, and dill in a small bowl. Stir in the Cheddar. Set aside.

Peel the zucchini and shred on the largest holes of a box grater. When peeling, feel free to leave a small amount of the green skin on. This adds flavor, texture, and nutrients.

Place the shredded zucchini in a colander lined with cheesecloth or a clean kitchen towel, and place over a large bowl to catch the juice. Sprinkle the zucchini with the salt and massage the salt into the zucchini, then allow the mixture to sit for at least 10 to 30 minutes. This will draw out excess moisture from the zucchini. Toward the end of this process, plug in and start preheating your waffle iron.

Once the time is up, gather the cloth or towel around the zucchini and squeeze out as much excess moisture as you can. Transfer the zucchini to a large bowl and stir in the eggs. Stir in the flour mixture and season with salt and pepper.

It's not recommended to taste your batter with raw ingredients at this stage, so I recommend taking a generous tablespoon of the batter and doing a test waffle to check for adequate seasoning. If the mini waffle tastes bland, add a generous pinch or two of salt to season and add more pepper to taste.

Spray the waffle iron with nonstick cooking spray and add a scoop of the zucchini mixture. Waffle irons differ, so you may have multiple square cavities or one large round/divided cavity. For each 4-inch square cavity, use a scant cup of zucchini batter; adjust according to your specific machine. Cook the waffles for 5 to 7 minutes, until golden brown on both sides. Serve with poached eggs and top with a spicy Choron (page 260)—think: tomatoey béarnaise.

*NOTE You can swap out an equal amount of gluten-free all-purpose blend successfully in this recipe, such as King Arthur Baking Company Measure for Measure.

ODE TO HOPE

HOPE, to me, is that period of time when things just start to awaken. When conditions are just right for early edibles to peak out of the ground and for farmers and home gardeners to get their hands dirty. When the plans you made during the fallow season start to come to fruition. It's spring, of course, but I'm calling it Hope because the timing of spring is different depending on where you live. In Vermont, true spring makes an appearance not with the vernal equinox but when almost everyone else is already sliding into summer. It's when I start stalking the aisles of my local co-op and farmers' markets for vibrant greens that were plucked from the ground just a few miles away and are juicy, crisp, and taste of sunshine versus the stuff that's been shipped in from thousands of miles away and tastes of regret and bad decisions.

Here in Vermont, our spring, our *Hope*, is when the sap flows from the maple trees, bringing sweetness to our world again as the snow melts. It's when the snows in the forest start to melt, creating pockets of moisture that invite new growth from fiddlehead ferns to morel mushrooms to wild ramps. In the garden, rhubarb is busting out and asparagus is pushing through. Peas and radishes thrive, as do heat-sensitive lettuces. Near our hammock, tucked in a sugar bush of maples, a stand of wild chive is the first thing to mark the start of our spring, like a toddler with permanent static-electricity hair. Hope is that time before the weeds take hold, where the tidying I put into the garden as the summer came to a close the year before becomes evident, as does the need to clean up if I didn't.

This is also the season when things can get pricey. Soil, compost, manure, seeds, tools, raised beds. All these are expensive. Sure, growing your own food, and specifically growing things that are impossible to find in a grocery store, can be cost effective. But things can go off the rails, and quickly. We've all heard about the $300 tomato. You buy a packet of seeds for a pittance. Even better, you can get some from a friend for free or from your local library (some book libraries also keep seed libraries!). But then, you buy a raised bed for the seeds. Then you buy the topsoil because any ol' dirt won't do (and it really won't). Then you buy the compost, because soil needs to be amended for optimal growing. Then you buy the tomato food. Then you buy the tomato cages. Then you buy the blacklight to spot hornworms that eat your tomatoes because you can't see them during the day and the blacklight makes them glow neon at night. And then you buy the miracle "all-natural" product that will protect against early blight. And then the one that combats late blight. And then there's blossom-end rot, what can you buy to protect against that? And then you need a way to water. Hose? Watering can? Water trolley? Rain barrel? That's all assuming you have the privilege of a bit of land to do these things. There is a way, but finding a way that isn't terribly expensive takes energy, too. Is it worth it? It really can be. It can be transcendent. Watching something grow from seed can transport you. That's what the season of Hope is all about: having faith that things will grow again. Even if it's just a seed in a little pot on your windowsill.

Krapfen

MAKES 14 DOUGHNUTS

Where New Orleans has Mardi Gras and King Cake, Austria and Germany have Fasching and *Krapfen*. Both celebrate the exultant time before the fasting period of Lent and both are all about some delicious yeasted treats. My mom adored Krapfen, a plump doughnut injected with jam (currant being Mom's favorite) and, as Fasching falls not far from her birthday, I honor the memory of my beautiful mom every year with a bouncy batch of her favorite winter treat.

1 batch Brioche dough (page 241), chilled

1 quart neutral oil, such as canola

1¼ cups red currant, apricot, or smooth jam of choice

½ cup confectioners' sugar

Divide the dough into 14 equal pieces. Flatten each piece with your palm, then draw the edges together to form a little parcel and pinch together the edges to seal. Place the dough, seam side down, on a counter and hold your hand over the dough in a clawlike cage, your palm gently resting on the top of the dough ball. Move your hand in a tight circle to tighten the ball and tighten the seam. Arrange the balls, a few inches apart, on a parchment-lined sheet pan, and cover loosely with plastic wrap. Allow the dough to rise at room temperature until the balls are puffed and jiggle when you shake the pan gently, about 2 hours.

Toward the end of the rise time, line a second sheet pan with paper towels and set aside. Pour the oil into a deep Dutch oven and heat to 350°F (180°C). Make sure to keep the oil at a consistent temperature. Too cool, and the doughnuts will start to absorb the oil into the dough and will be greasy; too hot, and the doughnuts will not expand and will burn.

Fry the doughnuts just a few at a time. Fry for about 2 minutes per side, or until golden brown on each side, using a slotted spoon or spider to turn. Remove the doughnuts and transfer to the lined sheet pan to cool. Repeat with the remaining doughnuts.

Fit a pastry bag with a ¼-inch-wide piping nozzle and fill with your jam of choice. If you are using a chunky jam, make sure to run it through a sieve to make sure it's smooth; otherwise, the chunks will clog the piping nozzle. Use a chopstick to create a "pilot hole" in the side of each doughnut. Pipe about 2 tablespoons of jam into each doughnut, then dust them with confectioners' sugar.

Scones with Clotted Cream

MAKES 16 SCONES

I make scones in the spring. They are the perfect "bridging" treat, managing to be both comforting with their tender crumb and creamy clotted cream on a cool March afternoon, yet bright with their punchy layer of fruity jam. Using the last of the jams you preserved the harvest season before will also get you motivated for the growing season ahead. And making homemade clotted cream will give you an authentic "teatime" experience without the international travel.

¾ cup (177 ml) whole milk

¼ cup (30 grams) granulated sugar

1 teaspoon freshly squeezed lemon juice

3 cups (360 grams) unbleached self-rising flour

1 teaspoon baking powder

Pinch of salt

Grated zest of 1 lemon

1 large hard-boiled egg yolk

8 tablespoons (113 grams) unsalted European-style high-fat butter, cold

1 teaspoon vanilla bean paste or vanilla extract

Unbleached all-purpose flour, for dusting

Egg wash (1 large egg whisked together with 1 tablespoon water)

Jam and Clotted Cream (recipe follows), for serving

Preheat the oven to 400°F (200°C). Line a half sheet pan with parchment. Set aside.

Pour the milk into a nonreactive cup, then add the sugar and lemon juice to the milk and stir. Set aside.

Whisk together the flour, baking powder, salt, and lemon zest in a large bowl. Push the hard-boiled yolk through a fine-mesh sieve into the flour mixture. Whisk to combine.

Use the largest holes of a box grater to shred the butter into the flour mixture. Use the tips of your fingers to work in the butter, making sure the butter stays cold. (You are using the cooked yolk and the butter to create tenderness in the dough: by coating some of the flour with the fat to form a barrier against moisture, you won't develop too much gluten once you add the milk mixture.) Continue to work the flour mixture until it resembles coarse cornmeal.

Create a well in the middle of the flour mixture and pour in the milk mixture, making sure to scrape out all the sugar. Add the vanilla and then, using a wooden spoon or rubber spatula, toss the flour with the milk mixture to just combine. Dust your counter with all-purpose flour and turn out the scone dough. Dust the top of the dough with more all-purpose flour and, using your hands or a rolling pin, press or roll the dough into a rough 4-by-8-inch rectangle, then fold it in half. Turn the dough and press or roll into a 4-by-8-inch rectangle, and fold in half. Turn and press or roll, and fold once more for a total of three folds and turns.

Press or roll the dough into a rough 1-inch-thick rectangle. Using a 2-inch biscuit cutter, cut out rounds, dipping the cutter into the flour and then cleaning off the cutting edge between cuts. Gently press the remaining dough together again to cut the remaining rounds. Place the scones on the prepared sheet pan, a few inches apart. Brush the tops of the scones with egg wash. Bake for 10 to 12 minutes or until the tops are golden brown and the scones feel set. Serve with jam and clotted cream.

recipe continues . . .

CLOTTED CREAM

MAKES 1 TO 2 CUPS

Clotted cream is the result of the process of heating heavy cream to the point that the fat from the cream "clots" together and separates from the milk. The texture is creamy and often a little grainy. It's essential for a traditional cream tea, where the clotted cream is dolloped onto a fresh scone and topped with jam. (That is, if you are in Devon, where the cream comes first. Not so in some other places that shall not be named.)

Both clotted cream and butter are the result of processes in which the fat in the cream is separated from the milk: with butter, the cream is agitated, whereas with clotted cream, the mixture is gently heated, resulting in very different (but equally delicious) products. I prefer to make clotted cream in a sous vide because (1) the temperature is constant and some ovens don't allow for such low temperature, and (2) the cream needs to be heated for 12 hours. I feel safer leaving a sous vide running overnight. If you do not have one, you can use the oven.

2 to 4 cups (473 to 946 ml) heavy cream*

Preheat a sous vide or oven to 170°F (76°C). If using a sous vide, place two jars or glasses in the water to create a stable platform for the dish with the cream.

Pour the cream into a heatproof baking dish. It's best when there is a large enough surface area so that the cream is not more than 2 to 3 inches deep. Place in the preheated sous vide or oven. If using a sous vide, place a tight-fitting lid on top of the vessel or cover tightly with plastic wrap, so water doesn't splash into the cream. Heat for 12 hours.

Carefully transfer the dish to the refrigerator and allow to cool for 12 hours. The timing is essential; you must allow the cream to heat and cool for the indicated amount of time. A yellow skin forming on the very top is normal. The "milk" that remains can be used for baking.

Once cool, use a spoon to skim off the thickened cream that formed on the top and press through a medium-mesh sieve into a bowl. Stir in a bit of leftover milk if the cream is too thick. Refrigerate, covered, for up to 2 weeks.

*NOTE Use cream that's been minimally processed. Do not use ultrapasteurized cream or whipping cream.

Lemon Crepes with Chantilly Cream

MAKES 10 CREPES

January is begging for brightness. The holidays are over. The days are short. If you're like me, you still have your tree up and lit so you can suck as much cheer out of that poor conifer as possible, but that carpet of dry needles ain't fooling anyone. So, you reach for anything that will bring a bit of sparkle to the shortest of days. And what do you know? Citrus just happens to be in season, and there's nothing like a little pucker to shake you out of that winter gloom. And even if you live in a cold clime, as I do, you can grow a mini lemon tree inside . . . or just go to your local grocer for a bag of sunshine.

1¼ cups (295 ml) whole milk

4 large eggs

¼ cup (50 grams) granulated sugar

2 tablespoons (28 grams) melted unsalted butter, plus more for the pan (if using)

Grated zest of 1 lemon

2 tablespoons freshly squeezed lemon juice

Pinch of salt

1 cup (120 grams) unbleached all-purpose flour

Nonstick cooking spray (if using)

Jam and Chantilly cream (recipe follows), for serving

Combine the milk, eggs, sugar, butter, lemon zest and juice, and salt in a bowl or blender. Whisk or blend to break up the egg. Add the flour and whisk or blend until fully combined, 30 seconds. Cover the batter and refrigerate for 1 hour.

Spray a nonstick skillet with nonstick cooking spray, or add a small knob of butter and melt over medium heat. Add a scant ½ cup of batter to the pan and swirl to coat. Cook until just set, 1 to 2 minutes. Flip and continue to cook for about 30 seconds more. Transfer the crepe to a large plate and set aside. Continue to cook the batter, ½ cup at a time, until all the crepes are cooked, stacking them one on top of the other.

Serve with your favorite jam or Peony Jelly (page 271) as a reminder that summer isn't too far away. A dollop of Chantilly cream won't be amiss, either.

recipe continues . . .

GOOD MORNING

CHANTILLY CREAM

MAKES 1½ CUPS

"Chantilly cream" is just another name for sweetened whipped cream. You can use either heavy cream, which has a fat content of at least 36 percent, or whipping cream, which must contain 30 to 35 percent fat but also contains whipping agents, such as carrageenan, to aid in the whipping. The higher fat content of heavy cream ensures that the cream will whip without added helpers present in whipping cream. No matter which one you use, make sure the cream is straight out of the fridge, otherwise you won't get it to thicken. I add cream cheese to stiffen and stabilize the cream; it also adds a bit of pleasing tartness and thickens it enough so it can be used as a topping on cupcakes or as a filling in cakes.

¼ cup cream cheese (optional)
¼ cup confectioners' sugar
½ teaspoon vanilla extract
Pinch of salt (optional)
1 cup cold heavy cream or whipping cream

If using cream cheese (which helps keep the cream from deflating), combine the cream cheese, confectioners' sugar, vanilla, and salt (if using) in the bowl of a stand mixer fitted with the whisk attachment and whisk until combined, then add the cream. Start the mixer on low speed at first and slowly increase the speed as the cream thickens. The cream cheese will allow you to whip a little longer and stiffer without the cream "breaking." If omitting the cream cheese, combine all the ingredients in the mixer and mix on medium-high speed until the cream reaches medium-soft peaks.

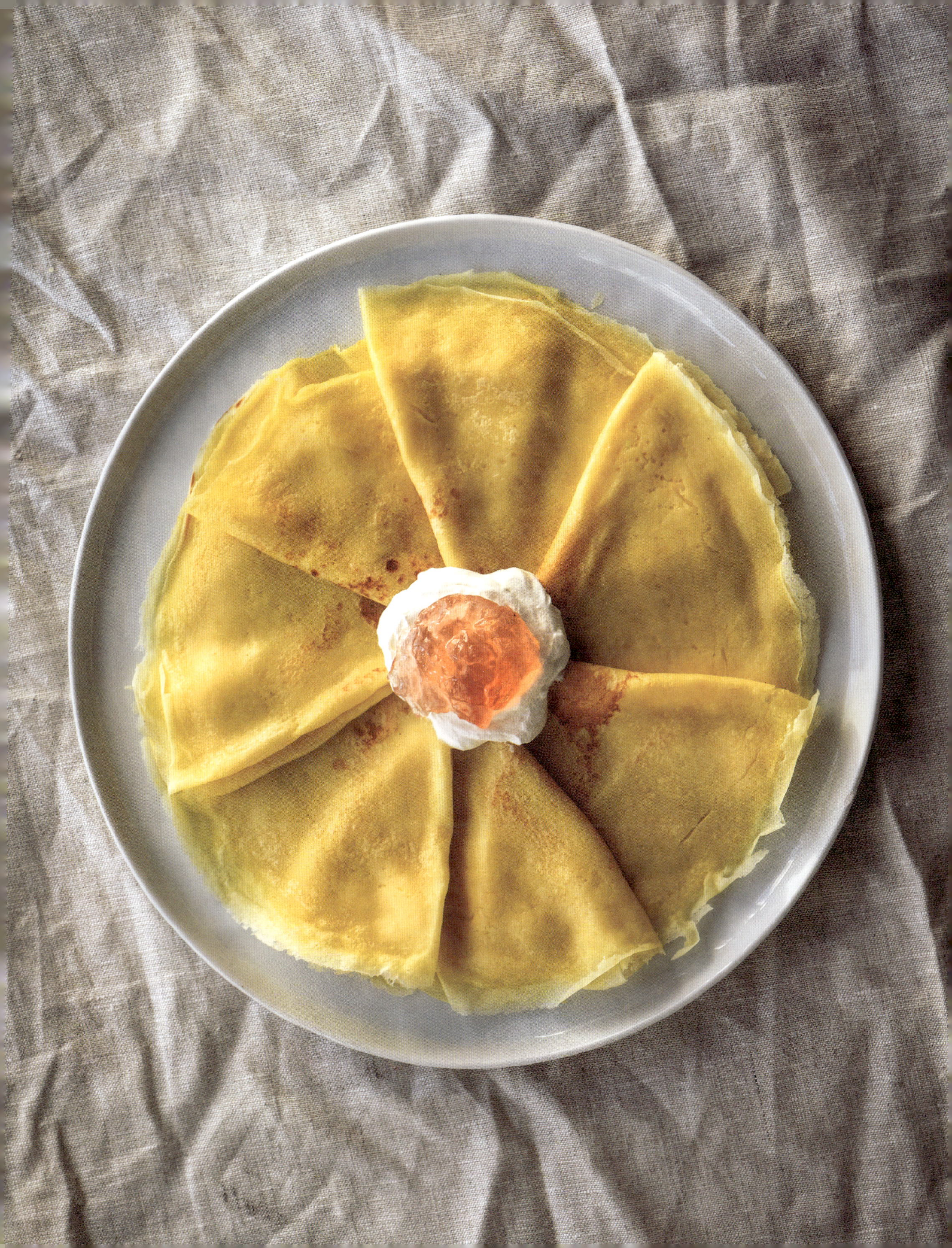

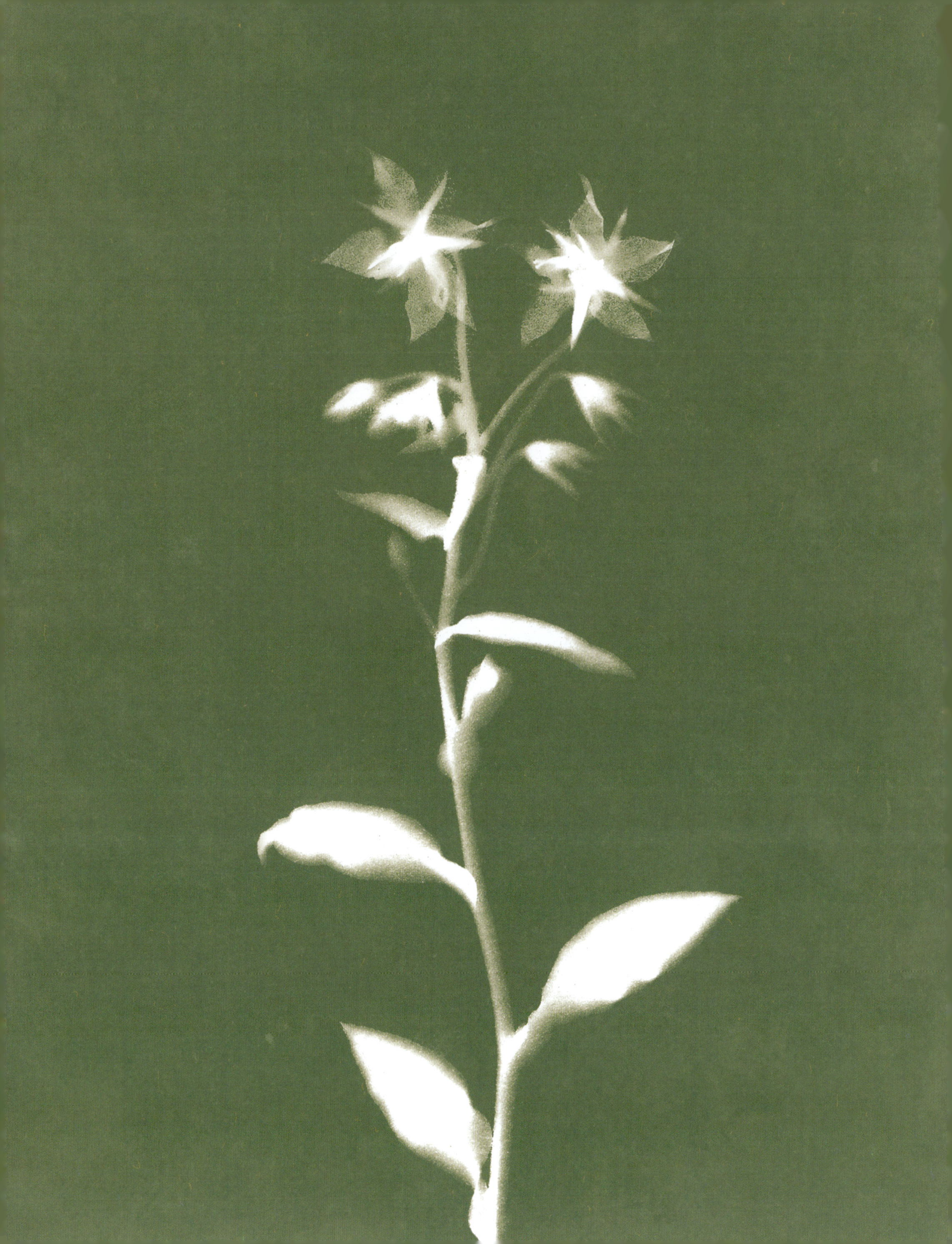

SOUPS, SALADS & SAMMIES

Creamy Roast Garlic Soup with Kale

SERVES 8

It's been close to six months since I harvested garlic in July, and it should still be in great shape. The papers should be intact and dry. The cloves, firm and juicy. But only just, depending on the variety and whether it's hardneck or softneck garlic. This is the time to use it up! Roasting the heads of garlic—you heard that right . . . heads—allows for deep garlic flavor without the sharpness of a finely chopped, raw garlic (see page 44). Just make sure, once you strip the tops of the heads, to keep a lookout for any green sprouts or "germs" in the middle of the cloves, which mean that the garlic is starting to go off. It's literally ready to move on with this life and make some new garlic in the ground. The potato, another long-storage veggie that's survived the winter, helps thicken the soup and lends creaminess as well. And kale is a fabulous green that can stand cold temperatures and survives in our greenhouse all winter long, adding a pop of color, nutrition, and zest to the soup.

4 heads garlic

4 teaspoons extra-virgin olive oil

1 medium russet potato, peeled and cut into ½-inch cubes

6 ounces pancetta or guanciale, cut into ¼-inch dice

1 medium sweet or yellow onion, finely chopped

5 cups low-sodium chicken stock or vegetable stock

½ cup heavy cream

1 bunch lacinato kale, ribs removed and discarded, torn into small pieces

Salt and freshly ground black pepper

½ cup shredded Gruyère

ROAST THE GARLIC

Preheat your oven to 350°F (180°C). Cut the tops of the stem ends of the garlic heads, exposing just the very tops of the cloves. Place each head on a square of aluminum foil, large enough to cover the head entirely, and sprinkle the exposed cloves with the olive oil. Wrap the heads in the foil and place on a half sheet pan. Roast for 45 minutes. Remove from the oven and allow to cool in the foil.

SOFTEN THE POTATO

Line a microwave-safe plate with a damp paper towel. Arrange the potato cubes in a single, even layer on the paper towel and cover with a second damp paper towel. Microwave for 3 minutes, or until they just begin to soften. Alternatively, arrange the potato cubes in a single, even layer on a parchment-lined sheet pan and bake for 10 to 12 minutes in a 350°F (180°C) oven to soften. Set aside.

MAKE THE SOUP

Place the pancetta in a Dutch oven and cook over medium heat until crisp and rendered. Using a slotted spoon, transfer the pancetta to a paper towel–lined plate. Remove all but 1 tablespoon of the pork fat in the Dutch oven, reserving the rest in a small jar for another use. Add the onion to the Dutch oven and sauté over medium heat until translucent and just starting to caramelize, about 10 minutes.

Squeeze the roasted garlic cloves out of their skins and into the Dutch oven. Stir in the stock and potatoes. Simmer over medium heat until the potatoes have completely softened, 10 to 15 minutes. Using an immersion blender, process the soup until smooth. Alternatively, carefully pour the contents of the Dutch oven into a blender and blend until smooth, then return the mixture to the Dutch oven. Add the cream and kale, stirring to combine. Simmer for 4 to 5 minutes to allow the kale to wilt. Season with salt and pepper to taste.

Serve topped with the reserved crispy pancetta, a sprinkling of Gruyère, and a generous slice of Crusty Bread (page 248).

ON GARLIC

THE BURN: Garlic is a complex little allium. It's been used as a culinary and medicinal ingredient since ancient times and, as we all know, is great for warding off vampires. But garlic doesn't always hit the same, does it? Sometimes, it's mild and flavorful. Sometimes, it's buttery and creamy. And sometimes, it buuuuuuurns. While different varieties of garlic will be more or less pungent (except for elephant garlic, which isn't really a garlic at all), they all contain two compounds that are responsible for garlic's famous flavor profile: alliin and alliinase. How they interact together and how you interact with the clove of garlic make all the different in taste and texture. In an uncut clove, the molecule alliin is just hanging around, minding its own business; so too the enzyme alliinase. But once you start slicing into that clove, its cell walls get broken and things get unleashed as the molecule and the enzyme are introduced to each other. The more chopping you do, the more interactions they have. So, the more you mince and chop the garlic, the more robust and "harsh" the flavor becomes. Mincing and then soaking in a weak acid mellows these interactions. Thus, if you need very finely processed garlic but want to cut back on the burn, hitting the chopped garlic with some lemon juice and letting it sit a bit will temper the bonds the two have created. On the other hand, if you roast whole garlic or whole cloves, the alliin is affected by the heat and transforms into a larger molecule, fundamentally changing how it will interact with the alliinase when it eventually does. When you smash or eat the whole roasted garlic clove, the result is sweet and mellow. So, the next time you see a recipe that calls for garlic, think about *how* you are meant to treat it: Chop into slices? Grate into a paste? Chop into small pieces? Roast it whole? Each method will elicit something different from those two compounds, and you are in charge of that journey now.

SCAPES: A scape is the long stem that emerges from growing hardneck garlic that, if not harvested, will bloom and set seed. There are two types of garlic, hardneck and softneck. Hardneck is known for having a more robust flavor; softneck is milder. Hardneck is suited for cold climates; soft, for warm. Hardneck has a shorter storage period, from 4 to 8 months, depending on how well you harvest, cure, and store the garlic, whereas softneck can be stored for 10 to 12 months (also based on how well you've done the job of harvesting, curing, and storing). That's the gist of it, but what I'm here to talk about is something that only a hardneck garlic can do: give you scapes. Scapes shoot out in early July (here in Vermont). This is where the allium would flower, if you'd let it. BUT DON'T YOU LET IT! The general rule is, you wait for the scape end to start making a second curlicue and then you snip it down, as close to the bulb end as possible, without harming the actual bulb. This does a few things: (1) It forces the plant to direct its energy to bulb growth rather than concentrating on seed generation (that stalk leads to a flower, which leads to seeds), so cutting it while the stalk is still curling and before it straightens out and blooms is key. (2) It gives you a tasty treat. Scapes are a bit like chives but sturdier, and bring with them a hint of the garlic underneath the ground. You can chop them up very finely as a garnish, as you would chives; you can puree them into a scape pesto; you can add them to stir-fries and all manner of dishes that benefit from a hit of garlic and onion; and you can dehydrate them and make a powder that will last for years. Making it is really quite easy, if time consuming.

MAKING SCAPE POWDER: I'm going to be totally up front with you on this. It took me 48 hours to fully dry out my scapes. I had them in a low oven, 200°F (95°C), the scape pieces sliced into 2-inch pieces, just riding along until they were dry enough to snap in half when cool. Is it safe to have your oven on while you sleep? I would not recommend it, so you can do this in waking-hour intervals. Or, if you have a dehydrator, use it. You can leave a dehydrator running safely while you are in a gentle slumber. Once fully dry, grind the pieces, about ½ cup at a time, in a blender or a small spice grinder, until the mixture becomes a powder. A food processor does not do this well, simply breaking up the pieces into shards rather than powdering them. Store in an airtight container and use as you would onion or garlic powder.

THE GERM: Garlic is ideally fresh and juicy as can be. Unfortunately, by early spring, grocery stores often only offer dried husks of allium that, when you pick up a huge head, are incongruously light and airy. They also often have started to sprout, with the green germ slicing through the middle of the clove. This is old garlic or garlic that's been stored in too long and in too humid an environment. The clove flesh is dry and doesn't shine with sharp juices as you slice through. And that green germ? That's a sign that all the sugars have been rerouted to feed the sprout and the flesh is left bitter. The garlic is finished being a culinary delight and is ready to be planted to regenerate into another bulb. That's right, each clove is, for all intents and purposes, a seed, and if you plant the clove, tip side up, in the late fall, you'll get a garlic bulb in the summer. But in the grocery store in spring, the cloves are confused and taking their regenerative life into their own hands by sprouting at the Kroger. And the garlic itself won't be as flavorful or juicy. However, if you grow your own, and I can't recommend it highly enough, you'll experience the beauty of incredibly fresh garlic.

Roasted Red Pepper Soup

SERVES 6

I grow red peppers. And onions. And potatoes. And garlic. And carrots. And tomatoes. And we tap our maples for maple syrup. All of them are easy enough to get from a grocer, but growing even one of these elements will bring a depth of flavor and sweetness that you just can't get from the anemic stuff on the store shelves. The next best thing is to gather the ingredients at a farmers' market, when everything is at the peak of ripeness, and make batches of this soup and freeze for cozy winter meals, served with a slab of Crusty Bread (page 248) or with a lush Croque Madame (page 28).

6 large red bell peppers (2½ pounds/1.1 kg)
2 tablespoons extra-virgin olive oil, plus more for drizzling
1 large onion,* roughly chopped
Salt
1 large carrot, peeled and cut into ¼-inch rounds
2 tablespoons cider vinegar
2 large paste tomatoes (canned San Marzano or fresh), roughly chopped
2 large garlic cloves, minced
1 tablespoon ginger paste*
1 teaspoon anchovy paste
1 large russet potato (1 pound), peeled and cut into ½-inch cubes
2 quarts low-sodium chicken stock
Leaves from 4 thyme sprigs
Freshly ground black pepper
1 tablespoon pure maple syrup

Place an oven rack in the highest position. Preheat the oven to 500°F (260°C) or the highest temperature possible. Line a sheet pan with aluminum foil; set aside.

Core the peppers and remove all the seeds. Place the peppers on their side on the prepared sheet pan, leaving a few inches between them.

Roast for 20 minutes, or until the pepper skins are charred on top. Remove from the oven and, using tongs, flip the peppers to expose the undersides that haven't been roasted; return the pan to the oven and roast for 20 minutes more.

Take the fully charred peppers from the oven and immediately bundle up the foil around the peppers to steam them. Allow to cool, wrapped up, at room temperature, then slip off and discard their skins and roughly chop the peppers. Place in a bowl and set aside.

Heat the olive oil in a large Dutch oven over medium heat. Add the onion and season lightly with salt. Cook until just translucent, 3 to 4 minutes. Add the carrot and cook, stirring often, until just tender, about 5 minutes.

Add the vinegar, scrape up any fond (the delicious brown, caramelized bits stuck to the pan) on the bottom of the pan, then add the chopped tomato and cook for about 5 minutes more to soften and reduce. Add the garlic, ginger paste, anchovy paste, and chopped red peppers and just heat through for a minute or two.

Add the cubed potato, chicken stock, thyme, and salt and black pepper to taste. Simmer over low heat until the potato is fork-tender.

Carefully transfer the contents to a large blender (I use a Vitamix, but any large blender will do) and add the maple syrup. Process until very smooth. Alternatively, you can use an immersion blender and process the soup directly in the Dutch oven. You can serve the soup in this slightly "rustic" state, or run it through a fine-mesh sieve for a more velvety texture. Serve the soup hot with a drizzle of olive oil.

*NOTE I use Rose de Roscoff, but you can use a juicy, sweet onion of your choice. To make ginger paste, peel ginger with a spoon and grate with a Microplane grater.

MY HARVEST KITCHEN

French Onion Soup (Soupe à l'Oignon)

SERVES 8

I was really close with my mom. Not with my dad. I don't think this is an unusual thing in some families, and definitely not unusual with my generation, X. But what I can appreciate now that I'm older is that my dad and I shared a love of food. My mother thought it the height of grotesquerie to anticipate dinner while having lunch, but my dad and I could find common ground in our love of discussing "what's coming next?" midbite. French onion soup, however, was something that my father loved that I simply didn't understand. It's not that I hated it; I thought it was perfectly "meh." But if it was on the menu, he'd order it. And even if I could smell badly scorched onions emanating from the bowl in front of him, he'd tuck in happily. My dad was not a man who would forgive a transgression in food (or a transgression of *any* kind, for that matter), but for French onion soup, he'd show the culinary forbearance of a saint. It occurred to me, after he'd passed and my sister Kathy and I were taking care of 90 years of his belongings in Alabama and looking for the Bronze Star he'd received serving during World War II, that, to him, French onion soup likely meant something altogether more than just soup. I imagined him as a 19-year-old boy, fresh out of high school, landing on the beaches of Normandy. I thought of that kid, the youngest of seven, away from the protective cocoon of his older sisters and mom for the first time in his life and surrounded by death and horror. And what it must have meant, after all that he must have seen and experienced, to have a meal that wasn't a US military ration but a dish made by a French family who were sharing their gratitude through what food they had. I decided that I wanted to taste what my father had tasted, something that was so memorable that just the hint of what once was would be enough to please him. I make the beef stock, I use cultured European butter, I grow my own onions to get as close to the original as I can, but I give you options to make it with less fuss. I only wish I could share it with him today, because I get it now.

ON CARAMELIZING ONIONS: Caramelized onions are an essential part of this soup. Many recipes describe the color as being dark brown, but don't go there, because the entire soup will taste of burnt onion. The onions should be golden brown and very sweet and soft. Red onions tend to take on a slightly gray cast, and this is absolutely normal. Bottom line: listen to French master chef André Soltner, of Lutèce fame: "Do not think for a minute that this is the notorious soup you get in Paris workingmen's cafés at five o'clock in the morning. . . . In those soups the onions are sautéed until they are black, and the soup is dark and bitter. Some people like it that way, which I can never understand." For that matter, I cannot imagine a war-torn family burning the precious few onions they have to spare. They would treat ingredients with care and reverence, not unlike a gardener who has spent close to a year growing those onions.

recipe continues . . .

FOR THE BEEF BROTH

5 pounds beef marrow bones

3 large carrots (1 pound), roughly chopped

3 large celery ribs (4 ounces), roughly chopped

2 leafy ends leek (8 ounces), roughly chopped

2 medium Rose de Roscoff onions* or 1 large yellow onion, roughly chopped

1 large thyme sprig

4 large garlic cloves, crushed

1 dried chili

2 bay leaves

1 tablespoon peppercorns

2 teaspoons kosher salt

1 gallon plus 2 cups cold water

FOR THE SOUP

4 tablespoons unsalted European-style high-fat cultured butter (or traditional American butter)

2 tablespoons reserved marrow fat

4 pounds onions, sliced into ¼-inch-thick half-moons*

1 teaspoon kosher salt

¼ cup dry sherry

1 cup dry French white wine

1 tablespoon pure maple syrup (optional)

Salt

TO SERVE

1 fresh loaf Crusty Bread (page 248) or baguette, cut into ½-inch slices

4 tablespoons unsalted butter

1 garlic clove, cut in half

4 cups shredded Gruyère

1 small bunch chervil or flat-leaf parsley leaves

*NOTE The broth is key to this recipe. Store-bought beef broth lining the shelves in cardboard containers cannot compare and can ruin the soup. Some markets offer high-quality frozen beef broth or stock, which is a fine substitute. Otherwise, if making a homemade beef broth is too time intensive, use a good-quality store-bought (or homemade) chicken stock.

MAKE THE BROTH

Preheat the oven to 400°F (200°C). Cover a sheet pan with aluminum foil and arrange the marrow bones, spaced evenly, on the prepared pan. Roast until the bones are deeply browned and the fat has rendered, about 1½ hours. Set aside 2 tablespoons of the rendered fat and then transfer the rest to a small glass jar and refrigerate for a later use.

Combine the carrots, celery, leeks, onions, thyme, garlic, chili, bay leaves, peppercorns, salt, and marrow bones in a large Dutch oven. Cover with the cold water. Bring to a boil, skimming up any foam that rises to the top, then lower the heat to maintain a very low simmer until the broth is reduced by half, 2½ to 3 hours. Measure out 8 cups of broth for the soup and freeze the rest for another use.

MAKE THE SOUP

If using a gas stove, place a heat diffuser over the burner to prevent hot spots and even the heat distribution; this will help keep the onions from burning since they'll be over the flame for a *long* time. Place the butter and the 2 tablespoons of reserved marrow fat in a large Dutch oven (you can use the same one you used for the broth, just clean it well) and melt them together over medium heat. Turn down the heat to low and add all the sliced onions. Season with the kosher salt and cook, stirring frequently, until the onions are golden brown and soft. This takes me 2 to 3 hours. Note: If you have two Dutch ovens, you can make the broth and the onions simultaneously. Alternatively, you can use a slow cooker for the onions at the lowest heat setting, making sure to stir occasionally, scraping the bottom as you go to take up any fond.

Once the onions are perfectly caramelized, whether using a stovetop or a slow cooker, add the sherry, increase the heat to medium, and scrape up any fond (the browned bits). Cook for about 5 minutes, then add the white wine and broth and allow to simmer for 30 minutes. Season with salt to taste and add up to 1 tablespoon of maple syrup for sweetness, if needed. (Rose de Roscoff onions are naturally sweet, but many recipes call for a touch of sweetener to make up for the lack of natural sugars in commercial onions.)

TO SERVE

Lightly butter both sides of each piece of bread. Brown on each side in a skillet over medium heat. Scrape both sides with the cut side of the garlic.

Preheat the broiler and place the oven rack at the highest position. Fill individual heatproof bowls with the soup, just ½ inch shy of the rim. Place a prepared bread "crouton" on top of each bowl of soup and sprinkle each with ½ cup of the Gruyère. Place the bowls on a sheet pan and allow the cheese to melt and brown under the broiler, 3 to 4 minutes. Garnish with chervil or parsley leaves and serve immediately.

> *****NOTE** For the soup, I use 16 Rose de Roscoff onions total. If you use onions traditionally found at grocery stores and farmers' markets, use an equal weight each of red, yellow, and Vidalia to get as close to the sweet complexity of the Rose de Roscoff. Keep yourself from slicing the onions too thinly. The amount of time it takes to patiently caramelize the onions can also disintegrate them to oblivion if they are sliced too thinly.

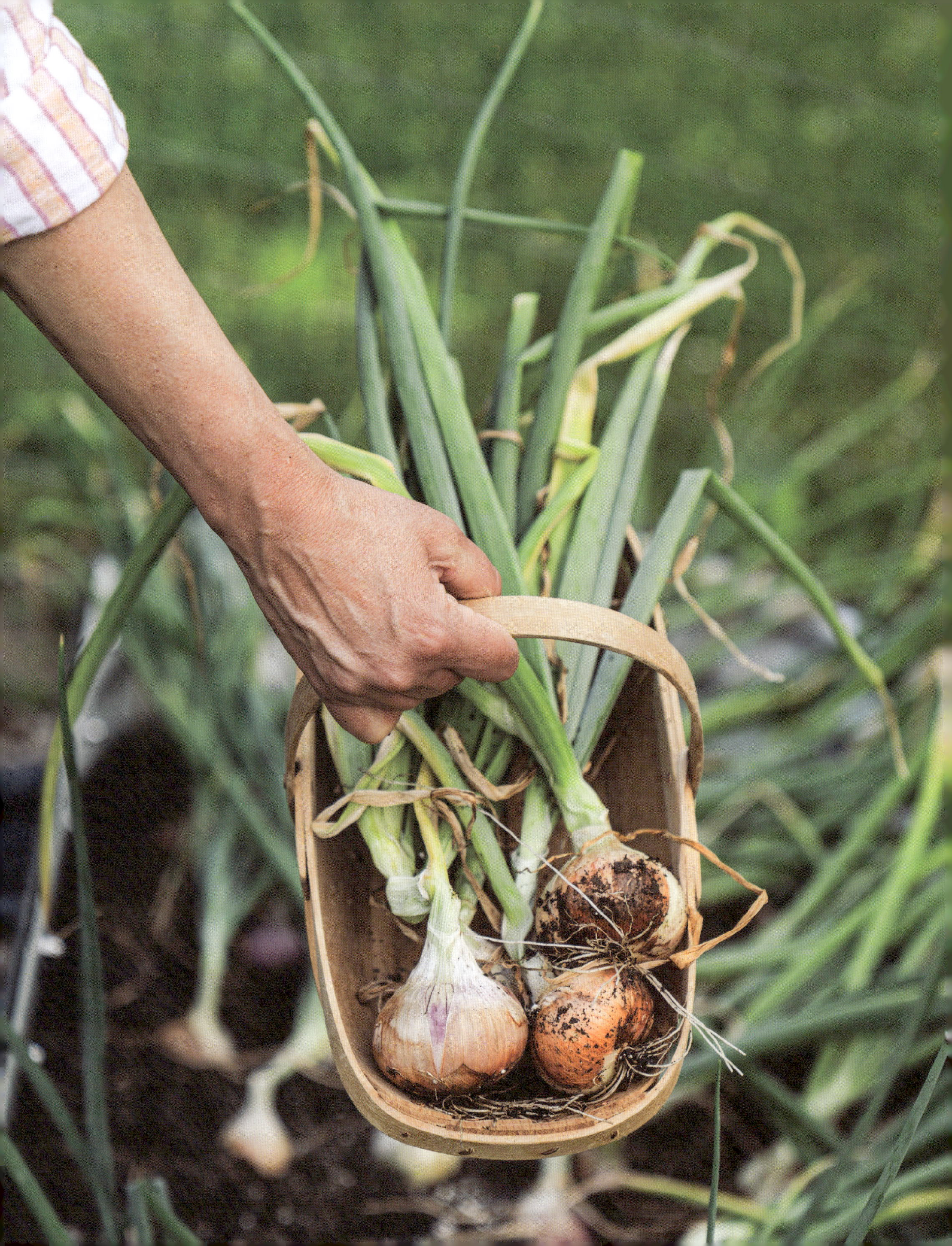

ON ONIONS

ONE of the most transformative things about gardening is growing things that will bring to life memories that have been long buried and dormant. My search for the perfect onion is the perfect example. In my journey of researching *soupe à l'oignon*, a.k.a. French onion soup, to re-create my father's transformative experience with French onion soup during WWII in France, I had to find just the right onion. The Rose de Roscoff onion, grown in Brittany and in great numbers, was what I was looking for. It turns out that Rose de Roscoff onions are also well known in the United Kingdom. Back in the day, beginning in the 1820s, farmers in the Roscoff area of Brittany found it easier and more profitable to get on a ferry to England to sell their onions, rather than take the questionable roads to market in France. They'd bring their harvest across the English Channel in July and sell their wares by carrying the onions around their neck in braided strings. In the UK, the French men who sold onions were called Johnny Onion. But I digress.

Gardeners who grow onions have a choice of growing "sets" or from seed. Sets are baby onions. They look like spring onions and, in fact, can be eaten as spring onions. You buy them at your local nursery in—you guessed it—the spring, you plant them in your garden plot, and in three to four months, you can harvest full-blown onion bulbs. The problem with sets is that your options are very limited, and Rose de Roscoff sets aren't available anywhere in the contiguous 48 states. However, I did find Rose de Roscoff *seed* available in Oregon, where their growing conditions matched those of France well enough that the onion grew there.

What are those conditions? In this case, we're looking at latitude. To grow onions, you need to know where in the world you are. To grow a Rose de Roscoff onion, you don't need to be in France, but you have to share a similar spring and summer growing season. In northern latitudes, such as France's, you grow "long-day" onions because the summer days guarantee you 14 to 16 hours of sun. I live in Vermont in a hardiness zone of 5a and that, no surprise, is situated in the northern latitudes, which meant I was in a suitable patch on this beautiful earth to grow the onion I needed. (Conversely, I cannot grow "short-day" onions, such as Vidalia, which require the shorter summer days of the south.)

In another very fortuitous twist, onion seeds must be started in the late winter to be able to harvest them in the summer. I, like many gardeners, get very antsy come late January. At this point, we've recovered from any disappointments our gardens wrought in the year prior and we're tired of rifling through seed catalogs. The danger in this very vulnerable state is that gardeners tend to start seeds far too early, chasing that green rush that comes from emergent shoots, and those plants have nowhere to go once they've outgrown their containers. Putting them out in the garden will lead to a very quick, frosty death. Starting onions scratches that itch and marks the start to my Hope season.

You start the seeds in flats, the gardener's version of a casserole dish. You sprinkle the seeds over a germination medium (not regular soil but something that's loose and sterile and formulated for the vulnerable seeds), you water, and you place it under a grow light. In the beginning, you treat the emergent sprouts like grass, giving them enough nitrogen and trimming the emergent stalks once they get a few inches tall. This makes them stronger and gives you something productive to do. By the time the ground is warm enough to work, your little onion seedlings will be gangly onion teenagers in need of getting out of the house and into their own little patch of dirt. At this stage, it's a waiting game. You need to water, of course. You need to switch up their diet with nutrients that will feed the bulb rather than the grassy stalk. And you need to ensure the soil not only has the nutrients but is loose enough that the bulb can easily expand. But other than that, your onions are left to the gardening fates.

I harvested my Rose de Roscoffs in July, almost six months to the day that I planted the very first onion seed. The bulbs had successfully emerged from the ground, some bigger than others, but all beautiful and round. The tops had dried slightly and fallen over, a sign that they were ready to be harvested. I grew more than 100 onions, their flesh gently striped with the most delicate pink. I requisitioned a metal metro rack and dragged it near a window in the lower barn that didn't see much direct light but would provide a nice cross-breeze. I hung the onions upside down between the metal slats, spacing them so that each onion would have its own space to dry properly, a process called curing that allows the outer skin to dry and to create a protective layer so that the onions store longer.

Ray aimed a fan at them, making sure they'd always have moving air to cure properly. When the tops had completely dried, I gathered sets of nine onions and braided their dry tendrils as if I were tending to the tresses of a child. I hung the onions in my kitchen and snipped a single allium from a bunch as needed. And once the leaves of our giant maples began to turn and the air took on a chill, I took down an entire braid, the one with the biggest and prettiest of the onions that I'd kept back for just this occasion, and I made the soup I'd been working on for over a year but for the first time with the very onion that held the memory of a boy who'd traveled across an ocean to land on a beach to fight for liberty and found a soup that lived in his memory until the day he died.

SOUPS, SALADS & SAMMIES

German Cucumber Salad

SERVES 4

The summers we spent in Germany were full of fabulous salads. Pasta salads. Tomato salads. Sausage salads (yes, sausage salad). And my favorite, cucumber salad. They came dressed with a simple vinaigrette or with a bit of yogurt dressing. It was a dish that even a sugar-obsessed, vegetable-rejecting kid like me loved. And guess what? You can use surplus zucchini in the exact same way!

2 large cucumbers or zucchini
1 tablespoon kosher salt
¼ cup whole-milk plain Greek yogurt
¼ cup crème fraîche or full-fat sour cream
2 tablespoons white wine vinegar
1 tablespoon Dijon mustard
1 teaspoon pure maple syrup
1 small yellow or sweet onion, finely chopped
2 tablespoons finely chopped fresh dill
Fine sea salt and ground white pepper

Wash the cucumbers and dry them. Gently peel, leaving some of the green on. With a chef's knife or mandoline, cut the cucumbers into very thin rounds. Place the cucumber slices in a colander over a large bowl and sprinkle with the kosher salt. Toss together to evenly distribute the salt. Set aside for 30 minutes, to allow the salt to pull excess moisture from the cucumbers.

Whisk together the yogurt, crème fraîche, vinegar, mustard, and maple syrup in a serving bowl. Stir in the onion and dill. Don't season with salt yet, even if you think the dressing needs it. The cucumbers will bring a bit of salt along with them, so wait to season until after adding the cucumbers.

Squeeze excess moisture from the cucumbers and add to the serving bowl. Toss to coat. Taste and adjust seasoning. Serve cold.

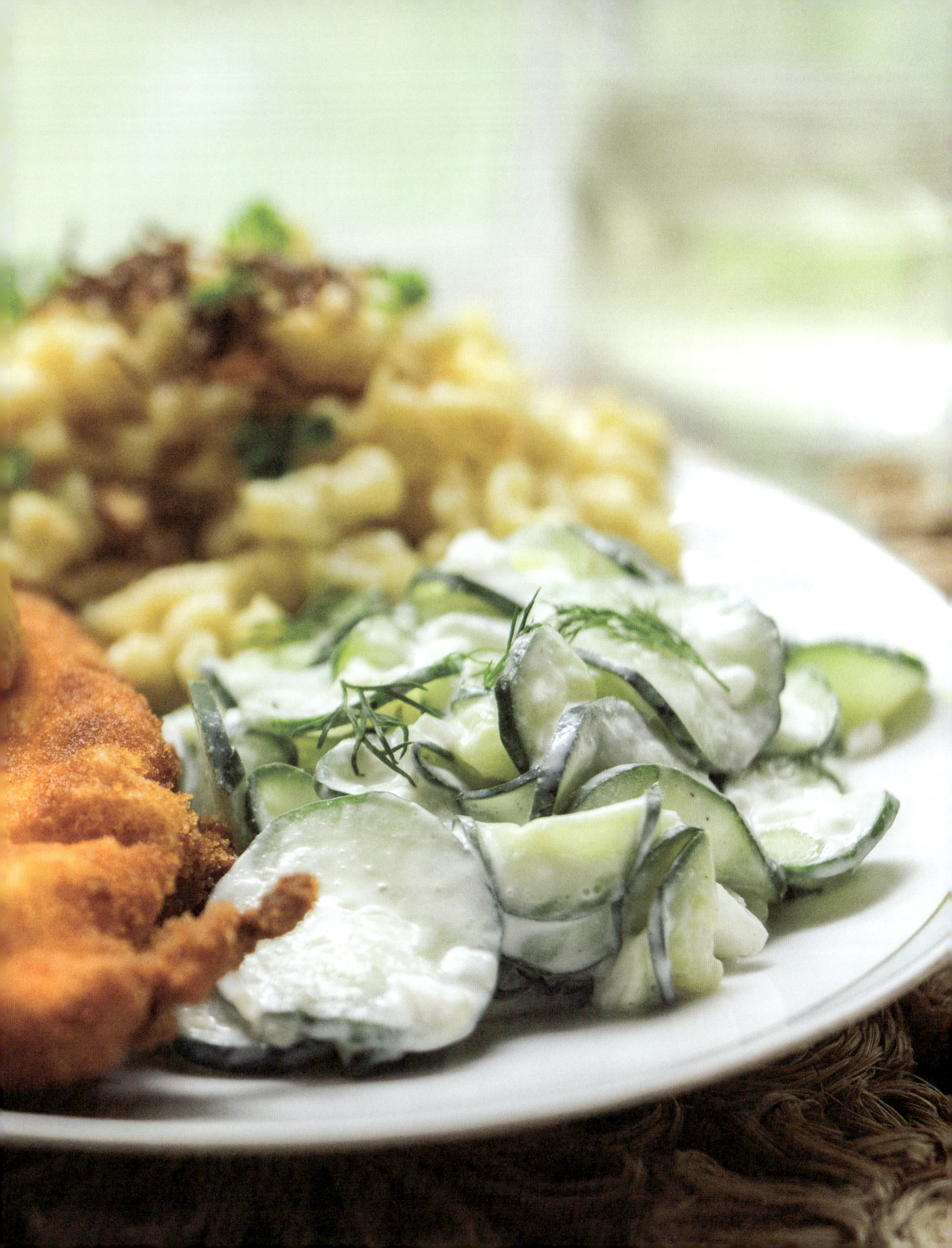

The Wicked Wedge with Buttermilk Dressing

SERVES 8

I am a fiend for a creamy dressing. Ranch and ranch-adjacent dressings, tangy buttermilk, a perfectly emulsified balsamic, a flavor bomb of a blue. Love 'em all. But my favorite? My "dry mix" buttermilk dressing. It utilizes a fabulous pantry staple, powdered buttermilk, so you can whip it up without having to source buttermilk at the last minute. You have all the ingredients available at home, and if you keep powdered buttermilk, you don't have to worry about wasting money on a large bottle, using only a small portion, and then tossing the rest when you discover it expired and hiding in the back of the fridge. It's a fabulous way to use dried herbs as well, including homemade scape powder, making the flavor both comforting and zingy. Grab a few compact heads of Boston Bibb from the garden, give them a quick rinse, slice in half, festoon with bright cherry tomatoes and some bacon, and your salad dreams have been made.

FOR THE BUTTERMILK DRESSING / MAKES 2 CUPS

- ¼ cup buttermilk powder
- 2 teaspoons dried parsley
- 1 teaspoon onion powder
- 1 teaspoon scape powder (see page 45)
- 1 teaspoon garlic powder
- 1 teaspoon dried dill
- 1 teaspoon mustard powder
- ½ teaspoon fine sea salt,* plus more if needed
- ½ teaspoon ground white pepper, plus more if needed
- 1 cup full-fat sour cream
- ½ cup mayonnaise
- ½ cup whole milk

FOR THE SALAD

- 4 heads Boston Bibb lettuce, cut in half
- 1 pint garden-fresh cherry tomatoes, halved
- 4 strips bacon, cooked and crumbled

MAKE THE DRESSING

Whisk together the buttermilk powder, parsley, onion powder, scape powder, garlic powder, dill, mustard powder, salt, and pepper in a small bowl, breaking up any clumps (mustard powder is notoriously clumpy).

Using a rubber spatula, stir in the sour cream, smashing the mixture against the side of the bowl to break up any herb clumps. Stir in the mayo and then whisk in the milk until smooth. Season with more salt and pepper, if needed. Cover and refrigerate for at least 15 minutes to blend the flavors and rehydrate the dried herbs and spices.

ASSEMBLE THE SALAD

Arrange the lettuce on a large platter and drizzle generously with the dressing. Sprinkle with the cherry tomatoes and bacon. Transfer the remaining dressing to a mason jar and have it handy for saucy minxes like me who like to reapply a bit of dressing as they go.

*NOTE You can use Herbamare herbed sea salt in lieu of traditional sea salt, as I do; it contains dried herbs for more flavor.

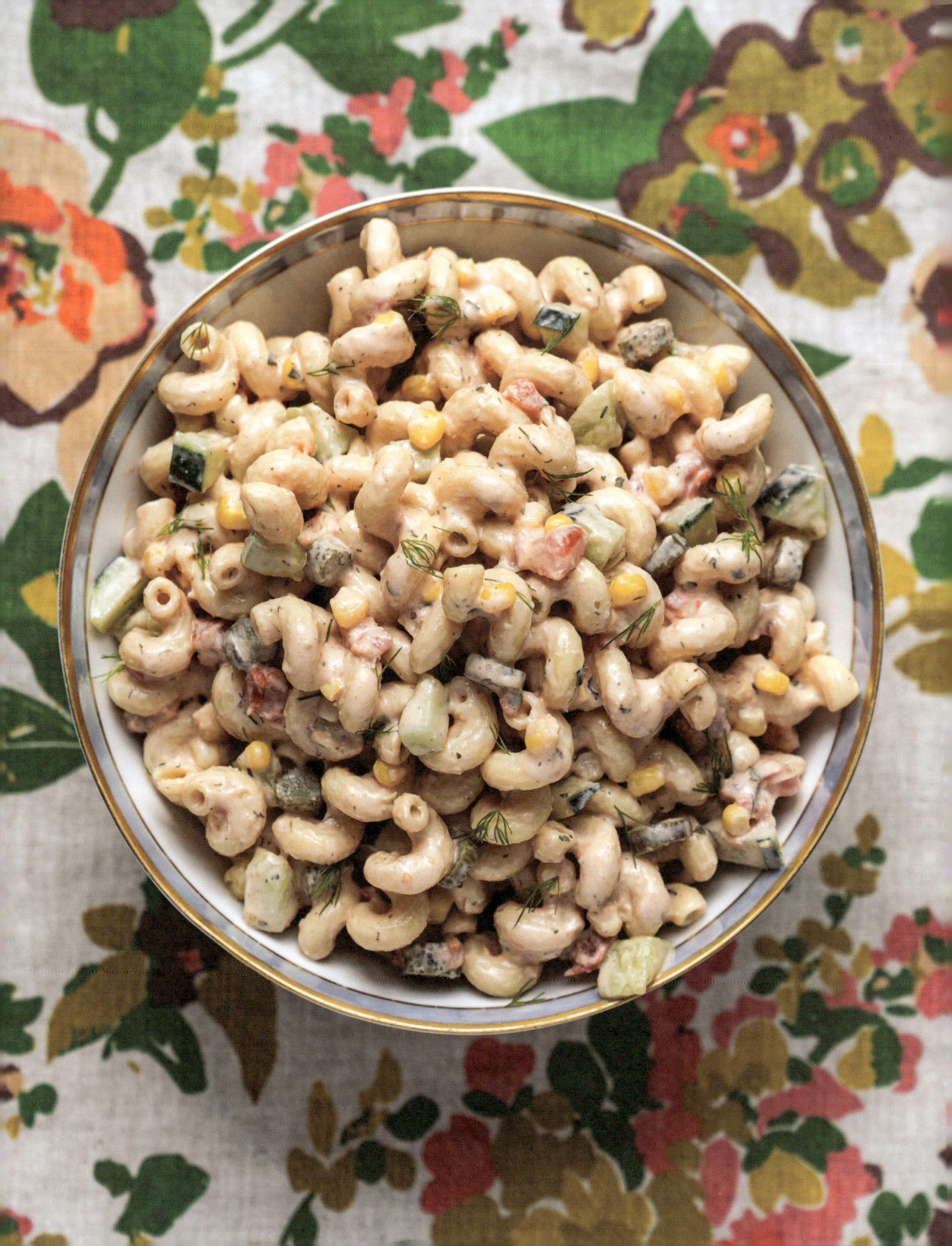

"Goat Cheese Party" Pasta Salad

SERVES 10 TO 12

In the 1990s, my sister and I shared a house in the Hollywood Hills. I was going to law school. She was getting famous. We thought we were hot stuff throwing house parties. Some well known people would come, but mostly nonfamous, nice people. Years later, I ran into someone who had the pleasure of attending a few of our shindigs. He said, and I quote, "Oh my god, do you remember your GOAT CHEESE PARTIES?!"

"Our *what*, now?" I asked.

"Your goat cheese parties! That's what we called them!"

Dear reader, where my sister and I thought we were throwing "bangers," we were, in fact, just filling people up with pregame goat cheese. While the rest of Los Angeles on Friday night was a den of late-night libation and excess, my sister and I had managed to corner the market on early evening wholesomeness with a side of goat cheese.

Why goat cheese? Well, we really liked it and we thought it was fancy. We put it in EVERYTHING. Pasta salads, lentil salads, bruschetta, skewers with watermelon. We treated goat cheese like salt: everything benefited from a little. And we'd festoon our really big dining table with trays, bowls, and platters of goat cheese–speckled offerings. To be fair, we also offered a buffalo mozzarella–heavy caprese salad, arranged on pattern-heavy Cottura pottery, for variety. But goat cheese was queen. The pasta salad really is a banger, though, and it features the best of the late-summer garden.

1 pound dried cavatappi pasta

1 cob sweet corn, shucked and kernels removed

¼ cup brine from a jar of cornichons

1 large cucumber, gently peeled with some of the green left on, sliced into ¼-inch rounds, then quartered

1 large beefsteak tomato,* diced

2 scallions, thinly sliced

12 cornichons (mini pickles), chopped into ⅛-inch rounds

½ batch Buttermilk Dressing (page 58)

4 ounces chèvre, a.k.a. goat cheese

Salt and freshly ground black pepper

Chopped fresh dill, for garnish

Cook the pasta according to the package instructions for al dente, drain, then transfer to a serving bowl. Immediately add the corn kernels and cornichon brine while the pasta is still hot. This will slightly "cook" the corn.

Once the pasta is cool, add the cucumber, tomato, scallions, and cornichons. Gently toss to distribute. Place the buttermilk dressing in a small bowl, crumble in the chèvre, then dress the salad with the mixture. Season with salt and pepper to taste. Top with fresh dill. Serve immediately or refrigerate for up to 3 days.

*NOTE I grow Johnson German tomatoes.

SOUPS, SALADS & SAMMIES

Salmon Panzanella Salad

SERVES 4

Panzanella is a bread salad. I don't know what else I need to say to sell this to you. It's as if this were tailor-made for me, a baking instructor who can't turn her head without running into half a loaf of stale bread with nowhere to go and a ready supply of parchment for baking the salmon, a method of cooking you can use any time you want to cook salmon without much fuss or mess. Combine that with an overflowing summer garden and a fillet of salmon hiding in the fridge and you've got a meal made in bready heaven.

1 pound salmon fillet
Salt and freshly ground black pepper
1 lemon, cut into thin slices
10 ounces stale Crusty Bread (page 248), cut into 1-inch cubes
¼ cup plus 2 tablespoons extra-virgin olive oil
2 tablespoons red wine vinegar
1 small cucumber, gently peeled with some of the green left on
1 large heirloom tomato, diced
1 medium red onion,* thinly sliced
2 cups baby arugula
1 bunch basil, leaves cut or torn into strips
¼ teaspoon baking soda
8 ounces French green beans, trimmed and cut into ½-inch pieces

Preheat your oven to 400°F (200°C). Place a half sheet of parchment on a sheet pan and fold in half lengthwise so that the folded piece measures approximately 9 by 6 inches. Unfold the parchment and place the salmon, skin side down, on one side of the parchment. Season with salt and pepper and arrange the lemon slices on top. Fold the other side of the parchment over and fold over the edges of the parchment to seal the salmon in.

Bake for 20 to 25 minutes, then remove from the oven and transfer the salmon in its paper to a cooling rack. Line the sheet pan with another piece of parchment and spread the bread cubes on the prepared sheet pan. Brush with 2 tablespoons of the olive oil and bake for 5 to 7 minutes to slightly crisp the bread. Remove from the oven and set aside to cool.

Whisk together the remaining ¼ cup of olive oil and the red wine vinegar, a generous pinch of salt, and a few pinches of pepper in a serving bowl. Cut the cucumber into ¼-inch rounds and add to the serving bowl, along with the bread, tomato, onion, arugula, and basil.

Fill a small bowl halfway with ice. Bring a medium saucepan of water to a boil and add the baking soda. Using a spider or slotted spoon,

MY HARVEST KITCHEN

add the green beans and cook until barely tender, about 3 minutes (the baking soda creates an alkaline environment in the water that will help keep the beans a vibrant green). Transfer the green beans to the ice bath to stop the cooking and cool them down quickly. Drain the beans and pat dry with a clean kitchen towel, then add to the salad in the serving bowl. Gently toss to coat the salad with the dressing. Using a fish spatula, carefully arrange the salmon on top of the salad. Serve immediately.

*NOTE I use Rose de Roscoff, but you can use a juicy, sweet onion of your choice.

MY HARVEST KITCHEN

Cold Soba Noodle Salad with Peanut Dressing and Soy-Marinated Eggs

SERVES 4

I'm very open about my unusual vegan macrobiotic upbringing. There was no hiding it when I was a kid; no one wanted to come play at my house because the snacks consisted of crispy seaweed strips and roasted tamari almonds. I do enjoy these things as snacks today. They just didn't appeal to the orange-cheesed and nuclear-bunker-snack-cake set of my youth. As it often happens, it takes a bit of growing up and worldly exploration to bring us back home to our taste buds' first encounters. Soba noodles, however, are a food I was on board with from the moment they graced our dinner table. It's easy enough to buy them at any ol' grocery store these days, but I'm partial to the homemade kind. They are far more rustic and way more toothsome, grabbing onto the peanut sauce with gusto. And while I *could* use buckwheat harvested from my cover crop, there is a distinct difference between what I mill at home and what has been expertly grown and milled for the sole purpose of making soba noodles. This is a nice way of saying, I tried it once but never again. Fortunately, there are artisan mills in the US that mill buckwheat flour expertly crafted for making these slightly bouncy, utterly delectable strands that make eating veggies an utter delight. So, if you find yourself staring at your overflowing garden beds, at your untouched CSA, or in your refrigerator and feeling really guilty about not vibing with the produce, make a batch of soba noodles, coat them with a dangerously addictive peanut dressing, and bring the veggies along for the delicious party.

FOR THE CHICKEN

2 boneless, skinless chicken breasts

Salt and freshly ground black pepper

1 tablespoon peanut oil

FOR THE NOODLES

4 cups (480 grams) soba-grade buckwheat flour, plus more for sprinkling

1 cup water, plus more if needed

or

4 servings premade buckwheat soba noodles*

FOR THE SALAD

2 cups shredded red cabbage

2 cups baby greens

1 cup julienned carrot

1 large cucumber, cut into ¼-inch rounds, then quartered

1 cup thinly sliced red onion, soaked in cold water for 20 minutes, then drained

2 tablespoons toasted sesame seeds

2 tablespoons Sichimi togarashi Japanese spice mix

2 Soy-Marinated Eggs (page 238), halved

recipe continues...

FOR THE PEANUT DRESSING

¼ cup smooth natural peanut butter

¼ cup water

3 tablespoons soy sauce

2 tablespoons rice vinegar

2 tablespoons sesame oil (spicy or mild, your choice)

2 tablespoons pure maple syrup

1 tablespoon freshly grated ginger

2 garlic cloves, grated to a paste with a Microplane grater

Salt

MAKE THE CHICKEN

Preheat the oven to 375°F (190°C). Pat the chicken dry with a paper towel and season liberally with salt and pepper. Heat the peanut oil in a large cast-iron skillet over medium-high heat. Place the chicken in the skillet and cook for 5 minutes. Turn the chicken over and immediately transfer to the oven. Bake for 25 to 30 minutes, until a digital thermometer reads 165°F (75°C). Remove from the oven and set the chicken aside on a cutting board, covering it with aluminum foil, to rest. Once cool, shred into bite-size pieces.

MAKE THE NOODLES

Sift the buckwheat flour into a large bowl. Add 1 cup of the water and gently massage it into the flour with your fingertips until the mixture forms small clumps. Press down on the mixture with your fist and "schmear" the mixture to compact it. Give the bowl a one-quarter turn and continue "schmearing" until all the dough is compacted. If the dough feels at all dry, sprinkle in more water, 1 tablespoon at a time, schmearing it in, until the dough forms a smooth disk when gathered and compacted with your hands. Transfer the dough to your work surface and knead until smooth, shiny, and no longer tacky, about 5 minutes. Compress the dough into a smooth disk, cover with beeswax wrap or plastic wrap, and refrigerate for 20 minutes.

Roll out the dough into a ⅛-inch-thick, large rectangle. Sprinkle well with buckwheat flour and fold in half lengthwise. Sprinkle again with buckwheat flour and fold in half again in the same direction. Using a long chef's knife, cut the noodles as thinly as you can. I tend to cut them more thickly than is traditional. Dust the strands with more buckwheat flour and divide the strands into four separate clumps.

To cook the soba, whether homemade or store-bought, fill two large bowls with cold water and add a cup of ice to one of the bowls. Bring a lightly salted quart of water to a boil in a large saucepan (it should be large enough to be able to lower a sieve with soba noodles into it). Place one serving of soba in a handled sieve and lower it into the water so that the noodles are fully submerged. If cooking freshly made, cook for 1 minute. If cooking from packaged, follow the packaging instructions. Remove the sieve from the pot, shake any excess water from the noodles in the sieve, then lower the sieve into the bowl of water without the ice. Use your fingertips to gently whirl around the noodles to rinse, about 20 seconds. Transfer to the bowl with the ice in the same manner, using your fingertips to whirl around the noodles to rinse them off. This helps keep the noodles from sticking together. Prepare the three remaining servings of noodles one by one, in the same manner. Set aside.

MAKE THE PEANUT DRESSING

Combine the peanut butter, water, soy sauce, rice vinegar, sesame oil, maple syrup, ginger, and garlic in a small bowl. Whisk together until smooth. Give a taste for seasoning and add salt as needed.

MAKE THE SALAD
Divide the cabbage, baby greens, carrots, cucumber, and red onion among the serving dishes. Top with shredded chicken and then the noodles. Drizzle with the dressing and sprinkle with togarashi and sesame seeds. Top each serving with half a soy-marinated egg.

*NOTE If using premade noodles, four servings may require two packages, as there are typically three servings in each package.

SOUPS, SALADS & SAMMIES

ODE TO THE HARVEST

SUMMER kicks in like a rocket in Vermont. One day, it's threatening to snow; the next, the dirt roads are quicksand from the thaw; and then, BAM! it's mid-June and everything is emerald green, it's humid, and I can't pick the tomatoes fast enough. It always feels the same, as if we didn't get to spend enough time with spring. There's no easing into harvest season; it just takes off into orbit whether you're ready for it or not. And I'm never ready.

The trick is not to panic. Tomatoes and zucchini are going to ripen all at once, so get used to the idea of eating tomatoes and zucchini for breakfast and then figure out how you're going to preserve the excess. This might seem like a very rural problem, and indeed I live and grow in a very rural state, but when I was a kid, we lived on a cul de sac in Arlington, Virginia, just across the river from the nation's capital. Everyone on 26th Street kept a neat lawn, some had lovely flowers, and there was even a koi pond behind the Witherspoons', but no one, not a single neighbor, grew vegetables. Except for my mom. In our tiny backyard, Mom grew squash, kale, radishes, and beets. She nurtured nasturtiums, that lovely flower that draws pests away from crops. In a time before CSAs, Whole Foods, and Pinterest gardening boards, my mom was harvesting bumper crops from our suburban backyard.

My mother died of cancer a year after I married. Three years before we made our way to Vermont from Los Angeles. Years before we found Freegrace Tavern, where I tend my gardens and run my baking school. Every day here, I think of her and how she lived her life exploring such interests as gardening, bricklaying, upholstery, and marathon running, not giving a fig whether it was "done" or acceptable. When I was a kid, I adored my mom but, in pure kid fashion, the things that made her unique and fantastically "my mom" were the things that often embarrassed me or things I simply didn't appreciate. But look at me now. My yearly harvest, my curiosity and delight at things that I grow and I can eat, are blessings from a mother who left us way too early. She'd have delighted in Freegrace as much as I do, and she'd be so thrilled that vegetable gardens are popping up all over suburbs and cities. I think of her when the panic of harvest starts to creep in, remembering that I am my mother's daughter and what a blessing it is to be alive and to appreciate the abundance. And then, I get cooking.

SOUPS, SALADS & SAMMIES

Cheffy Quinoa and Tuna Salad with Preserved Lemon Vinaigrette

SERVES 2

Sometimes, a tiny bit of effort in plating can transform a dish. I'm not saying that this scrumptious salad isn't full of flavorful delight when just dumped in a bowl and served. What I *am* saying is that plating things in an arty manner (1) is incredibly satisfying to do, (2) is visually impactful in a way that will make the salad taste *even better*, and (3) hides the fact that you may only have a few stray veggies that were harvestable from the garden (ahem), which can be an issue at the beginning and the end of the harvesting season or if your garden has simply not been at its best all season. There are only a few tomatoes that are truly red, a lone cuke is hanging on the vine, and a single radish has decided to go all Ledecky and has raced to ripeness before the others have even emerged as sprouts? Get cheffy with it! Grab a pair of culinary tweezers and make that plate shine as if you've earned a Michelin Star.

FOR THE DRESSING

½ preserved lemon (see page 269)

Juice of ½ fresh lemon, about 2 tablespoons

1 teaspoon Dijon mustard

½ teaspoon honey

Kosher salt and ground white pepper

½ cup extra-virgin olive oil

FOR THE SALAD

¼ cup shelled fresh peas

1 batch Perfect Quinoa (page 257), freshly made

1 cucumber, cut into thin strips with a mandoline or vegetable peeler

8 cherry tomatoes, halved

2 to 4 radishes, cut into paper-thin slices with a chef's knife or mandoline

Pea shoots

Edible flowers

1 (3.2-ounce) can albacore or yellowtail tuna in olive oil, drained

1 bunch fresh dill, ferny bits pulled from the stalk

MY HARVEST KITCHEN

MAKE THE DRESSING

Rinse the preserved lemon half really well; otherwise, the resulting dressing will be too salty. Seed and chop the rind into small cubes. Add the preserved lemon rind pieces, lemon juice, Dijon mustard, and honey, along with a small pinch each of kosher salt and white pepper, to a tall jar. Using an immersion blender, blend the mixture and then slowly drizzle in the olive oil. Alternatively, you can use a traditional blender. Taste for seasoning. Store leftover dressing in a sealed, clean jar in the refrigerator for up to 1 week.

MAKE THE SALAD

Add ice to a large bowl and stir in a few cups of cold water. Bring 2 cups of generously salted water to a simmer in a small saucepan, then add the peas. Boil for 1 minute, then immediately remove the peas with a sieve and transfer to the ice bath. Then, transfer the peas to a paper towel and gently blot to dry. Set aside.

Place a small bowl upside down in the middle of a large serving plate. Spoon the quinoa around the perimeter of the bowl and then, using a spoon or offset spatula, shape the quinoa into an even ring surrounding the bowl. Carefully lift up the bowl.

Coil the cucumber strips and carefully arrange around and on top of the quinoa. Using a culinary tweezer, place the cherry tomato halves, radish slices, peas, pea shoots, and edible flowers on the salad. Using a small offset spatula or a butter knife, slide large chunks of tuna on and around the quinoa ring. Drizzle the dressing onto the salad and garnish with fresh dill.

SOUPS, SALADS & SAMMIES

A NOTE FROM
MY KITCHEN GARDEN

A Bag Will Do

NOT EVERYONE HAS AN ACRE, OR EVEN a patch of grass, to create a garden. If we were to go by Pinterest and Instagram, you'd think the world was populated by prairie dress–wearing potager gardeners with shiplap-festooned homes and café-curtained henhouses. I know I am blessed to have the land I do, but for the love of Pete, please don't take a picture of me when I do my morning chores. My pajamas aren't photo-worthy. Add to that the chicken coop fencing that's falling apart and the tangle of knotweed I just can't eradicate. It's all about choosing your best angles and making sure the things you're ashamed of are just out of frame.

But say you have zero land. Maybe you have a windowsill. Perhaps a balcony. You may not have an Insta-perfect tableau, but who the hell cares; you can still grow something delicious if you know your hardiness zone and have the will. In fact, if you can haul a bag of topsoil upstairs, you can lie it flat on a balcony, carefully slit the middle open, and just plant seeds right in there. Poke a few tiny holes through the bottom for drainage and you've got a garden bed. Get a hardware bucket and plant potatoes inside. Find a hanging basket and grow cascading strawberries and cherry tomatoes that were bred to go all flopsy on purpose.

Gardening should not be gatekeeping. I once used a window box for asparagus and planted watercress in a rain swale. Luckily, gardeners are a generous bunch. If you can't find limitless bags of cash to build the ultimate garden, find your people, fellow growers, and they'll help you start your journey with saved seeds and extra grow bags. Also, keep an eye out for community gardens that build relationships and foodways, giving you access to knowledge and good soil.

SOUPS, SALADS & SAMMIES

Creamy Mustard Potato Salad with Broad Beans and Peas

SERVES 8

This potato salad contains not one, not two, but THREE of my favorite things to grow *and* eat: potatoes, peas, and broad beans. The joy I find in growing them almost matches how much I love eating them. You see, it's my opinion that you should love to grow the things in your garden and grow the things you love. I'm a sucker for a great potato, and I'm a goner when it comes to La Ratte potatoes. They are simply the finest of fingerlings: dense and creamy, flavorful and sophisticated. And broad beans and peas bring a bright green pop to the party and lend texture that's slightly similar to potato, leaving the onion in the mix to bring a skosh of crunch.

1 cup shelled fresh peas
3 tablespoons white wine vinegar
2 pounds fingerling potatoes*
1 tablespoon kosher salt
1 cup shelled broad beans or Windsor beans
1 small onion,* finely diced
¼ cup crème fraîche or full-fat sour cream
2 tablespoons extra-virgin olive oil
2 tablespoons whole-grain German mustard
1 tablespoon chopped fresh dill
Fine sea salt and ground white pepper

Combine the peas with 2 tablespoons of the vinegar in a large serving bowl. Set aside.

Halve the fingerlings lengthwise. Combine them with the kosher salt, the remaining tablespoon of vinegar, and 1 quart of water in a large Dutch oven or stockpot. Bring to a boil over high heat and cook until the potatoes are fork-tender, about 15 minutes.

Remove the potatoes with a spider or slotted spoon and allow to drain into the pot. Immediately add them to the bowl that contains the peas and vinegar and toss to coat. Set aside.

Combine 1 cup of ice and 1 cup of cold water in a small bowl. Bring the water in the pot back to a boil. Add the broad beans and boil for 2 minutes. Immediately drain and transfer to the bowl of ice water. Carefully squeeze one side of each bean until its green, inner bean pops out. Add the inner beans and onion to the bowl of potatoes and peas.

Combine the crème fraîche, olive oil, mustard, and dill in a small bowl and stir together until smooth. Add to the potato mixture and toss to coat. Season to taste with sea salt and white pepper.

*NOTE I grow and use La Ratte potatoes, and use a Rose de Roscoff onion.

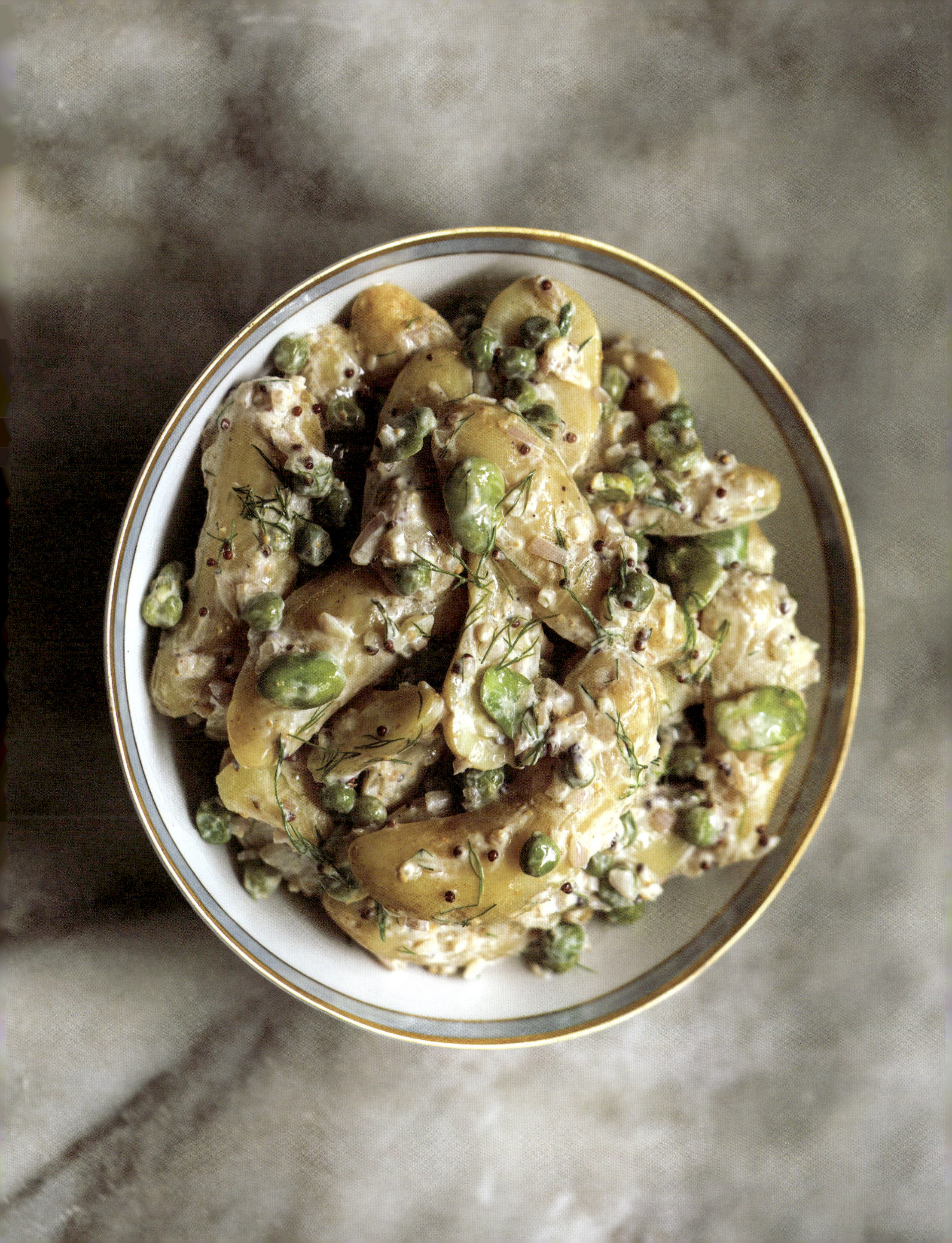

MY HARVEST KITCHEN

Sorrel, Spinach, and Barley Salad with Warm Bacon Dressing

SERVES 8

I don't think we praise winter salads enough. Summer salads get all the attention, with juicy veggies and tender greens just throwing themselves at us from every farmers' market and corner veggie patch. But I'm here to bring glory to the hearty wonder that is the warm winter salad, because it's more than just a side, it's a whole darn meal. And it's totally legit when it's warm, something we just wouldn't tolerate in the summer. And for those who are champing at the bit to grow something, anything, through the cold winter months, sorrel and spinach are the perfect greens to grow in a greenhouse or a cold frame during the hibernation season.

8 ounces uncooked bacon, diced

2 tablespoons cider vinegar

1 tablespoon whole-grain mustard

Kosher salt

1 cup uncooked pearl barley

10 ounces (about 9 cups) baby spinach leaves

1 cup common sorrel, torn into small pieces

½ cup pomegranate seeds

1 ounce blue cheese, crumbled

Cook the bacon in a skillet over medium heat, stirring often, until the fat is rendered and the bacon is crisp. Transfer the bacon to a paper towel and transfer the fat to a large bowl. To the bacon fat, add the vinegar and mustard, whisking to combine into a dressing. Season with kosher salt to taste. Set aside.

Bring 3 cups of water to a rolling boil in a large saucepan, stir in the barley, cover the pot, and lower the heat to low. Allow to cook, covered, for 25 to 30 minutes, until the barley is tender and the water is absorbed (if the barley is tender and some water remains, simply drain the barley in a sieve). Transfer the hot barley to the bowl of dressing, then add the spinach, sorrel, and pomegranate seeds. Toss to coat in the dressing. Top with the bacon and the crumbled blue cheese.

Aunt Sis's Tomato Sandwich

MAKES 2 SANDWICHES

This isn't as much of a recipe as it is a memory, a memory of an aunt who fed me a sandwich one stormy afternoon in her beach house on stilts overlooking the Atlantic Ocean on Alligator Point, Florida. And a tomato. Aunt Sis was my dad's older sister, and I think, of all my father's family, I favor her the most. She was the tallest and lanky. Wavy dark hair. She made candy. I have a pile of her recipes, mostly sweets. When she handed me a paper plate with a sandwich on it, I had very high expectations. I had assumed it would contain multitudes: bacon perhaps? Springy bologna? Gloriously orange plastic cheese? Alas, this sandwich had none of the things forbidden in my mother's kitchen, white bread notwithstanding. Instead, it was utter simplicity: two slices of fresh, squishy bread slathered with Duke's mayonnaise and, nestled within, a lightly salted, ½-inch thick slice of ruby red beefsteak tomato, one so big that it covered all but the very corners of the bread. I was dubious. I was disappointed. Suddenly, I wasn't very hungry. Tomatoes were a healthy thing. A fruit that masqueraded as a vegetable. I took a dainty, trepidatious bite. Juice ran down my chin. I'd barely nibbled the thing and it burst forth anyway, a medley of vegetal sweetness, creamy saltiness, and perfect bready squish. Aunt Sis watched, her eyes full of culinary wisdom and sparkling mischief. It stands as the most perfect sandwich I've ever eaten. It's the reason I grow German Johnsons, a type of heirloom Brandywine tomato, shaped like a beefsteak but elevating the sweetness and overall taste so beautifully that you'll never look at a tomato the same way again. This is as close as I've ever come to replicating Aunt Sis's sandwich, and reason enough to grow your own tomatoes.

1 very large and very ripe Brandywine-style, garden-fresh tomato

¼ cup mayonnaise

4 thick slices Brioche (page 241)

Salt and freshly ground black pepper

Slice the tomato horizontally into two slices between ¼ and ½ inch thick. Core and chop the remaining tomato into small pieces. Spread the mayonnaise on two of the slices of brioche, then center a tomato slice smack-dab in the middle of the mayo. Place smaller pieces of tomato on any empty bread real estate. Season with salt and pepper. Top with a second slice of bread. Eat immediately and with someone you love.

SOUPS, SALADS & SAMMIES

MY HARVEST KITCHEN

Summer Sandwich

MAKES 2 SANDWICHES

Growing up in Arlington, Virginia, the second you reach toddlerhood and graduate to complex solid foods, you're inducted into the world of The Italian Store. When I was a kid, there was only one. It was in Lion Village, down a few storefronts from Giant Supermarket, and, later, by the Starbucks. It has multiple locations now, but Lion Village will always be *the* Italian Store. And when you go to The Italian Store, you order the Milano. It has other wonderful sandwiches and, at least when I was a kid, had killer pizza, but the Milano is the entry into The Italian Store Life. Is it the two Italian hams *and* the Genoa salami that make it so addictive? Is it the soft provolone that's not a bit showy but, man, it's missed if it's not there? Or is it the combo of sweet *and* hot peppers, the lettuce, the onions, the oregano, all doused in the "special" dressing? Who's to say? I re-create some of that magic in the heat of summer, when things are busting loose in the garden, when a sandwich is just what you need. When the mercury rises, so do sweet memories of being a kid in the swamp heat of the D.C. suburbs with a Milano in hand and pepper juice running down my chin. I add some giardiniera to round out the veggie quotient, but otherwise, it's just like being in Virginia again. Heaven.

2 Ciabatta Rolls (page 246)
4 heaping tablespoons Giardiniera (page 267)
8 slices prosciutto
8 slices coppa ham
8 slices Genoa salami
6 slices provolone
1 cup shredded iceberg lettuce
½ cup Italian Sweet and Spicy Pickled Pepper Salad (page 266)
Red wine vinegar
Extra-virgin olive oil
Salt and freshly ground black pepper

Slice the ciabatta rolls in half and take out just a little of the "meat" of the buns inside to make more room for filling.

Spread half the giardiniera on each lower bun, then layer four slices of prosciutto, four slices of coppa ham, four slices of Genoa salami, and three slices of provolone on top of each lower bun. Sprinkle with the lettuce, then layer with the pepper salad. Season to taste with red wine vinegar, olive oil, salt, and black pepper. Lay on each top bun and press gently. Cut in half.

NOTE For a pure sandwich experience, keep your vinegar and oil in squeeze bottles to get the best control over the flow.

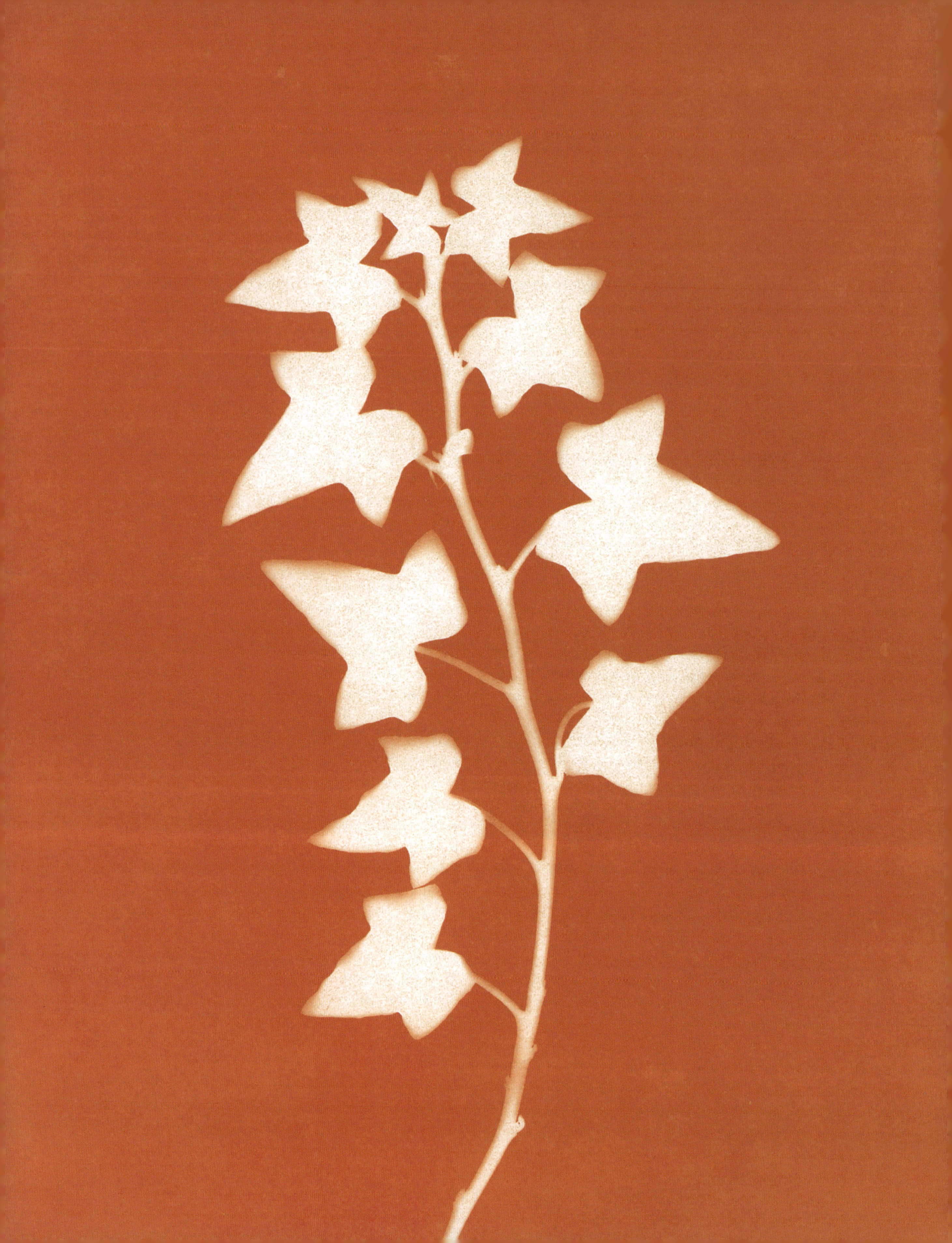

NIBBLES & SIDES

Lemony Labneh

MAKES ABOUT 1½ CUPS

I am a yogurt gal. Have been my entire life. Specifically, I'm all in for plain yogurt. My mom used to make it at home, just plain, before we went full macrobiotic. Back in the day, when Helga was creating probiotic goodness in our Arlington, Virginia, kitchen, the set of the yogurt was always on the looser side. Greek and Skyr hadn't yet made it over to the States. But now that we are blessed with the absolute luxuriance of yogurt that can hold its creamy shape, I will never look back. And if I can make it into a dip? Say no more.

12 ounces whole-milk plain Greek yogurt

Grated zest of 1 lemon

½ teaspoon freshly squeezed lemon juice

Pinch of salt

3 tablespoons extra-virgin olive oil

Line a large sieve with cheesecloth and set over a bowl.

Stir together the yogurt, lemon zest and juice, and salt in a bowl. Scrape the yogurt mixture into the cheesecloth-lined sieve and then fold the edges of the cheesecloth over the top of the mixture to cover. Refrigerate for 24 hours. The mixture will have stiffened considerably.

Transfer the labneh to a serving bowl and drizzle with the olive oil. Serve with pickled veg (see page 264).

NIBBLES & SIDES

MY HARVEST KITCHEN

Butter and Wine–Poached White Asparagus

SERVES 4

White asparagus is not a special varietal that emerges from the soil chalky white in the early spring. White asparagus can be *any* varietal, purple or green. You *make* it white by covering it with an opaque cloche or blackout fabric before there's a peep from the stalks coming from the ground. This prevents the spears from producing any chlorophyll and, therefore, any color. The reason it's so prized is that the taste is sweeter, less grassy, than its sun-soaked brethren. And if you cut the stalks and cook them in minutes, they are more tender than green or purple varieties. In my family, every Christmas Eve dinner will have a plate of pickled white asparagus, a sweet reminder of spring. I grow enough that I can enjoy the spears straight from the garden as well, peeking under my cloche to check on how high they've grown, snipping carefully with scissors, then back to the kitchen with my haul to make the freshest, sweetest, and most succulent bundle of asparagus in Vermont.

1 pound (14 to 18 stalks) white asparagus
6 tablespoons unsalted butter
½ cup white wine
Grated zest and juice of 1 large lemon
2 garlic cloves, smashed
Salt
1 cup panko breadcrumbs
2 tablespoons finely chopped fresh chervil or curly parsley
Freshly ground black pepper
2 tablespoons white wine vinegar

Using a vegetable peeler, gently peel the asparagus stalks just up to the floret. The outer layer of store-bought white asparagus can be a bit woody and stringy (fresh from the garden, it's supertender), so it's recommended that you peel a small portion of the outer membrane. Bend the stalk toward the end to snap off any wood ends (if just harvested, you don't need to peel or to snap off ends).

Combine 2 cups of water, 4 tablespoons of the butter, the wine, lemon juice (reserve the zest for now), and smashed garlic in a deep skillet. Bring to a simmer and season with salt. Add the asparagus and cook for 4 to 5 minutes, until tender, and then drain. Set aside.

Melt the remaining 2 tablespoons of butter in a separate small skillet over medium heat. Add the panko and cook, stirring with a wooden spoon, until it turns golden brown. Remove from the heat and stir in the chervil and the reserved lemon zest. Season with salt and pepper.

Arrange the asparagus on a platter. Drizzle with the vinegar and season with salt and pepper. Sprinkle the panko mixture over the asparagus.

Stuffed Grape Leaves

MAKES 80 TO 100

Leif Eriksson, every elementary school kid's favorite Viking, named the lands he visited in North America "Vinland," a.k.a. the land of wild grapes. Any gardening New Englander can attest to his observational rectitude by the ubiquity of wild grape vines squirreling their way through our landscape. After years of yanking and cursing at the things dragging down my lilac and elderberry branches, it took me struggling to open a jar of brined grape leaves (that had been packed in Greece in the last century, shipped across the ocean, and costing a Viking's plunder) to get it into my thick skull that the vines I had been wrestling with in my backyard were loaded with FREE GRAPE LEAVES. At a moment's craving, I can grab a basket, gambol out the back door to Mama Goose's coop where a male wild vine (wild grape vines are male and female) has nestled into the weathered barn boards and crawled up and over into my elderberry, and strip my nemesis of its precious greenery in minutes: a bit of backyard foraging laced with sweet, sweet revenge. My favorite filling for grape leaves is a meaty riff off Greek dolmas, those bright and succulent parcels that work beautifully as an appetizer but just as well as a full meal. Now, that's *delicious* revenge.

100-plus fresh grape leaves (choose the most tender of the large leaves that are a slightly lighter green), or one 16-ounce jar brined grape leaves

Salt

½ cup plus 5 tablespoons extra-virgin olive oil

4 large lemons

1½ cups uncooked long-grain white rice

2 large garlic cloves, minced

12 ounces 80/20 ground beef

Freshly ground black pepper

1 large yellow onion, roughly chopped

2 large eggs

1 cup fresh flat-leaf parsley, finely chopped

½ cup fresh dill, finely chopped

½ cup fresh mint, finely chopped

1 teaspoon kosher salt

½ teaspoon ground white pepper

4 cups low-sodium chicken stock

½ cup finely chopped fresh scapes (optional)

Rinse the grape leaves, whether fresh or brined, and remove the bottom stems.

For fresh leaves, fill a large bowl with ice water and set aside. Bring a Dutch oven of lightly salted water to a boil and, working in batches of seven or eight leaves at a time, boil the leaves for about 1 minute, or until they start to change to a darker, olive color. Remove with a slotted spoon and immediately submerge in the ice water. Repeat with the remaining leaves. Once finished, rinse and dry the Dutch oven, pour in 3 tablespoons of the olive oil to coat the bottom of the pot, and then line the bottom with a few of your rattiest and torn grape leaves to create a barrier between the Dutch oven and the stuffed grape leaves. You'll need about 12. Cut one of the lemons into very thin slices and place them on top of the leaves in an even layer.

recipe continues . . .

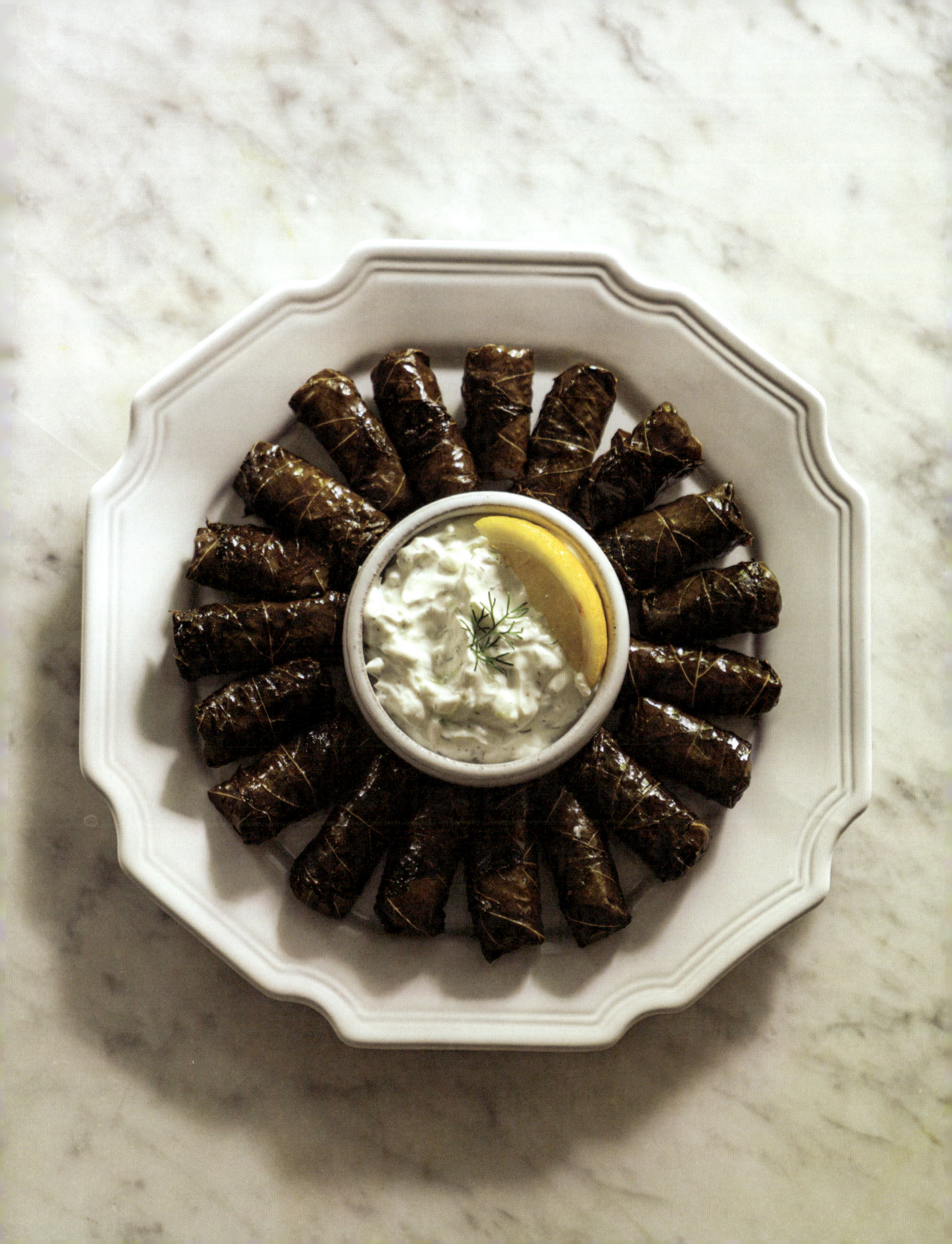

Rinse the rice in a fine sieve, using your fingers like a little claw to stir the rice as you rinse, to make sure every kernel gets a shower. Transfer the rice to a large bowl and cover with cool water. Allow to sit, covered, for at least 20 minutes. This is crucial, as you will be adding the rice to the filling uncooked. This process of rinsing and then soaking allows the granules to soak up a bit of moisture, ensuring that the rice is cooked perfectly along with the remaining ingredients.

Place the minced garlic in a small bowl. Zest and juice two of the lemons, and stir into the garlic. Set aside. (This process of combining a weak acid with the garlic mellows the "bite" of the garlic. See page 44.)

Spread the ground beef in a skillet and season with salt and pepper. Brown over medium-high heat until no pink remains. Transfer to a large bowl. To the same skillet, add 2 tablespoons of the olive oil and the chopped onion. Season the onion with salt and pepper, and sauté until translucent. Add to the bowl that contains the beef, and allow both to cool to room temperature.

Drain the rice and add to the bowl along with the beef, onion, eggs, parsley, dill, mint, garlic mixture, remaining ½ cup of olive oil, and the kosher salt and white pepper. Stir well to combine.

Pat the reserved grape leaves dry with a paper towel. Take a single grape leaf and lay it on a cutting board with the stem end toward you and the rib side up. Drop a scant tablespoon of filling onto the middle of the leaf but closer to the stem end. Wrap the leaf around the filling by folding the stem side up and over the filling, folding the sides toward the middle, and then rolling the package away from you to create a tight roll, like a mini cigar. Continue with the rest! Place each rolled grape leaf, seam side down, in a tight, even layer over the layer of lemons in the Dutch oven. Continue to add more layers of stuffed leaves on top of the first layer until all your stuffed grape leaves are arranged in the Dutch oven.

Place the chicken stock in a saucepan and bring to a boil. Carefully pour the hot stock over the stuffed grape leaves in the Dutch oven, making sure they are just covered with the stock. If they aren't, boil enough water to add to the Dutch oven so that they are all covered with liquid.

Take a heatproof plate, slightly smaller than the pot, and gently lay it on top of the stuffed grape leaves, to keep them from bouncing around and unwrapping as they are cooking. Over high heat, bring the stock to a boil and then cover the pot with the lid, lower the heat to medium-low, and continue to cook for 1 hour 15 minutes.

To serve, arrange on a serving platter and drizzle with a little extra olive oil, sprinkle with chopped scapes, if using, and serve with Tzatziki (page 262) and the remaining lemon, quartered. Store leftovers in an airtight container in the fridge for up to 2 weeks.

A NOTE FROM MY KITCHEN GARDEN

Grape Love

DOMESTICATED GRAPES ARE SELF-POLLINATING, OR HERMAPHRODITIC: THEY all make fruit and carry both the male and female plant "parts." Wild grapes, however, are either male *or* female; in fancy plant language that's *dioecious*. Bottom line is, you need both for fruit to develop. The majority of the vines on my property are male. There are two that are female and produce fruit. I grab leaves from only the males, and what little fruit appears on the female fruits, I make into jam in late summer (if I can beat the birds to the clusters). You'll find this need for male and female plants for successful fruiting in several plants, hardy kiwi being one. And in some cases, you simply need more than one of a type, such as with apples and plums (unless there are multiple varietals grafted to a single plant, so that the single tree produces different types of apples and, essentially, self-pollinates). I had a friend who planted a single Italian plum tree and assumed that she'd bought a faulty plant because it never flowered . . . until I explained that she needed another plum tree, any plum tree, for it to fruit. Most peach trees are self-pollinating and don't need another peach tree to bear fruit, but they'll bear even *more* fruit if they have a peachy friend. For wild plants, you just have to go with the flow and celebrate when you get some fruit—and make stuffed grape leaves when you don't. But if you're planning an orchard or a small fruiting garden, do a little research into what type of companionship each type of plant needs, if any, to live its best life.

Spring-Dug Parsnip and Cheese Soufflé

SERVES 6

A few crops overwinter, meaning that they hibernate in the ground during the winter months. The most obvious is garlic, whereby a single clove is planted in the late fall so that it may establish a healthy root system and then springs to action in, well, the spring. There's asparagus, a perennial whose crowns stay put in the same patch and gift us with lovely spears year after year. And then we have spring-dug parsnip, a root veggie you can (and should) harvest in the late fall after the first frost but that you can also leave to overwinter in the ground, where its starches are converted to sugars. That sweetness blends with its inherent nuttiness and, assuming they have survived critters and potential rot, parsnips are a wonderful treat when nothing else is on the go in New England. Blended together with some local sharp Cheddar, they make for a delicate and flavorsome soufflé that showcases the earthy sweetness of a veggie that's been hibernating all winter.

- 4 tablespoons unsalted butter, plus 1 tablespoon for soufflé dish
- ¼ cup unbleached all-purpose flour, plus a few tablespoons for soufflé dish
- 1 pound spring-dug parsnips, peeled and cut into ½-inch pieces
- 2 cups low-sodium chicken stock
- 4 ounces sharp Cheddar, shredded
- 2 teaspoons kosher salt
- 1 tablespoon creamy prepared horseradish
- 1 tablespoon pure maple syrup
- 1 tablespoon dried thyme leaves
- 6 large eggs, separated
- 1 teaspoon white wine vinegar

Place a rack in the middle of the oven and preheat to 400°F (200°C).

Butter an 8-cup soufflé dish, add a few tablespoons of flour, and turn the soufflé dish to coat the bottom and sides of the dish. Discard any flour not adhered to the butter. Set the dish aside in the refrigerator until needed.

Combine the parsnips and chicken stock in a large saucepan. Bring to a boil over high heat, then lower the heat to low and simmer, covered, until the parsnips are fork-tender, 10 to 15 minutes.

Using a slotted spoon, transfer the parsnips to a food processor (reserving 1 cup of the cooking liquid) and process until smooth. Transfer to a bowl and stir in the Cheddar and salt. Set aside.

Melt the 4 tablespoons butter in a saucepan over medium heat, add the ¼ cup flour, and whisk constantly until the mixture thickens and just begins to brown. Add the horseradish, maple syrup, and thyme, then pour in the cup of the reserved parsnip-cooking liquid, whisking constantly until the mixture has thickened, about 5 minutes. Remove from the heat and whisk in the cheesy parsnip puree.

In the bowl of a stand mixer fitted with the whisk attachment, or using a metal bowl and metal whisk, whisk the egg whites with the vinegar until they reach medium-stiff peaks. Make sure not to overbeat the egg whites—if they dry up and look "chunky," they will not fold into the remaining mixture properly.

Stir the egg yolks into the parsnip mixture until fully incorporated, then gently fold in the whisked egg whites in three batches. Pour the mixture into the prepared soufflé dish and bake until puffy and golden brown, 40 to 45 minutes. Serve immediately. The soufflé will slowly collapse if left too long before serving, but will still be delicious.

MY HARVEST KITCHEN

Homemade Ramp-Infused Farmer Cheese

MAKES 2 CUPS

In the first ephemeral days of spring, when the ramps and morels reveal themselves in the woodland, it's time to leave the winter hibernation behind and to strike out into the forest. Or into the backyard. Although ramps are most often found under dappled light in slightly boggy conditions, I have managed to cultivate these wild things along a ravine under my ancient apple tree on the back acre of our land. During the spring, when our local co-op offers ramps, they come with roots and bulbs intact. When foraging, however, I take just the leaves and a bit of stem, leaving the bulbs behind so that they can continue giving us vernal goodness each year. I buy what is acceptable at the co-op, use the stems and leaves for cooking, and plant the bulbs along the ravine to add to my growing patch. Add freshly foraged ramps to a surprisingly easy-to-make simple farmer cheese.

2 quarts organic whole milk
¼ cup distilled white vinegar
¼ cup finely chopped ramp leaves
1 teaspoon kosher salt

Line a large colander with a piece of moistened cheesecloth and place in a large bowl in the sink.

Pour the milk into a Dutch oven and bring to a gentle simmer (do not boil). The mixture should read 190°F (88°C) on a digital thermometer. Stir occasionally to keep the milk from scorching.

Remove from the heat and stir in the vinegar. The milk should immediately begin to curdle and form curds.

Allow the mixture to sit for 20 minutes without stirring. After the 20 minutes, gently stir in the ramps and then immediately pour the mixture into the lined colander. Draw the edges of the cheesecloth together and twist, squeezing to remove as much moisture as possible from the curds and into the bowl. The liquid is whey and you can drink it!

Keeping the cheese in the cheesecloth, transfer the "parcel" to a plate. Sprinkle the salt over the cheese, and then, using a spoon, gently mix to distribute the salt. Gather the cheesecloth again and gently use it to compact the cheese into a little wheel of cheese, 4 to 5 inches across. Tie up the cheesecloth with butcher's twine to create a tight bundle. Place in an airtight container. Eat within 1 week of making.

Creamed Spinach and Ramps

SERVES 4

Ramp season is ephemeral. Literally. This wild onion with deeply green, delicate leaves that taper into a grape-size bulb whose roots are barely tethered to the thawing forest floor, appears for only a few weeks in the spring. The timing is just right to coincide with the first baby spinach in the garden. Often, ramps are pureed into a pesto, but I find that using them in a recipe that can actually showcase their garlicky and oniony goodness while adding to the overall "bulk" is a lovely thing. And as the traditional flavor components that bring *zing* to the dish are often reaching the very tail end of their flavor and storing life when ramps show themselves, it's as if ramps are waving at you from the forest floor, saying, "Put me in, coach!"

4 tablespoons unsalted butter

1½ pounds fresh baby spinach, cleaned

8 ounces ramp leaves, cleaned and chopped into thirds

2 tablespoons unbleached all-purpose flour

Pinch of freshly grated nutmeg

1½ cups heavy cream

½ cup low-sodium chicken stock

1 cup crème fraîche or full-fat sour cream

2 ounces aged Cheddar,* finely grated with a Microplane grater (about ½ cup)

Kosher salt and freshly ground black pepper

Melt the butter in a Dutch oven over medium heat. Add the spinach and ramps, stirring and turning over the leaves with a wooden spoon so that they wilt evenly. Sprinkle with the flour and nutmeg, turning the spinach and ramp mixture continuously to incorporate the flour so that no dry clumps remain. Add the heavy cream and chicken stock, stirring to combine, then lower the heat and continue to cook, stirring occasionally, until the greens are incredibly soft and the cream has thickened, about 45 minutes.

Remove from the heat and stir in the crème fraîche, then sprinkle with the Cheddar and season with salt and pepper. Serve immediately.

>*NOTE Instead of Cheddar, you can use the same amount of Parmigiano-Reggiano, as is traditional in this recipe, but I enjoy using a local ingredient that brings a similar punch of salt and creaminess.

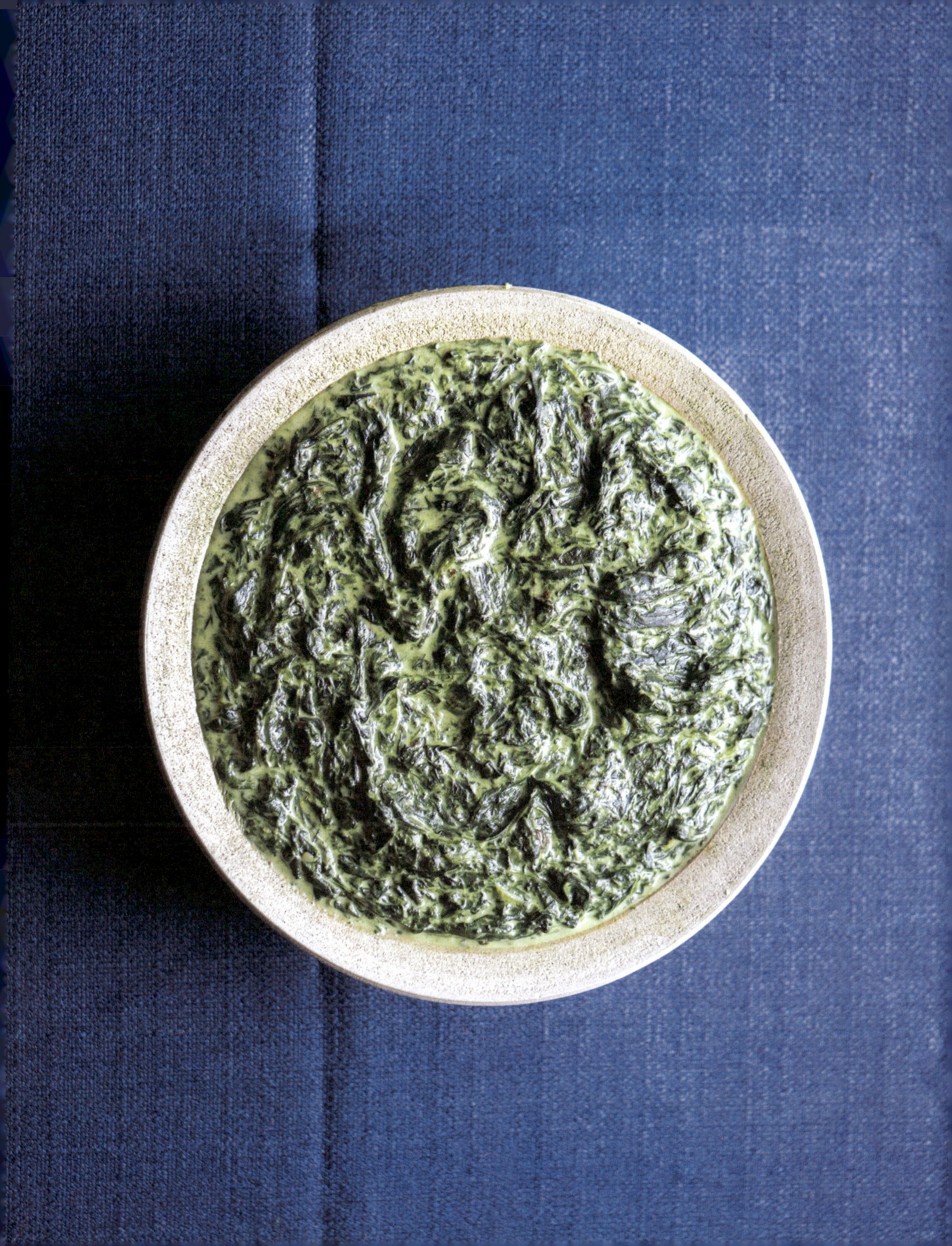

MY HARVEST KITCHEN

French Tomato–Goat Cheese Tart

SERVES 10

One of the wonders of early September is that with the unrelenting drumbeat of back-to-school, off to college, schedule schedule schedule, there are also sweet heirloom orbs piled up, waiting for you. When all the relaxation of summer has ended and the stress of new beginnings overwhelms, give yourself this gift. This tart. Make a quick pâte brisée crust, slice up a sweet onion, grab a handful of herbs and some tomatoes, slice up a creamy wheel of soft goat cheese, and you're in heaven.

FOR THE PÂTE BRISÉE

1½ cups (180 grams) unbleached all-purpose flour

½ teaspoon sea salt

8 tablespoons (113 grams) unsalted butter, very cold

1 large egg

1 tablespoon cold water

FOR THE FILLING

3 or 4 heirloom tomatoes, plus a handful of cherry and/or spoon tomatoes

1 small sweet onion

1 tablespoon Dijon mustard

Kosher salt

4 ounces soft French goat cheese, such as Bucheron, cut into four or five ¼-inch slices

Leaves from 3 thyme sprigs

Leaves from 3 oregano sprigs

2 tablespoons honey

2 tablespoons extra-virgin olive oil

MAKE THE PÂTE BRISÉE

Stir together the flour and sea salt in a medium bowl. Using the largest holes of a box grater, grate the butter into the flour mixture. Using the tips of your fingers, work the butter into the flour until the mixture resembles cornmeal. Whisk together the egg and cold water in a small bowl, then pour over the flour mixture. Use a rubber spatula to toss the dry and wet together, then use the spatula in a slicing motion to slice through larger wet clumps. Use your palm or fist to compress the dough and "schmear" to compact the dough. Gather the dough into a smooth disk. Cover with plastic wrap and refrigerate for at least 20 minutes to overnight.

MAKE THE FILLING

While the dough chills, preheat the oven to 400°F (200°C). Slice the heirloom tomatoes into ¼-inch rounds and cut any cherry tomatoes in half. Slice the onion into ¼-inch rounds.

Roll out the dough into a 12-inch round. Line a 9-inch tart pan with the dough. Spread the mustard on the bottom of the tart shell. Arrange a layer of onions and then place the large tomato slices on top, close together but not overlapping. Top the tomato slices with the goat cheese slices and then scatter the top with cherry tomato halves. Season lightly with kosher salt. Sprinkle with half of the herbs and drizzle with the honey. Bake for 20 to 25 minutes, until the edges of the tart shell are golden and the goat cheese has taken on some color. Remove from the oven, drizzle with the olive oil, and sprinkle with the remaining herbs and spoon tomatoes.

ON TOMATOES

TOMATOES come in two types: determinate and indeterminate. Determinate plants are smaller, bushlike, and usually need just a bit of staking to keep them upright. They are the perfect tomato plants for containers, living happily on a sunny balcony or any small space. Determinate tomatoes also fruit all at the same time. Think of it as "one and done": they set fruit in one go and the harvest is singular. This is great if you have a plan for tomatoes, because you'll have all you need when they ripen simultaneously.

Indeterminate tomatoes keep growing for as long as the weather and pest/disease conditions allow. A 7-foot-tall indeterminate tomato plant is not an unusual thing in my garden, as long as I stake it properly. And that's the thing: you need a support system that can, well, support, a plant that will grow up and out and then bear weight of fruit on its branches. Speaking of fruit, it's a constant flow of flowers, fruit set, and ripening. There's no single time period to account for when everything ripens. If you plan well, you can get tomatoes for months. In Vermont, it's not unheard of to get a frost before tomatoes fully ripen, so I make sure to start my tomatoes *very* early indoors and continue to pot up, so that by the time my plants are hardened (that's a period of time spent acclimating vulnerable seedlings that have been safe inside. I take 10 days, increasing plants' time outside by an hour until they can safely spend an entire day outside; otherwise, they can be sunburnt), they are already setting fruit and starting to ripen in June. It takes a boatload of work, and I tend to lose track of what plant is what variety of tomato as I get lazy from all the repotting, but that works itself out once I see the tomatoes.

Issues arise on all tomatoes, though, no matter how vigilant the gardener. There is early blight, late blight, blossom-end rot (caused by too much water, too little water, or both), and hornworm. That's just a few of the problems. Sometimes, it's easy enough to fix by mulching with straw or, as I do, dry grass from a mow. This keeps water from splashing on the leaves and causing fungal infections. Be careful to keep ahead of the problem by eradicating any blighted foliage. If it's very dry, make sure to water more frequently to prevent blossom-end rot, but that rot can also occur with too much rain, which is tough to fix unless you can control the weather. And for hornworms—creatures that are virtually impossible to see in the daylight and can munch through a plant in a day—you can get a blacklight and have a little party after dark. Hornworms glow in the dark like neon ravers and are easily picked off by hand. Because the hornworm transforms into fabulous sphinx or hawk moth, also known as the hummingbird moth, I've come to carefully pluck them from my main harvest plants and transfer them to "volunteer" tomatoes (tomatoes that I didn't purposefully plant in that growing year but happen to self-seed from a tomato I wasn't able to harvest in time). These plants tend to grow in a bed that I've since rotated, growing another non-nightshade crop, so I keep the plant for the hornworms and don't concern myself with the damage.

You'd think after reading all this that I'd never grow another tomato again. Au contraire! I tend to grow more tomatoes every year, not including my volunteers. Even with the inevitable issues, I still get a great crop of tomatoes that I use to make sauces and salsas. And then I freeze pounds for use in the hibernating times, when sweet summer tomatoes are but a distant memory in the garden but just waiting to bring back their full flavor after a quick thaw.

Ugly Tomato Cheesy Bean Dip

SERVES 12

When tomatoes are at the end of the season and there are disparate varieties looking worse for wear from blight or excess (or lack of) rain but there's enough that look superjuicy, there's always that question of what to do with tomatoes that are so ugly you are tempted to just toss them out for the squirrels and birds. But there's another solution: cut off what's not working and roast the rest for an unbelievably yummy end-of-season dip. I choose to cook my favorite beans from scratch, but you can use canned beans to make this even zippier. Roasting the tomatoes brings out their complexity and utter sweetness and allows you to pluck off any skins before you work them into the mixture.

- 1 pound dried white beans, or two 15-ounce cans cannellini beans
- 1 pound superripe tomatoes
- 1 medium onion, finely chopped
- 4 garlic cloves, thinly sliced
- 2 tablespoons chili crisp
- ¼ cup extra-virgin olive oil
- 8 ounces cream cheese
- Salt and freshly ground black pepper
- 4 cups baby spinach
- 10 ounces low-moisture mozzarella, shredded
- 4 ounces sharp Cheddar, shredded

If using dried beans, soak them in water in a large bowl for a minimum of 2 hours to overnight. Make sure the water covers the beans by at least 2 inches. Drain the beans and cook per the package instructions. Once cooked, drain but keep ½ cup of the cooking liquid. If using canned beans, drain all but ½ cup of the liquid. Set aside.

Preheat the oven to 450°F (230°C). Line a sheet pan with a silicone baking mat. Place the tomatoes on the prepared pan, flesh side down if you are using pieces, and toss with 2 tablespoons of the olive oil. Roast for 20 minutes, or until the tomatoes are very soft. Remove from the oven, leave the oven on, and using tongs or culinary tweezers, pluck the tomato skins from the flesh. Place the roasted tomato flesh in a bowl. Set aside.

Heat the remaining 2 tablespoons of olive oil in a large ovenproof skillet or enameled braiser over medium heat and sauté the onion until just translucent, about 5 minutes. Add the garlic and continue to cook for 2 more minutes. Add the tomato flesh and cook out any excess juices, about 5 more minutes.

Add the cream cheese to the skillet and, using a wooden spoon, break up the block into smaller pieces and stir until the cream cheese has melted. Add the chili crisp, beans, and reserved bean liquid. Stir to combine and season to taste, and then fold in the spinach and cook until wilted, about 2 minutes. Sprinkle with the mozzarella and Cheddar, then bake for 10 minutes, or until the cheese has melted and is slightly browned. Serve with hearty slices of Crusty Bread (page 248). For a great breakfast, serve with fried eggs and some homemade Corn Tortillas (page 254).

NIBBLES & SIDES

MY HARVEST KITCHEN

Käse Spätzle
(Mini Dumplings and Cheese)

SERVES 4 TO 6

German cheese dumplings are better than mac and cheese. Better is relative, so don't yell at me! I'll tell you why I love one more than the other, in one word: texture. When you make a fresh batch of spätzle, draining the tender dumplings, and then adding them to a pan sizzling with butter, you add a gentle, caramelized crisp to the outside but the inside is still tender. The taste is well, comforting, just like a noodle but with the added benefit of the gentle caramelization adding depth of tastiness that's brought about by adding that *texture*. Then, you quickly add a soft, mild, yet flavorful cheese that melts quickly and coats perfectly without being gloopy. A pinch of nutmeg just makes everything sing, and then topping with crispy onion doubles down on flavor and texture. Top with a bright sprinkling of parsley fresh from the garden and, if you're feeling jaunty, add a bit of crispy bacon. You can thank me later.

FOR THE SPÄTZLE BATTER

¾ cup (180 ml) lukewarm water (98 to 110°F [36 to 43°C])
2 large eggs
1 teaspoon fine sea salt
2 cups (240 grams) unbleached all-purpose flour

FOR THE CRISPY ONION

1 large sweet onion, such as Vidalia, finely chopped
2 cups neutral oil, such as canola
Pinch of kosher or fine sea salt

FOR THE SAUCE

2 tablespoons unsalted butter
½ cup heavy cream
4 ounces soft mild cheese such as Monterey Jack, shredded
Pinch of freshly grated nutmeg
Herbamare herbed sea salt or fine sea salt
Ground white pepper

1 small bunch flat-leaf parsley, leaves roughly chopped

MAKE THE SPÄTZLE BATTER

Combine the water, eggs, and salt in a large bowl. Add the flour and stir with a wooden spoon until smooth. Cover and allow to rest for 10 to 15 minutes.

MAKE THE CRISPY ONION

Place the chopped onion in a large, deep skillet and just cover with the oil. Cook over high heat until the onion is golden brown, about 10 minutes. Pour the onion and oil through a sieve over a heatproof vessel. Drain the onions well, reserving 1 tablespoon of the onion oil for this recipe (you can keep the rest to use for another recipe), and immediately transfer the onion to a clean paper towel and sprinkle with salt. When cool, store in a resealable plastic bag.

COOK THE SPÄTZLE

Bring a large stockpot of water, seasoned with a generous pinch of salt, to a high simmer

recipe continues . . .

over medium-high heat. Place your spätzle lid on the pot, or use your spätzle maker of choice or a potato ricer with the largest holes. Using the flat side of a bowl scraper, scrape about ½ to 1 cup of the batter through the holes and into the water. Allow the spätzle to cook about 2 minutes; they should have risen to the top. Use a strainer or spider to drain the spätzle and transfer to a dish. Repeat in batches until all of the batter is used. Toss the spätzle in the reserved tablespoon of onion oil.

MAKE THE SAUCE
Melt the butter in a large, clean skillet. Add the cooked spätzle and cook, stirring, over medium-high heat until they get a little crisp and brown on some of the edges. Lower the heat to medium and add the cream. Stir to coat and then add the cheese, stirring until melted. Season with the nutmeg, Herbamare, and white pepper. Transfer to a serving bowl, then top with crispy onions and a bit of parsley.

NOTE The dumplings will start to absorb moisture from the cheese as it cools, drying out the sauce. If you need to reheat the spätzle and the sauce has dried out, add about ¼ cup of water to reliquefy the cheese as you are reheating. Adding a small amount of water helps to rehydrate the cheese and make it smooth again.

Leeks Vinaigrette

SERVES 4

The summer after I graduated from college, the same summer I worked in the gardens of Giverny, I had my first leeks vinaigrette. My best friend Christine and I were backpacking around Europe and we stayed with her friend Freddy and his family in Lyon. We had dinner outside, and his mother served us a casserole dish with incredibly unexciting giant leeks. I was still a vegetarian at the time (having been raised vegetarian then vegan but transitioning back to dairy), and our poor host didn't quite know what to do with me and my dietary demands. She made a French summer staple with a board of gorgeous cheeses and bread to round out the meal. I wasn't convinced it was for me, but the leeks dish went down effortlessly. It managed to be both punchy in flavor yet elegantly simple.

8 medium leeks

Salt

3 tablespoons red wine vinegar

1 tablespoon Dijon mustard

Freshly ground black pepper

⅓ cup extra-virgin olive oil

Chopped fresh tarragon, for garnish

Trim the root end of the leeks and then slice the leeks lengthwise, starting at the leaf end and down toward the root end but not cutting all the way through. Rinse the leeks, using the spray nozzle of your faucet (if you have one) to remove any sandy dirt, then place the leeks in a large bowl of water to soak for 5 minutes and dislodge any extra dirt or sand. Do this a few more times, rinsing with the spray nozzle and soaking so that you've rinsed and soaked four times total.

Fill a rondeau or wide saucepan with water and a generous pinch of salt. Bring to a hearty simmer and add the leeks. Simmer until tender, 8 to 10 minutes. Using tongs, gently transfer the leeks to a cooling rack set over a sheet pan.

Whisk together the vinegar and mustard in a small bowl. Season with salt and pepper and then slowly pour in the olive oil while vigorously whisking to emulsify the vinaigrette.

Place the leeks in a serving dish and, while still warm, coat with the vinaigrette, 1 tablespoon at a time, allowing the leeks to absorb the vinaigrette. Sprinkle with tarragon and serve at room temperature.

Summer-to-Fall Focaccia

SERVES 8

"Summer" is relative; you can make this recipe *any* time. But when my garden and farmers' market are overflowing with bright veggies just waiting to be turned into edible art, I tend to make this recipe often.

FOR THE DOUGH*

700 grams water
700 grams unbleached all-purpose flour
300 grams unbleached bread flour
55 grams extra-virgin olive oil
15 grams sea salt
7 grams (1 packet) instant yeast

TO FINISH

Nonstick cooking spray
6 tablespoons extra-virgin olive oil
Medley of vegetables to decorate

MAKE THE DOUGH

Pour 650 grams of the water into a large bowl. Add both flours and mix with a wooden spoon or Danish dough whisk until the flour and water are completely combined. (You may need to use your hands a bit.) Cover and allow to sit at room temperature for 30 minutes to 1 hour. This process is called *autolyse* and allows the flour to hydrate and gluten to be produced without mechanically mixing. The other ingredients in the dough interfere with the flour's getting full access to the water, so they are left out at this stage.

Add the remaining 50 grams of water, the 55 grams of olive oil, and the salt and yeast. Use your hands in a pincerlike manner to incorporate the ingredients into the dough. This can take a few minutes. Alternatively, you can use a mixer on low speed for this process. The water and oil will slop around for a bit without combining, so be patient.

Allow the dough to sit at room temperature, covered, until doubled in size. This will take from 45 minutes to 2 hours, depending on the temperature of the room and the temperature of the dough. Once doubled, keep covered and refrigerate the dough overnight, about 8 hours. This rest creates loads of flavor.

Spray a sheet pan lightly with nonstick cooking spray and then add 3 tablespoons of the finishing olive oil to the surface, spreading with a pastry brush or your hands. Add the dough and use your fingertips to spread the dough. It doesn't need to fill the entire space as it will continue to expand outward and upward during the proof. Spread the remaining 3 tablespoons of olive oil over the top of the dough.

Place the veggies decoratively on top of the dough and cover loosely with plastic wrap. Allow to proof at room temperature until doubled in size, about 1 hour. During this time, preheat the oven to 375ºF (190ºC).

Bake for 20 to 25 minutes, until the dough is golden brown and crisp on the top and bottom.

*NOTE For accuracy, please weigh the dough ingredients.

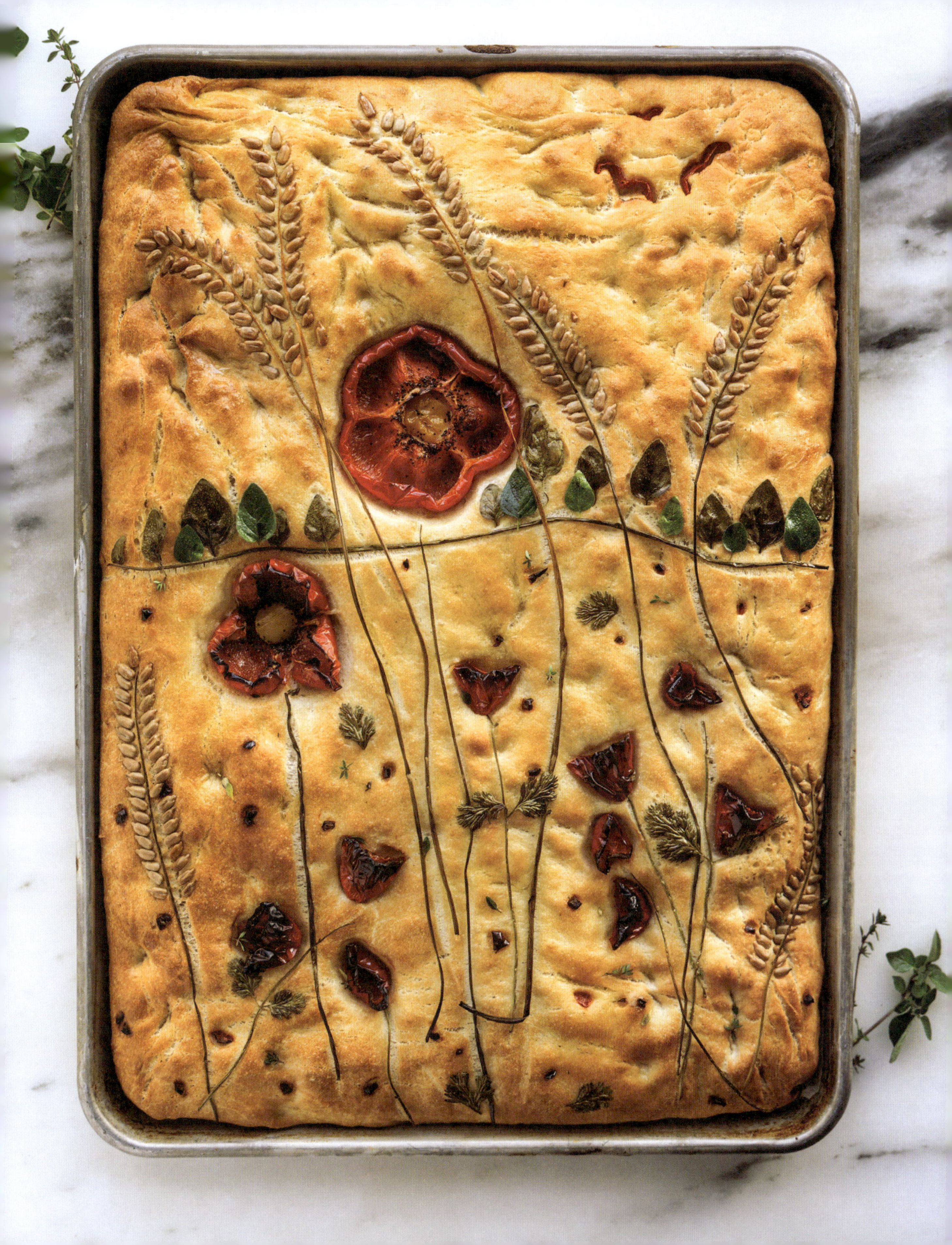

MY HARVEST KITCHEN

Upside-Down Leek Tart

SERVES 12

As with onions, I sow seeds for their cousin, the leek, inside in late winter. Harvested in August and kept in a cool, dark place, they store incredibly well. If you find yourself in possession of seeds in the summer and want to get to planting ASAP, you can plant seedlings in the late summer or early fall and, like garlic, allow them to overwinter in the ground for a spring harvest. What's also great about leeks is that you don't have to grow them yourself; you can find beautiful specimens in the grocery store all year long because of their nimble growing season. Which is perfect for this tart that's a staple in the cooler months in our house but works just as well on the dinner table in late spring or summer.

2 tablespoons pure maple syrup

1 tablespoon unsalted butter, at room temperature

3 ounces sharp Cheddar, shredded

4 ounces cream cheese, cold

1 teaspoon dried thyme

1 teaspoon red pepper flakes

Kosher salt

3 large leeks, root ends and dark greens removed (save for stock), cut in half lengthwise

One 3-ounce package prosciutto, 5 to 6 slices total

Unbleached all-purpose flour, for dusting

½ batch G's Zippy, Flaky Pie Dough (page 239), cold

Fresh thyme leaves, for garnish

Preheat the oven to 400°F (200°C). Line a half sheet pan with a silicone baking mat or with parchment. Smash together 1 tablespoon of the maple syrup and the butter in a small bowl, then schmear the mixture into a rough 13-inch square on the prepared pan. Set aside.

Place the Cheddar in a small bowl and crumble the cream cheese over it. Use your fingertips to combine the two. Sprinkle with the dried thyme, the red pepper flakes, and a pinch of salt, and toss with a spoon to distribute the additions. Drizzle the remaining tablespoon of maple syrup over the mixture and toss again.

Trim the leeks to about 10 inches long and arrange them, cut side down, over the maple-butter mixture on the sheet pan. Drape the prosciutto over the leeks and then evenly sprinkle the cheese mixture over the prosciutto.

On a flour-dusted work surface, roll out the pie dough to a rough 13-inch square and trim with a very sharp knife into a 12-inch square. Dock the dough with a fork, poking holes all over the dough, and then drape the dough over the leeks. Bake for 40 to 45 minutes, until the pastry is golden brown and puffed.

Remove from the oven, place a large serving platter over the tart and, using oven mitts, invert the tart onto the platter. Remove the sheet pan and then carefully peel off the silicone mat or parchment. Top with a sprinkle of fresh thyme and season with kosher salt. Serve warm or cool.

Creamed Savoy Cabbage

SERVES 4

I love Savoy cabbage for its sweet delicacy. I also love to grow it, because, while it differs in flavor from traditional green cabbages, it still grows in a tight ball, keeping all of its leaves close, so that any critters interested in a snack are a bit limited in what they can get to. Savoy doesn't have the keeping quality that its cousins have; once harvested, it has to be used within two weeks. Traditional cabbage, on the other hand, can be kept quite happily in the crisper for up to two months. If you only can get your mitts on traditional green cabbage, it is a perfect substitute. In that case, I'll often add a teaspoon of maple syrup to make up for the slight loss in subtle sweetness.

1 large head Savoy cabbage or green cabbage (2 pounds)

4 tablespoons unsalted butter

1 large yellow onion, finely chopped

Salt

½ cup low-sodium chicken stock

½ cup heavy cream

1 tablespoon unbleached all-purpose flour

1 tablespoon creamy horseradish

1 teaspoon pure maple syrup (optional)

Ground white pepper

Remove and discard the outer leaves of the cabbage, then quarter, core, and cut into ½-inch strips.

Melt the butter in a Dutch oven over medium heat, add the onion and a generous pinch of salt, and sauté until translucent. Add the cabbage, sprinkle with the flour, and another generous pinch of salt, and cook, stirring occasionally, until reduced by half and beginning to caramelize, 10 to 15 minutes.

Stir in the chicken stock and scrape up any fond from the bottom of the pan. Cover and lower the heat to low. Cook for 5 more minutes.

Stir together the heavy cream, creamy horseradish, and maple syrup (if using) in a small bowl. Remove the cabbage from the heat and stir in the cream mixture. Season to taste with salt and white pepper. Serve alone or stir into gently browned Sour Cream Spätzle (page 115).

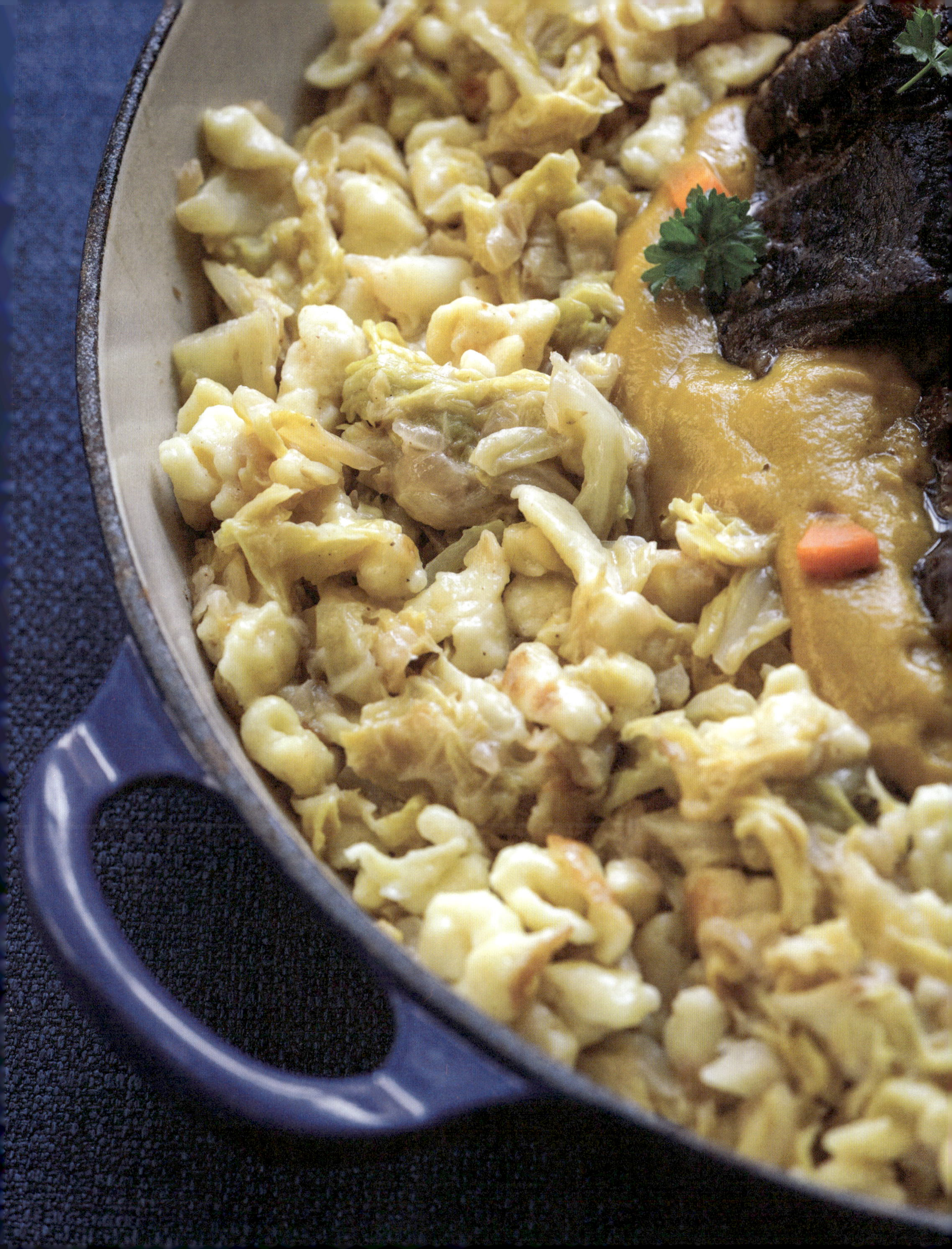

MY HARVEST KITCHEN

Sour Cream Spätzle

SERVES 6

Spätzle are often described as German pasta or as little dumplings. When they are made with quark or, in this case, with sour cream, they definitely lean toward dumplings. The soft cheese makes them incredibly tender. Although quark is traditional, it's not the easiest ingredient to find in the States. Sour cream, on the other hand, is readily available and provides the creaminess, fat, and gentle nudge of tartness that makes these little dumplings irresistible. You can eat them as is or fry them up a little with butter to add another layer of texture and caramelized flavor. And if you're feeling jaunty, fry them up and then fold them into Creamed Savoy Cabbage (page 112).

1 cup plus 1 tablespoon (240 grams) full-fat sour cream

4 large eggs

Salt

2 cups (240 grams) unbleached all-purpose flour

TO FRY (OPTIONAL)

2 tablespoons unsalted butter

Combine the sour cream, eggs, and a generous pinch of salt in a bowl and whisk together until smooth. Add the flour and stir with a wooden spoon until smooth. It should be the consistency of a thick pancake batter. Cover and refrigerate for 30 minutes.

Bring 2 quarts of lightly salted water to a hearty simmer in a stockpot over high heat. Using a spätzle maker (there are multiple types and all work well) or a potato ricer (using the largest opening plate), press the batter into the simmering water. Allow the dumplings to rise to the top, 2 to 3 minutes, before skimming them off and transferring to a large bowl. Once all the dumplings are cooked, eat immediately or fry them if you like: In a large skillet, melt the butter over medium-high heat. Gently fry the dumplings until they just start to take on a bit of golden-brown color.

Eggplant, Squash, Zucchini, and Tomato Casserole (Tian)

SERVES 4

At the end of the movie *Ratatouille*, the big dish finish is a *tian*, not a ratatouille. I'm sorry. It's true. Ratatouille, though containing many of the same ingredients, is prepared with more rusticity and contains peppers. A tian calls for the ingredients to be cut in the round and layered in a spiral (in a round dish) or in rows. You'd think that rusticity would signify "less time," but I've found just the opposite. It's faster and easier to go with the natural contours of the vegetables by cutting them into rounds. When you start cubing to specific sizes, things can get persnickety. The benefits of keeping it in the round makes for quicker prep work and, in the end, a more beautiful (and delicious) dish.

1 cup Fresh Tomato Pomodoro Sauce (page 261)
½ cup extra-virgin olive oil
2 medium-large zucchini (1 pound), cut into ¼-inch rounds
2 medium-large yellow summer squash (1 pound), cut into ¼-inch rounds
2 medium eggplants (1 pound),* cut into ¼-inch rounds
Salt and freshly ground black pepper
1 tablespoon fresh thyme leaves
1 tablespoon fresh oregano leaves

Preheat the oven to 450°F (230°C). Spread ½ cup of the pomodoro sauce in the bottom of a 2-quart round casserole or earthenware dish. Set aside.

Heat 3 tablespoons of the olive oil in a large grill pan or skillet over medium-high heat. Add the sliced vegetables, in batches—don't crowd the pan—and cook until both sides have a bit of golden brown and have softened slightly, 45 seconds to 1 minute on each side. Transfer to a parchment-lined sheet pan as they are finished.

Layer the cooked vegetables in overlapping circles in the prepared baking dish, starting at the outer edge and working toward the center and alternating between zucchini, yellow squash, and eggplant. Sprinkle each round with a bit of salt, a bit of pepper, and a sprinkling of thyme and oregano. Drizzle with the remaining tablespoon of olive oil and top with the remaining ½ cup of pomodoro sauce. Bake until the tian is heated through, about 20 minutes.

*NOTE Grow or look for more slender varieties, such as Japanese eggplant.

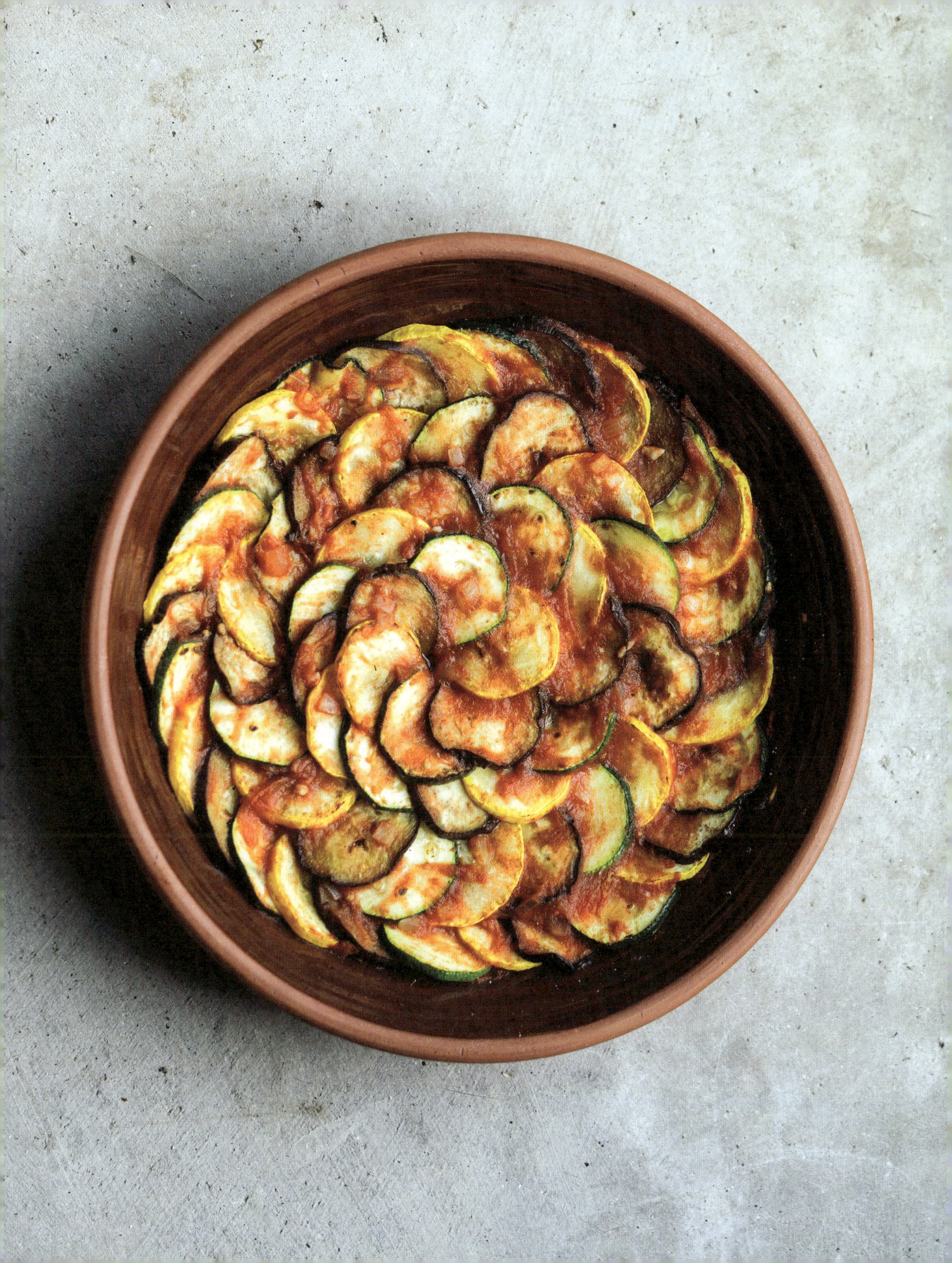

Green Mountain Arancini

MAKES 18 TO 20 ARANCINI

Arancini are what leftovers are meant to be: better than the original. Don't get me wrong, I love risotto, but I love leftover risotto turned into arancini more. Because I'm a good Vermonter and never without a 5-pound block of sharp Cheddar in the fridge, I tuck Cheddar cubes, instead of mozzarella, inside my arancini. I know this is blasphemy, but it's *so* good, *so* flavorful. You can, of course, use the cheese that makes you happy, but I will never go back to anything but Cheddar. I serve these during football season, heating up some Fresh Tomato Pomodoro Sauce (page 261) that I've stored in the freezer for this very occasion. It's Hope season, people, and breaking out last year's fresh tomato goodness will be just the nudge you need to do right by your tomato seedlings so you're never without a frozen batch of glorious pomodoro sauce *next* football season.

FOR THE RISOTTO

- ¼ cup extra-virgin olive oil
- 4 tablespoons unsalted butter
- 1 small onion, finely chopped
- 1½ cups uncooked risotto rice
- ½ cup dry white wine
- 4½ cups low-sodium chicken stock
- ¼ cup shredded aged sharp Cheddar
- Kosher salt and freshly ground black pepper

FOR THE ARANCINI

- 4 ounces sharp Cheddar, cut into ½-inch pieces
- 1 quart neutral oil, such as canola
- 2 cups panko breadcrumbs
- ½ cup unbleached all-purpose flour
- 2 large eggs
- Fresh Tomato Pomodoro Sauce (page 261), for serving

MAKE THE RISOTTO

Heat 2 tablespoons of the olive oil and 2 tablespoons of the butter in a skillet over medium heat. Add the onion and cook, stirring occasionally, until just translucent, about 5 minutes. Stir in the rice and white wine, and cook, stirring occasionally, over medium-high heat until the wine has almost entirely been absorbed by the rice.

Add the stock, ½ cup at a time, stirring occasionally, only adding the next ½ cup of stock once the first portion has been absorbed by the rice. Cook, stirring occasionally, until the rice is creamy and al dente (or to your textural preference). Stir in the ¼ cup Cheddar and season to taste with kosher salt and pepper. Transfer to a bowl, allow to cool to room temperature, then cover and refrigerate overnight. Alternatively, spread the mixture on a parchment-lined sheet pan, cover with plastic wrap, and refrigerate for 1 to 2 hours to bring the temperature down more quickly.

MAKE THE ARANCINI

Line a half sheet pan with parchment. Scoop ¼ cup of cooled risotto and flatten it into a 3-inch disk. Place a cube of Cheddar in the middle and gather the outer edge of the risotto disk up and over to completely encapsulate the cheese. Gently roll in your hands to create a perfect little ball. Place on the prepared sheet pan and continue in this manner with the remaining risotto and cheese. Refrigerate to firm up, covered loosely with plastic wrap, for 30 minutes to 1 hour.

Pour the oil into a Dutch oven or deep stockpot. Heat to 360 to 370°F (182 to 188°C), using a digital thermometer to keep tabs on the heat, making sure it doesn't dip below 350°F (180°C) or above 370°F (188°C).

While the oil is heating, process the panko in a food processor to create finer crumbs, or transfer it to a resealable plastic bag and use a rolling pin to crush the pieces into a finer powder. Transfer the crumbs to a shallow bowl, place the flour in a second shallow bowl, and whisk the eggs and transfer to a third shallow bowl. Set up your dredging station with the bowls lined up in the following order: flour, eggs, panko.

Dredge the balls in flour first, then roll in the eggs to coat. Transfer to the panko, pressing gently with your hands to adhere the crumbs to the sides of the balls. Fry the balls a few at a time, making sure they have room between them, lowering them into the oil with a spider or large slotted spoon. Fry for 5 to 6 minutes, until deep golden brown. Transfer to a paper towel to cool slightly. Serve with the pomodoro sauce for dipping.

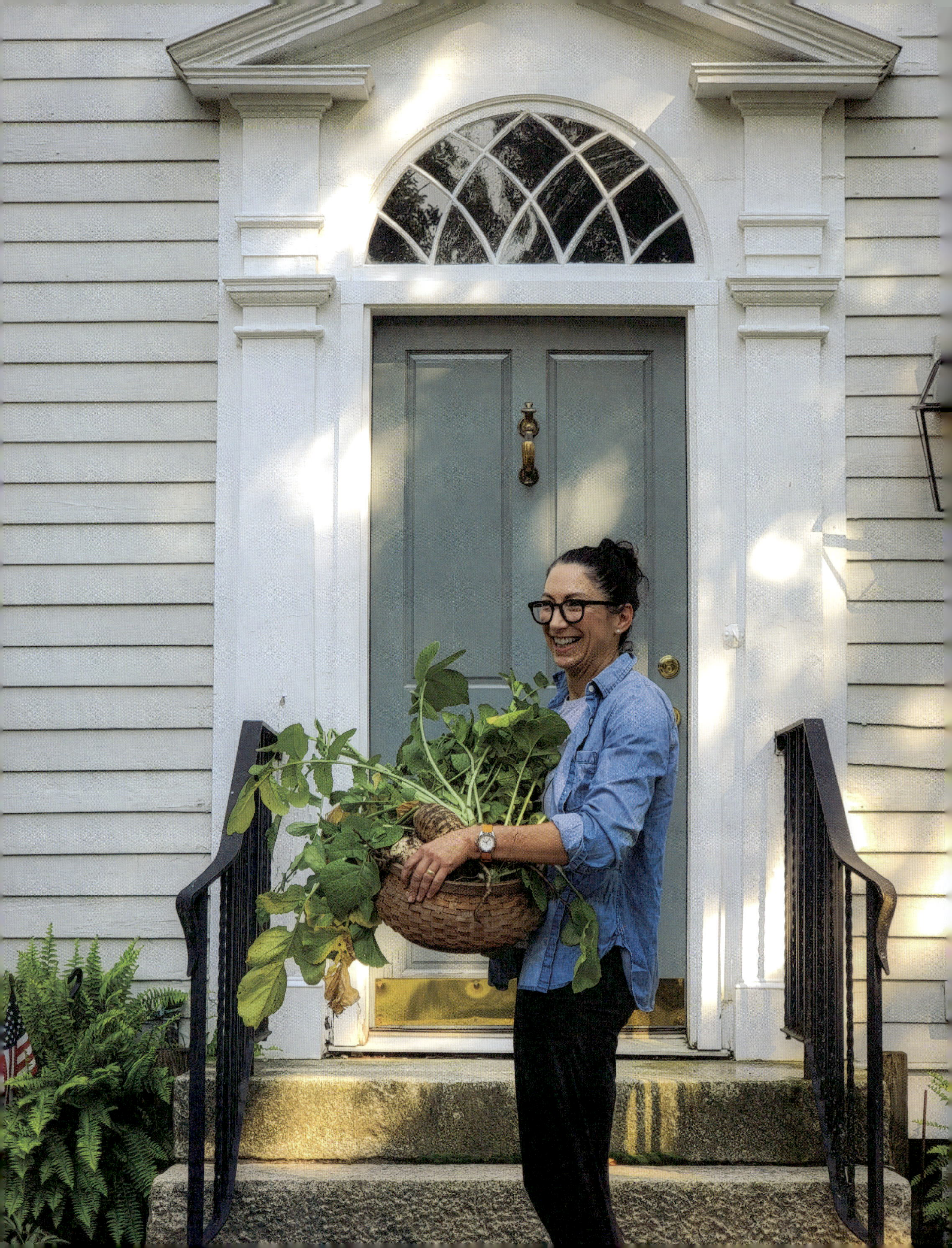

A NOTE FROM MY KITCHEN GARDEN

Top 10! Things I Love (and Loathe) to Grow

AS A PASTRY CHEF AND BAKING instructor, the question I'm asked most often is, "What's your favorite thing to bake?" and my response is always, "How dare you make me choose between my babies?" I really do feel guilt when confronted with such a choice. When it comes to gardening, on the other hand? I'll tell you exactly what I love to grow. I list them in order of preference, even. I'll also tell you what I hate growing. No guilt.

1. **POTATOES AND ONIONS AND GARLIC:** All three are things I love to eat and often. And I find them most delicious when I grow them myself. They all possess a type of magic in the growing. The potatoes bide their time underground, sending up tomato-like plants (more on this later) but, all the while, multiplying and producing delicious spuds out of view. They are also incredibly easy to grow in containers, allowing you to layer the seed starts up on top of one another, maximizing space and fun. When you harvest, it's like emptying a clown car. Onions find their magic in their long evolution. They start out tiny and grasslike. Next, they look like leeks, just straight up and down. And then, all of a sudden, the bulb starts to show just under the soil and then rises to the top. What a lovely gift after all that time. And garlic, especially hardneck, similarly starts underground in the late fall and then sends up gorgeous scapes, and then the single seed clove you planted in the fall reveals itself as a full, glorious head of garlic, individual cloves magically separated. And I get to grow exactly the varieties that please me and that are otherwise impossible to find in the store.

2. **RADISHES:** Can't get enough of radishes. Love them so much. They are fabulous straight out of the ground, all by themselves. Magnificent on a gorgeous slab of bread with butter and a pinch of salt. Glorious roasted. Also, very easy to grow and you can eat their greens. 10 out of 10. No notes.

3. **CARROTS:** Like potatoes, onions, and garlic, carrots bring their magic underground. You can leave them in the ground up until the first frost. In fact, you should, because they gain a bit of sweetness from the shot of cold. And the colors! So many beautiful colors.

4. **TOMATOES:** I grow a lot of tomatoes. Tons, actually. All kinds. Heirloom, paste, cherry, spoon. I love to eat them, I love to grow them . . . until I don't. The problem is that tomatoes invariably get hit with some kind of blight in Vermont (and everywhere else, for that matter). But what I *do* love about them is that there's nothing like a perfectly ripe tomato just off the vine. And if you have the good fortune of a bit of dry weather in the last days of ripening, you'll manage to concentrate the sweetness. If you are growing in containers (or a greenhouse), you can control this more easily.

5. **BROAD BEANS:** Broad beans grow fast and furious, and they do well in a range of temperatures. They also produce multiple harvests in one growing season; in fact, they keep sending up new shoots throughout the summer. The beans themselves are as delicious as they are beautiful, but they do take a bit of work in extracting from both the pod and the outer skin. And the plants themselves, while beautiful with their snapdragon-like flowers, are prone to aphid activity, so have some insecticidal soap spray ready.

6. **BEANS AND PEAS:** These two, including broad beans, are considered nitrogen fixers (if you inoculate with a powder that actually keeps the nitrogen in the ground). That means they rejuvenate the soil. That's reason enough to grow them. Peas are edible at multiple stages of their growth cycle as well. Their shoots are adorable and tasty and, of course, the peas themselves are sweet and delightful fresh, and then when dried, they are used for split pea soup (although this is a pain because you need a lot of peas to make a pot of soup). Beans, the vining type, join peas in making a garden just beautiful. They scale tall structures and pepper it all with lovely flowers. And then the ornamental pods just lend so much joy, swinging like little ornaments on trellises. And they are both delicious. Anything that brings me joy in the way of surprise (growing underground!) or beauty (flowers!) is a winner, in my book.

7. **CORN:** I don't eat a ton of corn, but I sure like to grow it. I make sure to grow the exact types I enjoy the most. Because my plot of corn is always small, I take time to hand pollinate, to ensure I get a decently filled cob. And once the cobs start filling out, I get old (but clean) socks that I'd otherwise throw away and I slip them over the cobs. This deters deer and other critters from completely decimating your crop. Not to worry, though. The sock is over the husk, not touching the corn.

8. **SQUASH:** I have a love/hate relationship with squash and with cucurbits in general. It's very satisfying to watch them vine and twine, flower, and grow. It's very depressing to watch them grow and get annihilated. There are so many things that love to mess with squash. There are the vine borers and cucumber beetles that are very promiscuous and will demolish all curcurbits, not just cucumbers. There's powdery mildew and downy mildew. There's gummy stem blight and bacterial wilt. And then there's Mildred, the groundhog who's intent on getting her five a day and exclusively in my vegetable patch. She especially likes taking buck-toothed chunks from my squash. Yet, after all this, if I can get only one decent fruit off the vine, I'm perfectly happy having gone through the drama.

9. **ASPARAGUS:** Asparagus is great because, once you plant it, it keeps producing for years, as it's a pretty hardy perennial. You do need to keep the patch weeded and nourished, but that's pretty much it. They are pretty dependable, and you'll never have eaten a more delicious asparagus than one just snipped from the patch. The bummer is that their season is very short and, once done, the patch just sits there—you can't plant anything else in that location. But once spring rolls around and it's one of the only things producing, all is forgiven.

10. **BEETS:** I hate beets. Beets hate me. I don't like eating them. They don't like growing for me.

11. **BRASSICAS:** This may be surprising because brassicas, whose genus includes cabbage and Brussels sprouts and broccoli, includes a host of things I love to eat. I adore cabbage. And I'm pretty good at getting them to grow. No problem with seed germination. Easy transplant to the garden. Steady growth and plant formation. Then, WORMS! That, to me, is the life cycle of a brassica. It's all going great and then those cute little white cabbage butterflies and the brown cabbage moths start fluttering around and laying their eggs on the brassicas, and then the loopers and cabbage worms are suddenly the size of a toddler. At first, you don't see them. They are all as green as the cabbage (and also why I grow more red cabbage than anything, so I might see them), but then your eyes adjust and they are *everywhere*. It's nightmare fuel, quite frankly. Yes, you can cover the rows. Yes, you can pluck them off. Yes, I've done all the things, but what a pain in my tush. Does that mean I don't grow brassicas? No—I cycle through types, depending on how devastating the last year's trauma was. But even a thing I hate to grow is still something I manage to eke joy from, and that pretty much sums up what I love about growing food.

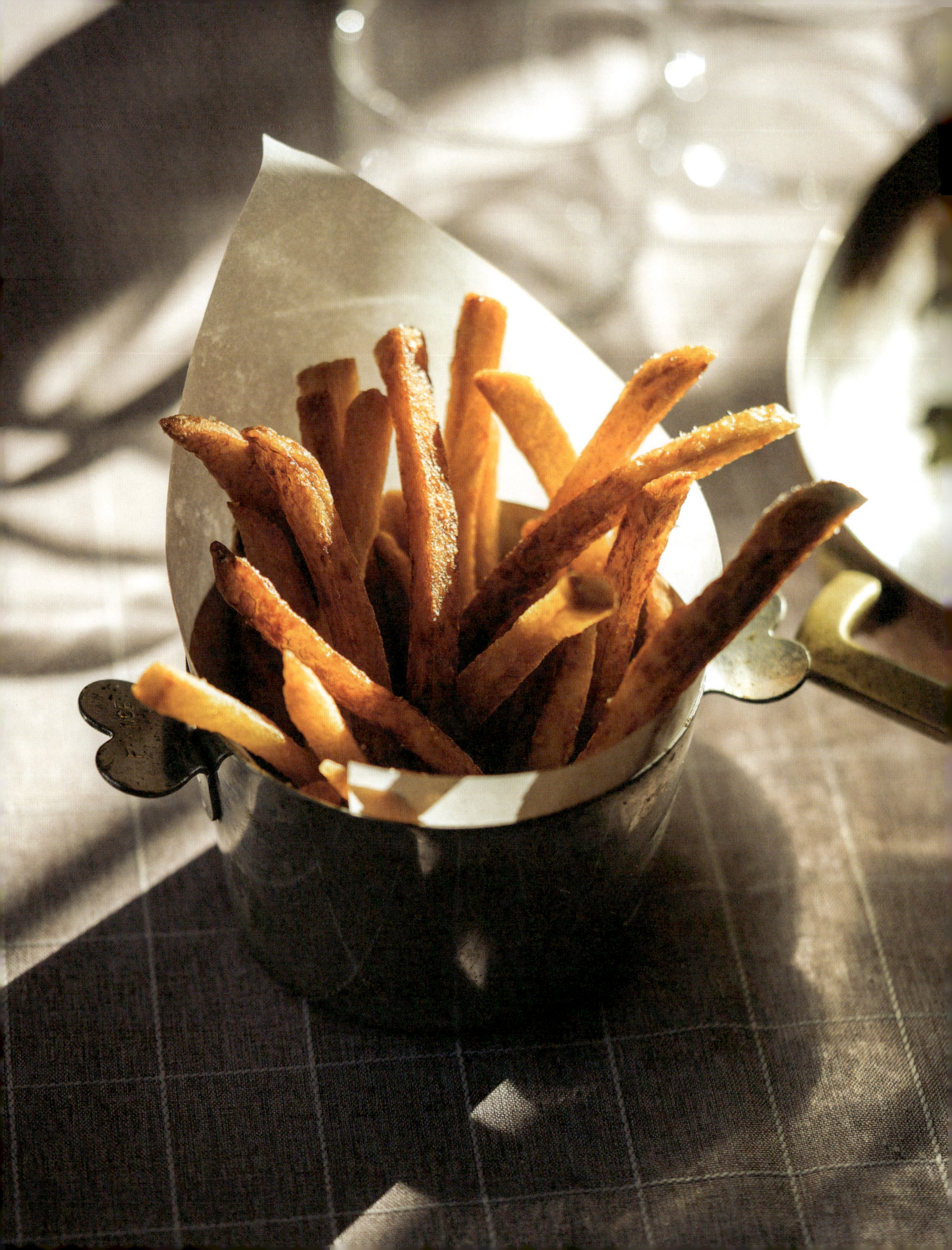

Brined and Twice-Fried Fries

SERVES 2 TO 4

January is a great time to play in the kitchen, using up root veggies that are tucked away in cool, dark corners. Making these perfectly crisp fries using a little mad science is just the ticket. A salty brine seasons the potato, deepens flavor, and draws moisture from the starchy nuggets. Parfrying and then deep-frying ensures that you end up with perfect, crispy fries that stay crispy longer.

1 cup kosher salt
6 cups water
2 tablespoons pure maple syrup
4 russet potatoes
Peanut oil, for frying

Combine the salt, water, and maple syrup in a large Dutch oven. Stir until the salt is completely dissolved. Peel the potatoes and slice, lengthwise, into ¼-inch-thick slices. Then, turn and cut into ¼-inch sticks. Submerge the potatoes in the brine, cover with the lid, and refrigerate for 2 to 3 days. A Dutch oven takes up quite a bit of room, so I'll often put it in an outbuilding or three-season porch, where it stays just a bit warmer than it is outside, so that the mixture doesn't freeze.

Pour the potatoes into a colander, then rinse them with cold water. Pat the potatoes dry with paper towels.

Place the Dutch oven over low heat to dry the interior of the pot. Pour the peanut oil into the pot to a depth of just halfway. Heat the oil over medium-high heat until it reaches 320°F (160°C). Place a cooling rack on a sheet pan and line the rack with paper towels. Fry the potatoes for 1 to 2 minutes and then immediately transfer to the prepared rack.

Bring the oil to 350°F (180°C) and fry the potatoes again for 3 to 4 minutes, until golden brown and crispy. Serve immediately with some spicy Garlic Aioli (page 263) or smothered in gravy and cheese in a comforting poutine (see page 126).

Poutine

SERVES 4

Living in Vermont, just hours away from the Montreal border, we deeply appreciate the soul-satisfying goodness of a hot poutine. If you've never had the pleasure, you must rectify that huge error and whip up a batch as soon as you've brined a few potatoes and procured a batch of cheese curds.

FOR THE GRAVY

- 4 tablespoons unsalted butter
- ¼ cup unbleached all-purpose flour
- ¼ cup full-fat sour cream
- 1 tablespoon caper juice
- 1 tablespoon capers
- 1 tablespoon Dijon mustard
- 1 teaspoon tomato ketchup
- 2 to 3 dashes Maggi brand liquid seasoning or soy sauce
- 3 cups beef broth
- Salt

- 1 batch Brined and Twice-Fried Fries (page 125)
- 12 ounces fresh cheese curds

MAKE THE GRAVY

Melt the butter over low heat in a Dutch oven and whisk in the flour. Cook, stirring with a wooden spoon, until the mixture just begins to brown. Add the sour cream, caper juice, capers, Dijon, ketchup, and Maggi. Stir to combine, and simmer until the mixture just begins to thicken. Slowly add the beef broth, stirring constantly. Increase the heat to medium-high, bring to a hearty simmer, and reduce the mixture by half. Season to taste with salt.

ASSEMBLE THE POUTINE

Line a serving platter with the hot fries. Top with the cheese curds and drizzle with gravy.

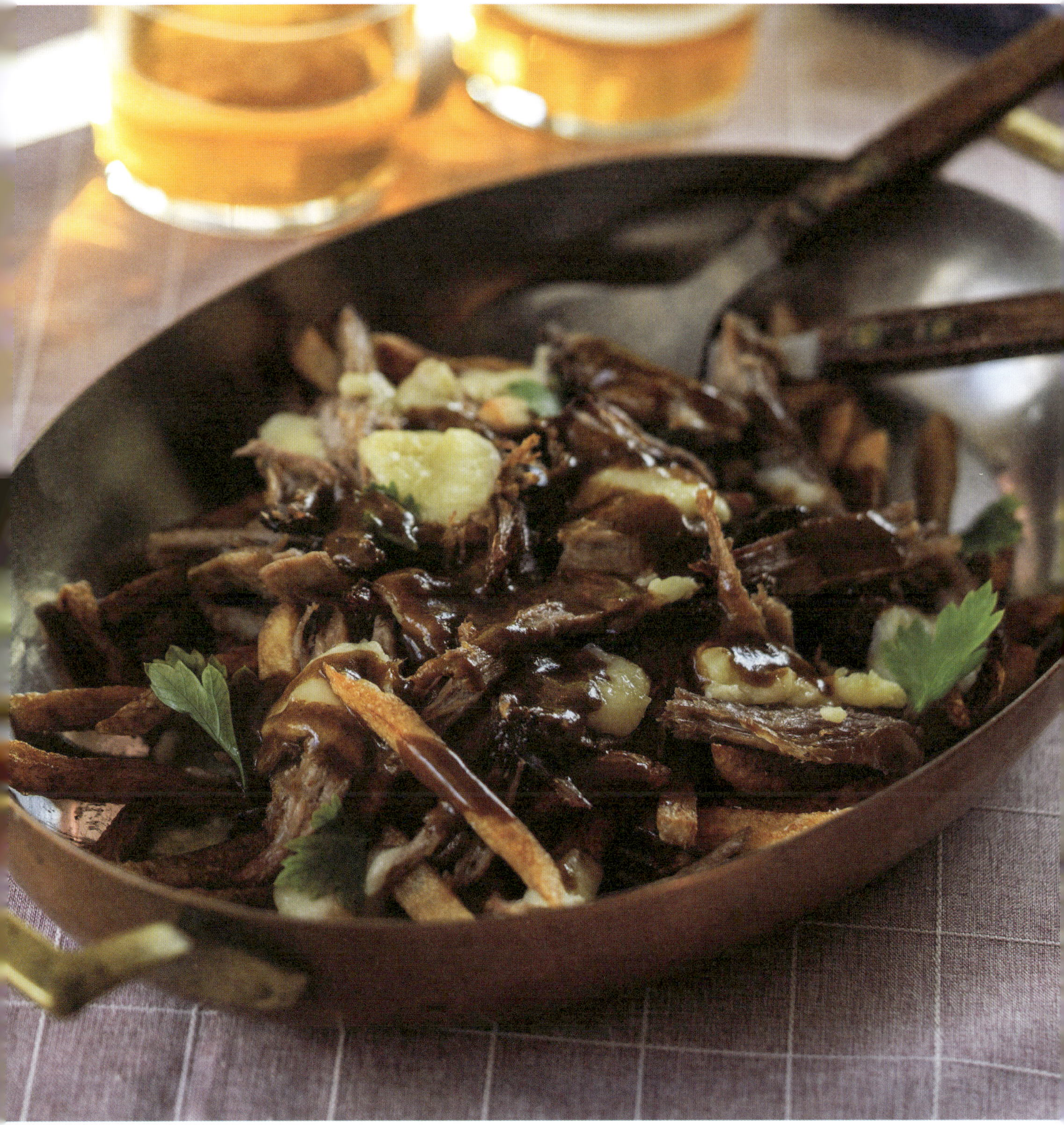

Potato Pavé

SERVES 8

Pavé, in French, translates to "paving stone." Rest assured that potato pavé takes on only the shape of the rectangular paver and not the texture. In fact, these potatoes are utterly transcendent in both taste and texture, managing to be both outrageously tender and shatteringly crisp. Did I also mention they are creamy? And if you add aromatics, they carry with them herbaceous brightness. If you grow your own potatoes, you would never imagine as you dig those weird tubers from the ground that they'd one day become such an elegant and delicious beauty.

1 cup heavy cream
2 tablespoons unsalted butter
2 tablespoons rendered pork fat
Leaves from 4 thyme sprigs
2 garlic cloves, crushed
3 pounds russet potatoes (3 or 4 large potatoes), peeled
Salt
Ghee, for frying

Preheat the oven to 350°F (180°C). Line a loaf pan with parchment so that the parchment hangs over the edges. Set aside.

Combine the cream, butter, pork fat, garlic, and thyme leaves in a saucepan. Simmer over low heat until the fats have melted and the mixture is infused with thyme, about 5 minutes. Pour the cream mixture into a large bowl. Remove the garlic. Set aside.

Using a mandoline (I use Dash brand Safe Slice mandoline) or a sharp chef's knife, slice the potatoes into very thin slices and transfer to the bowl with the cream mixture.

Line the bottom of the prepared loaf pan with potato slices, overlapping as you go, until you have two layers. Ladle 2 tablespoons of the cream mixture over the potatoes and sprinkle with salt. Continue layering, overlapping, ladling with the cream mixture, and sprinkling with a little salt every two layers. Once all of the potatoes have been added, pour any leftover cream mixture over top of the potatoes. Fold the overhanging parchment over the top and then cover the pan with aluminum foil and bake for 1 hour. Remove the foil and pull back the parchment, and bake for another 30 minutes, or until the top of the pavé is golden brown and a sharp paring knife easily slices through the potato layers. Remove from the oven and allow to cool completely.

Fold the parchment back over the exposed top of the potatoes. Cut a piece of cardboard so that it fits on top of the potatoes and then place a few unopened 15-ounce cans on top of the cardboard, to compress the potato layers. Refrigerate overnight.

The next day, preheat the oven to 300°F (150°C). Line a half sheet pan with parchment. Set aside.

Remove the weights and the cardboard, then carefully lift the potatoes from the loaf pan, using the parchment (if it's sticking, gently heat the sides of the loaf pan with a hair dryer or heat gun to loosen the fats). Transfer to a cutting board and slice the potato block into eight equal slices.

Melt 2 tablespoons of ghee in a large nonstick skillet over medium heat and, using kitchen tongs, add the pavé slices, cut side down. Cook in batches, adding ghee as needed, until all sides of the pavé are a crisp, golden brown. Transfer to the prepared sheet pan and finish by heating through in the oven for about 10 minutes. Serve immediately. Goes beautifully as a side with Schweinebraten (German Pork Roast) (page 179).

Cheesy Potatoes (Pommes Aligot)

SERVES 6

If you've ever stirred your mashed potatoes to oblivion and ended up with gummy spuds, this is the recipe for you. You're *supposed* to work these taters to the point that they give you a full-on cheese pull. Think of these potatoes as a cross between cheese fondue and pureed potato, with a heavy emphasis on the cheese. Using dense potatoes, such as my favorite, La Ratte, is crucial to the overall texture, making them creamier. And using an Alpine, midsoft, young cow's milk cheese is also a must. Anything too dry and funky won't give you the requisite silken stretch or the mild cheesiness. The official cheese for this dish is Tomme de Laguiole or Tomme d'Auvergne, not easily sourced in the States, and if you are able to find it, plan on its being very spendy. To replicate both the cheese pull and the mild profile, I tossed the need to hunt down an obscure French cheese and admitted that being a purist isn't always the best approach. So, I turned west, toward Monterey, to the cow's milk cheese that's supple and mild with hints of butter. And its melting quality? Can't be beat. Am I a culinary heretic for using Monterey Jack? Probably. Did I want to go even further and go pepper Jack and name this "Jalapeño Popper Potatoes"? You betcha.

2 pounds waxy, dense potatoes,* such as La Ratte or Yukon Gold

4 garlic cloves

Salt

8 tablespoons unsalted European-style high-fat butter, cut into tablespoon-size pieces, at room temperature

1 cup heavy cream, warm

12 ounces mid-soft, mild cow's milk cheese, such as Monterey Jack, Comté, or fontina

*NOTE For La Ratte potatoes, if small, use them as is; don't worry about the skins. For larger potatoes, make sure they are uniform in size and, if large, cut accordingly.

Combine the potatoes and 2 of the garlic cloves, crushed, in a Dutch oven and cover with cold water. Add 2 tablespoons of salt and bring to a boil. Cook until tender, 20 to 25 minutes. Drain.

Cut the whole potatoes in half. Press the potatoes and cooked garlic through a fine drum sieve or a potato ricer on the finest setting, into a saucepan. Using a Microplane grater, grate the remaining two garlic cloves into the potato mixture. Add the butter.

With a wooden spoon or rubber spatula, stir the mixture over medium-low heat to incorporate the butter and garlic. While constantly stirring, slowly add the warm cream. If, at any point, the potato mixture is beginning to form a skin at the bottom of the pan, lower the heat. Continue to stir until the cream is completely incorporated.

Still stirring, add the cheese, ¼ cup at a time. Continue to stir until the mixture is very *very* smooth and it holds together in a big cheese pull when you lift it with a spoon. Give it a taste and season with salt, if needed. Serve immediately in the pot you used to cook it in or, if transferring to a serving dish, make sure the dish is very warm; otherwise, the mixture will set. Serve while still very warm with hearty meats, such as Ray's Bone-in Rib Eye (page 150) or flavorful sausages.

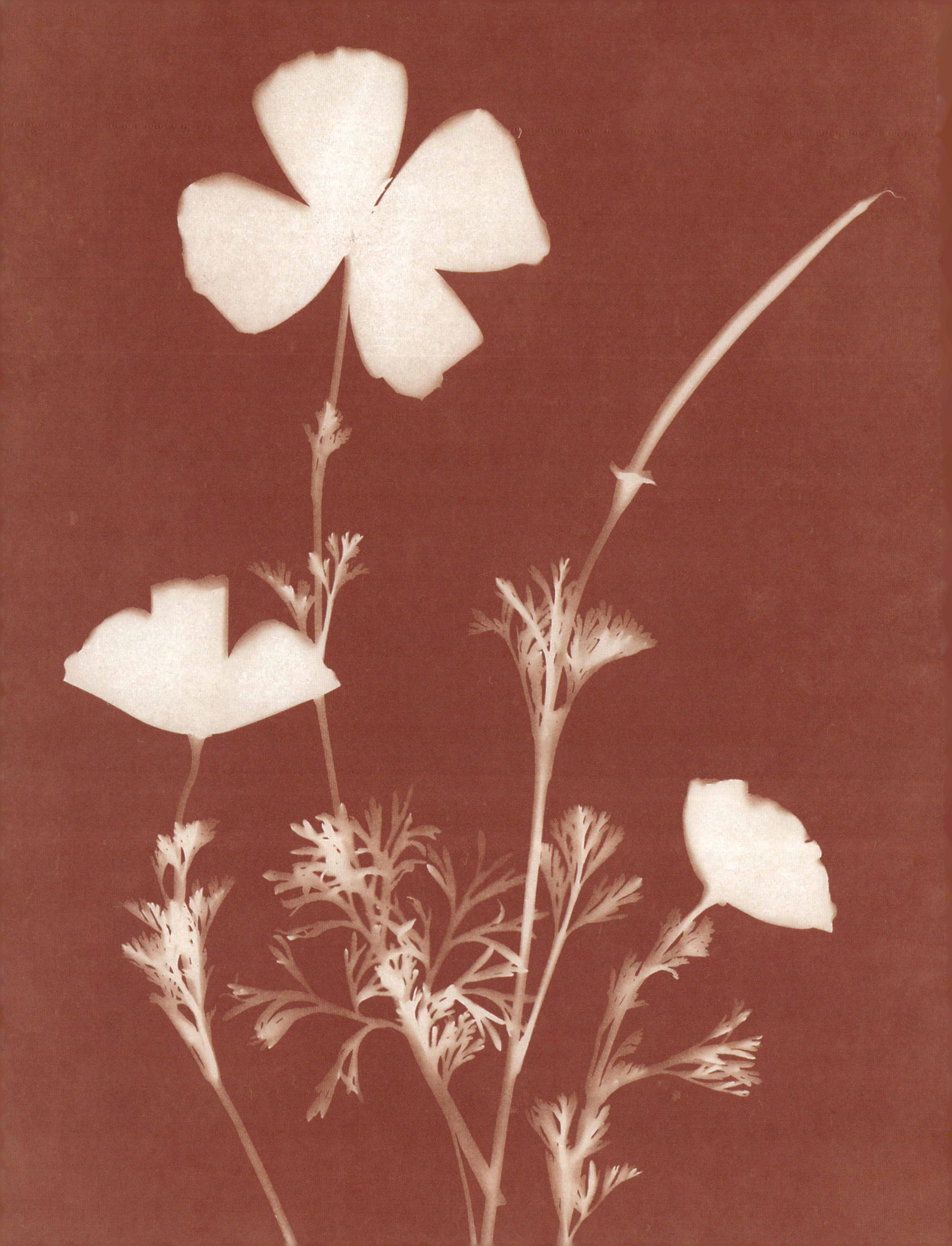

FEASTS

ON FORAGING

IF I foraged for morels and only ever found two a year, I'd be a happy woman. My favorite way to find a morel—or, really, any wild-growing, unexpected delicacy—isn't when I schedule a time to go foraging but when it stumbles across my path when I'm not even looking. For instance, on the patchy grass drive leading up to our barn, a lone morel was waiting for me as I trundled by, schlepping a 50-pound bag of manure. I spotted it out of the side of my eye. I immediately dropped the bag on my foot, but that was okay because I didn't drop it on the morel.

It was that way, too, with the sweet white grapes I spotted twining their way up my butternut tree. I'm used to wild grape vines inundating my plants, and when I spotted this insanely long stinker, at least 20 feet long, dangling from one of my favorite trees, I got ready to grab on to it, yank it from its purchase on the branches, and uproot it. And then I saw grapes.

Mind you, wild grapes are normally small and deep, dark purple. But these were that lovely light green of store-bought grapes and the size of marbles. They were really high up. But being the gleeful and devil-may-care forager that I am, I grabbed an apple ladder and set it in a stable crotch in the tree and then shimmied up to the grapes. I popped one in my mouth. It was sweet. It was seedless! It was one of the sweetest treasures I'd ever found, and I hadn't even been looking for it.

Other similar finds include the watercress I spotted just noodling around in a drainage ditch, the wild asparagus along the river, and a chicken-of-the-woods mushroom waving at me from the highest reaches of a tree but not so high that I didn't clamber up to grab it. Some found and foraged things appear with regularity, things that I've not planted and don't necessarily want around, but I'll pluck and eat happily nonetheless, including grape leaves for stuffing, stinging nettle for ravioli, and wild mint for mojitos.

I forage after years and years of experience (and not poisoning myself). Without knowing exactly what it is you're looking for, I do not recommend striking out on your own and putting what you *think* is an edible into your mouth. But there's a solution and it doesn't require time specificity: you can grow mushrooms indoors and at any time. Specialized kits provide the housing, the substrate, and the spores to grow your own shrooms any time. For someone who grew up hating mushrooms, this is a big step forward in my culinary maturity.

All that in mind, though, nothing can compare to running into a morel in the most unexpected place.

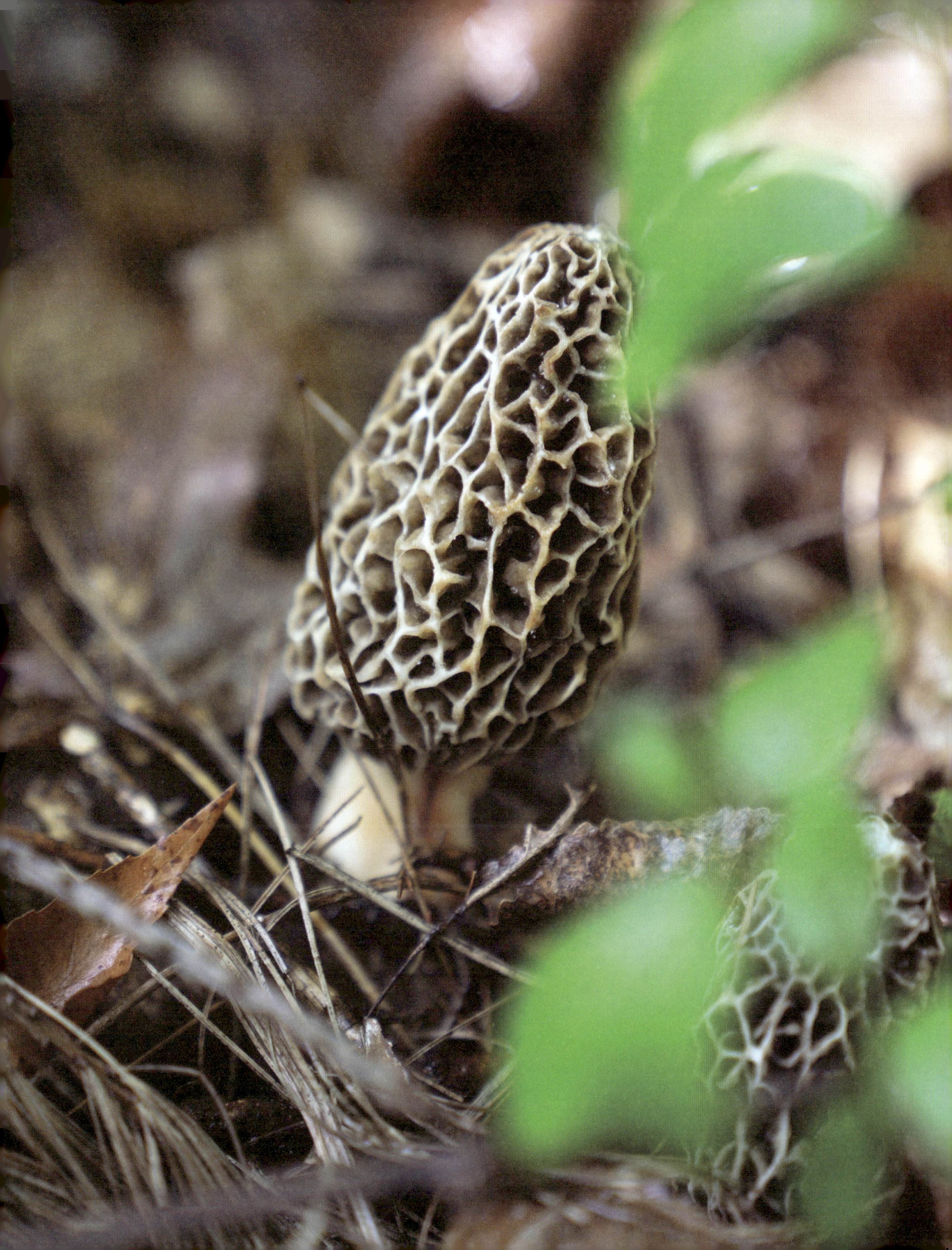

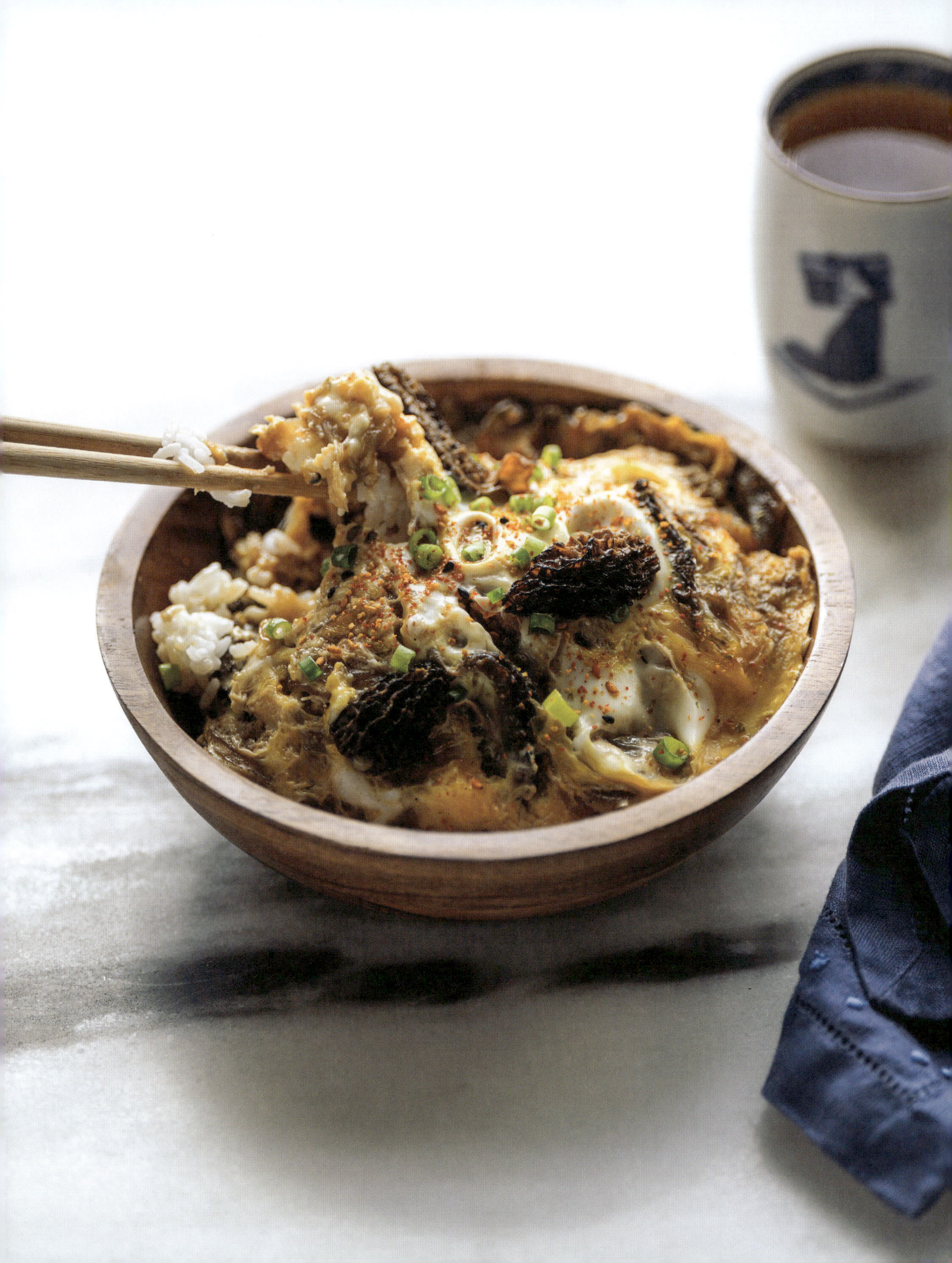

Tamago Don with Morels

SERVES 1

When Ray and I lived in Los Angeles, our favorite restaurant was called Mishima. It was a temple of Japanese comfort food, with rice bowls and hot soups aplenty. One of our favorites was the *tamago don*, a bowl of seasoned rice topped with silken egg and caramelized onions. The relationship between the two, sweet onion and creamy egg, is an equal partnership and, paired with morel and rice, is a meal for which I have the ingredients waiting in the yard or my pantry. The restaurant has since closed and we've moved from California, but I miss the casual atmosphere and stupendously nurturing food that warmed our bellies. It turns out that tamago don is very well suited to Vermont, especially when spring arrives and the hope of warmer days is upon us but the chill isn't yet ready to leave. Enter a few morels from the forest and a couple of eggs from the chicken coop, and lunch or dinner is served!

¼ **cup water**

1 **tablespoon soy sauce**

1 **tablespoon mirin**

1 **teaspoon pure maple syrup**

½ **teaspoon dashi powder**

¼ **yellow onion, finely sliced**

2 **fresh morel mushrooms,* quartered**

2 **large eggs**

½ **batch Perfect Japanese Short-Grain Rice (page 256)**

½ **spring onion, finely chopped**

Kosher salt

Togarashi

Combine the water, soy sauce, mirin, maple syrup, and dashi powder in a small skillet. Add the yellow onion and morels and bring to a simmer over medium-high heat. Cook until the onion is translucent and soft. Gently whisk the eggs together in a small bowl, then slip the eggs into the pan over the onion and morels. Do not agitate or stir. Cover the skillet to cook the eggs, about 1 minute, or until cooked to your desired set.

Fill a bowl with a generous scoop of rice and carefully transfer the egg mixture onto the rice. Top with spring onion and season with a bit of kosher salt and togarashi.

> ***NOTE** Alternatively, you can use dried morels: rehydrate in warm water for 10 minutes, drain, and pat gently with a paper towel, then chop.

Spring Risotto

SERVES 4

How do you emphasize that spring has sprung? Make green risotto with spring vegetables! With ramps and asparagus in season for such a short time, a creamy risotto is the perfect playground for them to be showcased. Add some tender peas and Windsor beans to the party and you'll have greens of every shade to herald the vernal season.

4½ cups low-sodium chicken stock

1 small bunch fresh flat-leaf parsley, stems and leaves separated

1 bunch ramps (about 12 leaves)

1 bunch fresh asparagus (about 12 stalks), woody ends trimmed and reserved, cut into 1-inch-long pieces

¼ cup extra-virgin olive oil

4 tablespoons unsalted butter

1 small onion, finely chopped

1½ cups uncooked risotto rice

½ cup dry white wine

1 cup shelled fresh peas

1 cup shelled broad/Windsor beans, blanched

Grated zest and juice of ½ lemon

Salt

4 small chicken breasts

Freshly ground black pepper

¼ cup freshly grated Parmesan

1 cup arugula

Thin lemon wedges, for serving

Bring the chicken stock to a simmer in a medium saucepan and immediately add the parsley stems, ramps, and the woody trimmed bits of asparagus. Simmer for 2 minutes and then, using an immersion blender, process the mixture to create a vibrant green sauce. Run through a sieve into a medium bowl or a large Pyrex measuring cup. Set aside.

Heat 2 tablespoons of the olive oil and 2 tablespoons of the butter in a large skillet over medium heat. Add the onion and cook, stirring occasionally, until just translucent, about 5 minutes. Stir in the rice and wine and cook over medium-high heat, stirring occasionally, until the wine is almost entirely absorbed.

Add the green stock, ½ cup at a time, stirring occasionally. Only add the next ½ cup of stock once the first addition of stock has been absorbed by the rice. After about 20 minutes, when the rice's exterior is starting to soften but the middle is still is opaque, fold in the tender asparagus pieces and the peas. Continue to add the remaining stock, ½ cup at a time, stirring occasionally, until the rice is creamy and al dente (or to your textural preference). Stir in the broad beans and the lemon zest and juice. Season with salt to taste.

Heat the remaining 2 tablespoons of oil and remaining 2 tablespoons of butter in a large skillet over medium-high heat until shimmering. Season the chicken breasts with salt and pepper and cook on each side for 3 to 4 minutes, until just golden brown and the interior temperature of each breast reads 165°F (73°C) on a digital thermometer. Slice each breast into four or five pieces.

Plate the risotto into four shallow dishes and sprinkle with Parmesan and arugula. Top each with sliced chicken and serve with a lemon wedge.

Green Mountain Pradonara (A Nontraditional Carbonara)

SERVES 4

This recipe is an exercise in timing. First, I wait until the hens just start laying again. Second, I wait until the second round of peas has started to emerge while the first have already started to pod, so I get the benefit of both the edible tender shoots and the actual peas. As for the making, you have to have your elements going at just the right time. First, you start rendering and crisping the guanciale. Then, you start the pasta. As the pasta's going, you bring a small saucepan of water to a simmer. And then you do the pastry chef's carbonara dance, a jaunty jig that mimics the making of a sabayon sauce, but porky and savory. You have to catch the sauce at just the right time, once it's thickened but not so thick that the eggs start to coagulate. Since this is savory, there's no sugar to help protect the proteins, which would allow this sauce to spend more time over heat. And then it has to be March 6. Because that's my birthday, and this is what I make myself to celebrate another year 'round the sun.

8 ounces guanciale or pancetta

Salt

12 ounces bucatini or spaghetti

6 large egg yolks

3 ounces aged Vermont Cheddar,* finely grated, plus more for garnish

⅓ cup fresh shelled peas

4 to 8 fresh pea shoots

Freshly ground black pepper

From the guanciale, trim any bits of fat that look at all yellow; the outer layers of guanciale that appear yellow may be rancid and need to be trimmed. (This is not unusual. You simply need to trim the sides.) Cut the rest into slightly smaller than ½-inch cubes.

Render and crisp the guanciale in a large skillet over medium-low heat, stirring often. The guanciale will reduce in size by almost half, will be deeply golden brown, and a good deal of the fat will have rendered, leaving you with up to ⅓ cup of liquid pork fat.

Transfer the crisp cubes to a paper towel–lined plate, using a slotted spoon or spider. Pour the fat into a measuring cup. You'll need ¼ cup total for this recipe. Keep the rest in a small jar in the fridge for up to a week or freeze in a freezer bag for up to a month, for other uses.

Bring lightly salty water to boil in a large braiser or rondeau. Add the pasta and cook according to the package instructions. By cooking the pasta in a shallower amount of water, instead of in a large stockpot, you concentrate the pasta water, making for a creamier final sauce.

While the pasta cooks, fill a saucepan with just over an inch of water and bring to a simmer over medium heat. Whisk together the egg yolks and Cheddar in a metal bowl large enough to later sit atop the saucepan.

Once the pasta is al dente, use tongs to transfer it to a colander, leaving the pasta water in the braiser. Measure out ½ cup of the pasta

MY HARVEST KITCHEN

water and, while whisking constantly, slowly trickle the pasta water into the cheese mixture. Place the bowl over the simmering water in the saucepan and whisk until the cheese has melted. Then, while whisking constantly and *vigorously*, slowly pour the rendered guanciale fat into the mixture. Continue to whisk until it just starts to thicken and the temperature reads 150°F (66°C) on a digital thermometer. Immediately add the peas and then the pasta to the sauce and, using tongs, turn the pasta over in the sauce to coat. The sauce should be smooth and shiny. If it starts to look dry, immediately add a tablespoon of pasta water at a time, whisking constantly, to bring the sauce back.

Capture about a quarter of the pasta with large culinary tweezers or tongs and twirl on a large serving spoon to make a neat little nest. Transfer to a plate and garnish with guanciale cubes, pea shoots, grated cheese, and pepper. Serve immediately.

*NOTE If you want to be traditional, substitute pecorino romano for the Cheddar.

MY HARVEST KITCHEN

Sous Vide Lamb Chops

SERVES 8

Lamb is expensive. It's also pretty lean. Leaner than, say, a rib eye. It's really easy to overcook and dry it out. And that would be a shame, both for your wallet and for your taste buds. My magic trick to make sure it's perfect? Sous vide. Sous vide is a technique of cooking whereby you vacuum pack (either with a vacuum sealer or the old-fashioned way, through water displacement) the ingredients and then cook them in a circulating water bath that regulates the temperature to such exactitude that the meat is cooked perfectly from edge to edge. Sous vide machines aren't crazy expensive, and they are small enough to store in a drawer. And newer tech ovens often have the feature built in. Schmancy restaurants rely on the tech for good reason: you are assured of a perfect outcome.

2 pounds rack of lamb (2 racks total)
Kosher salt and ground white pepper
4 thyme sprigs
2 garlic cloves, thinly sliced
4 tablespoons unsalted butter
2 tablespoons neutral oil, such as canola

Preheat the sous vide to 130°F (54°C) for medium rare. This is the fine-dining restaurant standard temperature and will create the most tender results. However, there are plenty of eaters out there who are put off by medium rare, so if you prefer medium, preheat the sous vide to 140°F (60°C). You lose a bit of tenderness, but the sous vide helps retain juices in the lean meat.

Generously season the lamb racks with kosher salt and white pepper. Place 2 tablespoons of butter on each rack and then lay two thyme sprigs and a sliced garlic clove on each.

Place each rack in a separate resealable plastic bag, slowly lower each bag into the preheated water bath using the water displacement method, and seal completely. Alternatively, if you have a vacuum sealer, individually seal each rack and place in the preheated sous vide.

Cook for 1 to 4 hours. Do not cook longer than 4 hours or less than 1. During this time frame, the meat will be cooked perfectly to the temperature you set and won't overcook.

Remove the lamb racks from the sous vide and pat dry with paper towels.

Heat the oil in a cast-iron skillet or large, heavy-bottomed skillet over medium-high heat until it shimmers. Place one lamb rack in the pan, meat side down, being careful as the oil will splatter. Brown each side for 45 to 50 seconds, until deeply golden. Remove from the pan and repeat with the second rack.

Using a very sharp chef's knife, slice in between the bones to make individual chops. Serve immediately with a drizzle of Chermoula (page 259).

ON NETTLES

IT is a universal truth that soil needs amending. You can't just reuse the same soil, year after year, putting in the same plants, and expect everything to thrive. Different plants need different nutrients, and all plants draw nutrients from the soil. It's the common practice of farmers and home gardeners alike to rotate crops for this reason. Heavy feeders, such as corn, need to move on to a patch that was just vacated by "givers," such as beans and peas, that fix nitrogen in the soil and leave the earth better than they found it. And every year, no matter what's been grown, I add compost and manure to boost what might be lacking. Running a baking school, cooking a lot, and writing cookbooks (like this one!) leads to a fair amount of compostable material. I pretty much have an endless supply. But sometimes a little boost is needed, something extra, and that's when I brew a stinging nettle tea.

Stinging nettle grows all over our property. It grows especially happily near our chicken coop. I do control it for the sake of my sanity, because the stuff is painful. Rub against it just a bit and the sting, the prickle, the numbness that follows is tremendous. If you encounter enough of it, it can make you numb. In fact, a hiker once went to get a drink of water in a stream and needed to be evacuated for fear of having been bitten by a deadly spider or snake; her legs had become numb and immobile. Turns out, she'd stomped through a thicket of stinging nettle on her way to get a drink and they'd given her what for. Knowing this, you might think it lunacy to consume nettles, but if you take care, wearing very long gloves, you can harvest it, because it can't be ignored that stinging nettle is also famously packed with nutrients, for both humans and plants. For humans, a little blanching of the leaves first is necessary to rid it of its sting.

To use nettles as a fertilizer, I snip the plant at the base, adding the whole plant, except for roots, into a bucket. (This should go without saying, but I wear *really* long gloves for this.) I then take my long loppers and cut up the pieces into smaller chunks. I pour in water almost to the top of the bucket, leaving about an inch of space from the top, and put the bucket in a sunny place to brew, making sure it won't be easily knocked over. Every day, I take a long stick and stir the mixture. It gets stinky and foamy but that just means it's working. After about 10 days, I run the mixture through a big sieve or a bit of old muslin into another bucket, discarding the plant bits into the compost pile and keeping the "tea." The stuff lasts for up to six months, and a little goes a long way. Dilute before using at a ratio of 1 part nettle tea to 10 parts water. Nettle tea is full of nitrogen, chlorophyll, iron, and potassium, and is great for plants that are "heavy feeders," such as fruit trees, shrubs, leeks, brassicas, cucumbers, and squash. (Jury's out on whether it's okay for tomatoes and roses; both are heavy feeders but aren't so keen on the high levels of iron in the mixture.) Pour the tea around the roots and your free fertilizer will start working its magic. Just make sure to wear your gloves.

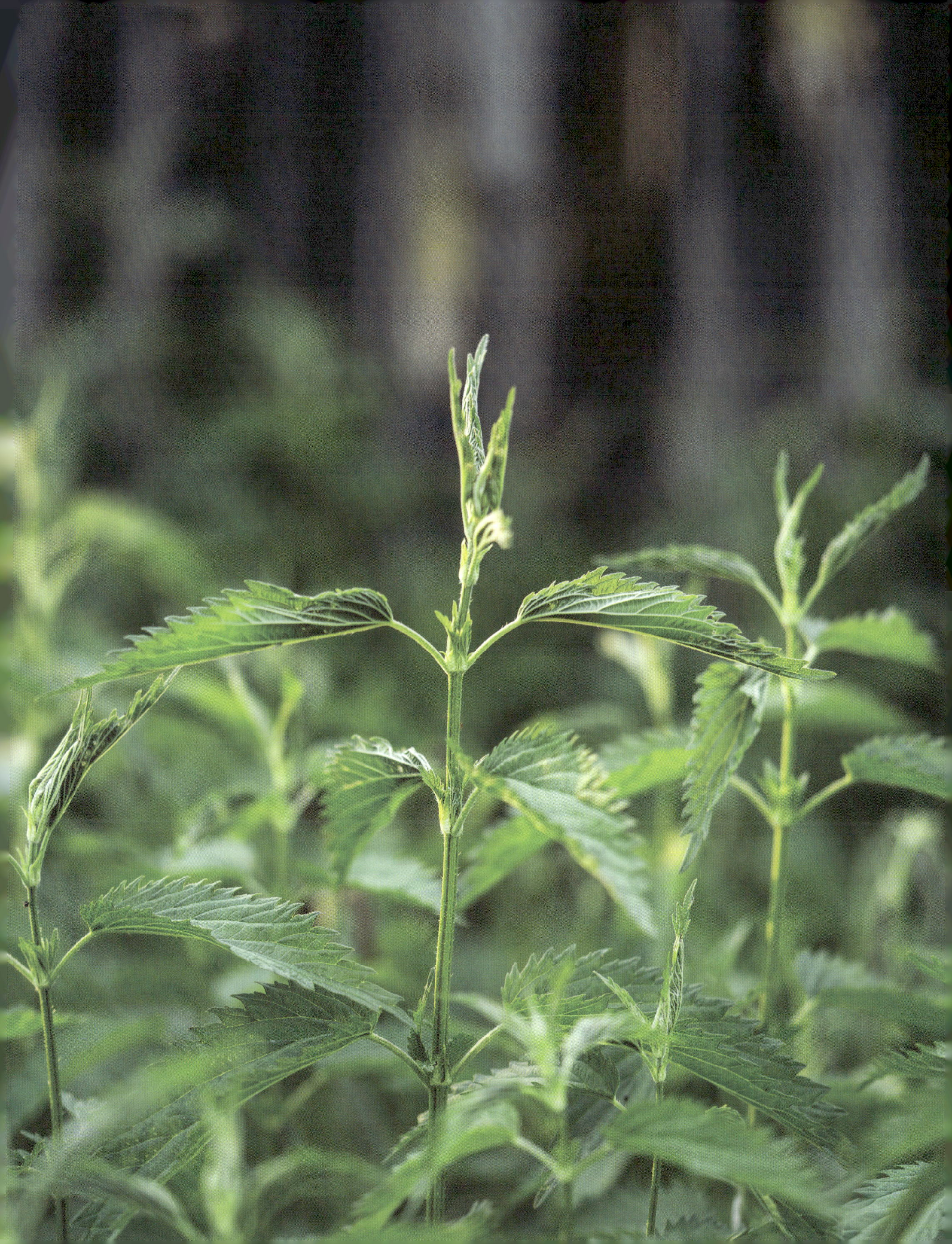

MY HARVEST KITCHEN

Stinging Ravioli

SERVES 4

One of the first plants to pop up in the spring, one that I haven't planted but makes itself at home everywhere on our property, is stinging nettle. Brush past it unawares, and you'll get a painful sting. You can harvest the most tender, new leaves and blanch them for a few minutes. This removes the sting and preserves their wonderful, herbaceous flavor and color.

- 1 cup blanched stinging nettle leaves, cooled
- 2 large eggs, at room temperature
- 2 large egg yolks
- 2 tablespoons extra-virgin olive oil
- 2 cups (240 grams) unbleached all-purpose flour, plus more for dusting
- 2 cups (240 grams) unbleached durum flour
- ½ teaspoon fine sea salt
- 1 batch Homemade Ramp-Infused Farmer Cheese (page 95) or 2 cups ricotta cheese, drained of excess liquid

Place the blanched stinging nettle in a food processor and process until pureed. Add the whole eggs, egg yolks, and olive oil, and pulse until just incorporated.

Stir together the all-purpose and durum flours with the salt in a large bowl. Make a well in the middle of the flour mixture and add the nettle mixture. Using a flexible rubber spatula, fold the nettle mixture into the flour mixture until the dough just comes together. Dust a work surface with flour and knead the dough by hand until it becomes a smooth ball, about 8 minutes. Wrap the dough in plastic wrap and refrigerate to relax the dough, at least 30 minutes and up to 2 hours.

Cut the dough in half and roll out to a depth that will fit through the largest opening of a pasta machine. Roll out the dough through the machine, fold in half, and run through the machine again. Do this three or four more times, or until the dough is very smooth and supple. Cover the dough and then process the second piece of dough the same way.

Cut each piece in half again and roll each piece into long sheets to the second-to-thinnest setting on the pasta machine, making sure that no matter how long the pieces are, they are at least 4 inches wide. Pipe ramp-infused farmer cheese in 2-inch strips along one long side of the dough, leaving a ½-inch gap between strips. Gently wet the exposed edge of the dough with water and then fold the dough over the filling, pressing along the edge to seal and then pressing in between the strips of farmer cheese. Trim the long edge with a fluted pastry cutter or a sharp chef's knife, then cut between the piped pieces, pressing the sides of the dough to seal the filling into the little ravioli.

Bring a large pot of lightly salted water to a gentle boil (too rapid a boil, the ravioli will burst). Cook the ravioli for 3 to 5 minutes, until they float to the top. Drain.

Serve topped with the last of your Fresh Tomato Pomodoro Sauce (page 261).

Korean BBQ Ssams (Lettuce Wraps)

SERVES 6

In one of my little indoor gardens, tucked away in a corner of the kitchen island (alongside my sourdough starter), I grow hot peppers, Sweety Drop peppers, and next to the peppers, perilla. Perilla is a cousin of Japanese shiso, and they're both cousins of mint. It has a touch of herbaceous bitterness that cuts through the fattiness of beef. Perilla offers hints of anise, and the leaf itself is beautiful. It's a boon to both your meal and to my kitchen corner. The leaf, in its early growth, isn't big enough for (my) wraps, so I tuck it into a crispy piece of romaine. Meant to be taken in one bite, a *ssam* should be a flavor explosion each time you shove one into your gob. That unassuming leaf goes a long way in bringing the party to your taste buds.

FOR THE KOREAN BBQ SPICE BLEND

½ cup gochugaru
½ cup smoked Spanish paprika
¼ cup fine sea salt
¼ cup garlic powder
¼ cup ground cumin
2 tablespoons cayenne pepper
2 tablespoons maple sugar
2 tablespoons mustard powder
2 tablespoons freshly ground black pepper

FOR THE BEEF

2 tablespoons neutral oil, such as canola
1 tablespoon plus 2 teaspoons sesame oil
½ cup soy sauce
1 small pear or firm apple, cored and shredded with its skin
2 tablespoons Korean BBQ spice blend
1 pound skirt steak, cut thinly *against* the grain

FOR THE WRAPS

2 heads romaine lettuce
6 perilla leaves
Rice
3 garlic scapes or scallions, thinly sliced
2 teaspoons toasted white sesame seeds
Pickled vegetables (page 264)

MAKE THE KOREAN BBQ SPICE BLEND

Stir all the ingredients together in a bowl, then store in an airtight jar. This will make more than you need but can be used as a dry rub on meats and veggies.

MAKE THE BEEF

Combine the neutral oil, 2 teaspoons of the sesame oil, the soy sauce, the shredded pear, and the Korean BBQ spice blend in a large bowl. Add the beef and toss to coat. Cover with plastic wrap and refrigerate for at least 1 hour.

Heat the remaining tablespoon of sesame oil in a large skillet over medium-high heat. Add the beef, leaving the marinade in the bowl, and cook for 2 minutes on each side, for a total of

MY HARVEST KITCHEN

4 minutes. Transfer to a plate. Add the marinade to the skillet and reduce over medium heat for 3 to 4 minutes. Remove from the heat and add the beef to the marinade. Toss to coat, then arrange the beef in a serving bowl.

MAKE THE WRAPS

Serve along with a platter of the romaine and perilla leaves, a bowl of rice (see page 256) sprinkled with the scapes and toasted sesame seeds, and a bowl of pickled vegetables (see page 264). Let your guests assemble their own parcels of goodness!

Ray's Bone-in Rib Eye with Scape Chimichurri

SERVES 2

Ray loooooooooves his rib eyes. Any ol' rib eye won't do. We travel 30 minutes to Brownsville Butcher & Pantry in Brownsville, Vermont, to make sure the meat is local and up to his standards. We try to time things out just perfectly for optimal steak goodness, and that all depends on whether he's going to grill or panfry. Either way, the important part is to dry brine the steaks at room temperature for 40 minutes. This gives the salt time to penetrate the meat and go through a cycle of moisture extraction and what I call "redeposit." Salt is hygroscopic, so if you grill or panfry within a few minutes of seasoning, the salt will have sucked up moisture from its position on top of the meat, and the moisture it's sucking up will settle on top. As the salt starts to fully dissolve and intermingle with the moisture, it starts to brine the meat, traveling down into muscle fiber and tenderizing and seasoning as it goes. For a thick rib eye, this takes time. If you remember to do this ahead of time, you can season a steak and leave it in the fridge, uncovered, overnight on a cooling rack. The chimichurri adds a lovely kick to the proceedings, bringing brightness and a bit of texture to the succulent meat.

2 large bone-in rib eyes
Salt and freshly ground black pepper

FOR THE CHIMICHURRI
1 tablespoon red pepper flakes
¼ cup dried oregano
10 garlic scapes, finely chopped, or 2 tablespoons scape powder (page 45)
2 tablespoons scalding-hot water
½ cup red wine vinegar
½ cup finely chopped fresh cilantro
½ cup finely chopped fresh flat-leaf parsley
1 shallot, minced
¾ cup neutral oil, such as canola or avocado
Salt and freshly ground black pepper

FOR COOKING THE STEAK
2 tablespoons neutral oil, such as canola or avocado
2 tablespoons unsalted butter

Forty minutes before cooking, dry brine the steaks: liberally season the steaks with salt and pepper and place on a plate, uncovered, at room temperature to allow the seasoning to penetrate the meat.

MAKE THE CHIMICHURRI
Stir together the red pepper flakes, dried oregano, and the scape powder (if using) in a heatproof bowl. Add the hot water, whisk, and allow to sit for 5 minutes to hydrate. Whisk in the vinegar, cilantro, parsley, shallot, and fresh chopped scapes (if using). Then, continue to whisk while slowly adding the oil. Whisk in salt and black pepper to taste.

COOK THE STEAK
Heat the 2 tablespoons oil in a large cast-iron or stainless-steel skillet over high heat until shimmering. Add the steak and cook for 30 seconds,

MY HARVEST KITCHEN

and then flip. Cook for 30 seconds more on the other side, then flip. The flipping allows for more even cooking and a better finished color. Continue to cook and flip the steak until it has almost reached your desired temperature (use a digital thermometer; see Note). At this point, add the butter and baste the steak. Remove the steak and allow to rest for 10 minutes.

Serve with the chimichurri, Creamed Spinach and Ramps (page 96), and Pommes Aligot (page 130) for an elevated steakhouse meal.

NOTE Internal temperature guide for beef:
rare: 120 to 130°F (40 to 54°C),
medium rare: 130 to 135°F (54 to 57°C),
medium: 135 to 145°F (57 to 63°C),
medium-well: 145 to 155°F (63 to 68°C),
well done: 155 to 165°F (68 to 73°C).

OK OK Burger

MAKES 4 BURGERS

Combine an Oklahoma onion smash burger with a bit of Raymo's family, the Okamatsus', Japanese flair, and you've got the OK OK burger. The patty combines both an 80/20 ground chuck and a bit of ground pork, a tip of the hat to the Japanese nod to Western cuisine via the Hambagu. It's seasoned with a bit of powdered kombu and soy for a lightly umami backbone, and then there's a dash of togarashi for spice. Sweet onions get smashed into the patty, providing the Oklahoma side to the burger party, along with a couple shingles of American cheese. Crisp lettuce and pickle round out the textures and flavors, making this a burger bursting with flavor and fun. It's more than okay. It's OK OK.

½ cup Japanese mayonnaise

¼ cup ketchup

2 tablespoons hot sauce (Sriracha or Frank's RedHot)

12 ounces 80/20 ground beef

4 ounces ground pork

1 tablespoon togarashi

2 teaspoons powdered kombu

1 tablespoon soy sauce

4 black sesame Brioche buns (page 241) or regular buns

1 large sweet onion, sliced into paper-thin half-moons

8 slices American cheese

12 bread-and-butter pickles

8 crisp lettuce leaves

In a small bowl, whisk together the mayonnaise, ketchup, and hot sauce to make the "burger sauce." Cover and refrigerate.

Place the beef and pork in a bowl, then gently break apart and mix to combine. Sprinkle with the togarashi, kombu, and soy sauce, gently working the mixture to incorporate them. Once the ingredients are evenly distributed, divide the mixture into eight 2-ounce patties. Pat each firmly into a ball and then pass each neat sphere back and forth from one hand to the other. This allows you to get rid of any air pockets that might cause the patty to break apart when you smash it. You want them compacted, unlike how you might handle a traditional burger patty.

Slice the buns in half horizontally and arrange on a plate. On each bun bottom, add a tablespoon of burger sauce (more or less, depending on your taste).

Heat a cast-iron or stainless-steel griddle over high heat. Preheat for at least 5 minutes, to get it scorching hot. Place two patty balls on the griddle at a time and, using a burger weight or a very large, flat metal spatula, flatten the patties. Top one patty with a mound of onion (one-quarter of the total). Re-smash the burger with the onion to embed the onion into the patty. Allow the patties to cook for about 1 minute, or until the edges begin to brown. Use a very stiff metal spatula or a bench scraper to *really* scrape up the patties. You want to get all the goodness up and, as you haven't greased the skillet or griddle, they will stick. But sticking is what allows browning (i.e., flavor) to really happen. After flipping, immediately put a slice of cheese on each patty. Cook the non-onioned patty for 30 seconds more and the onioned patty for 1 minute more. Place the onioned patty on top of a bottom bun, cheese side up, and then place the second patty on top of that. Top with pickles, a drizzle of burger sauce, and 2 leaves of lettuce. Top with the second bun (feel free to dress the top bun with more burger sauce or condiments of choice). Cook the remaining patties and assemble the remaining three burgers.

Saturday Night Meatballs

MAKES 15 MEATBALLS

I think a lot about the culinary journeys of American food. How an Indian naan might take on local Louisiana Cajun flavors, how German kuchen takes on the Dakotas' pie shape, how an Italian marinara simmers its way into a New York Nonna's gravy. There's so much about necessity matched with memory and heart that permeates America's food. We love nostalgia, but we're also practical and, well, a bit rebellious when it comes to food. My meatballs are no different. I love a tender meatball. I'm also terrible at keeping track of what I don't have in the fridge. For instance, I will be convinced that I still have ground pork in the meat drawer, and I cannot imagine a day where there isn't a hunk of Parmigiano-Reggiano hiding somewhere. But often, my best-laid dinner plans are almost thwarted when I realize none of those things exists within the confines of my fridge. So, I do what Americans do: I improvise. And, sometimes, I end up with a really happy accident. That's exactly how my Saturday Night Meatballs came to be. I thought I had Parmigiano. I didn't. I *did* have sharp Vermont Cheddar. The garlic, onion, and herbs are always a guarantee because I grow them in very large quantities, so I'm never without. That's all to say, this is now my go-to recipe, and it's deliciously inauthentic. You can swap in Parmesan for the Cheddar if that's what you have (or what you want to use), and feel free to just use beef. This is *your* Saturday night, after all.

2 cups ½-inch-cubed stale white bread
¼ cup whole milk
¼ cup chicken stock
2 large eggs
2 large garlic cloves, finely chopped
1 teaspoon crushed red pepper flakes
¼ cup fresh oregano leaves
1 cup finely shredded sharp Cheddar
2 tablespoons extra-virgin olive oil
1 large yellow onion, finely chopped
2 teaspoons kosher salt
1 pound 80/20 ground beef
1 pound ground pork
Kosher salt and freshly ground black pepper

Combine the bread, milk, and chicken stock in a large bowl. Toss to coat the bread. Stir in the eggs, garlic, red pepper flakes, oregano, and Cheddar cheese. Set aside.

Heat the olive oil in a large skillet over medium heat. Add the onion and sprinkle with the kosher salt. Cook, stirring often, until translucent, about 5 minutes. Remove from the heat and allow to cool.

Break up the ground beef and ground pork, add to the bread mixture, then add the cooled onion. Use your fingers to gently combine the ingredients. The mixture will be mushy. This is normal! Take about a tablespoon of the mixture from the bowl, then cover the bowl and refrigerate the mixture while you preheat the oven to 350°F (180°C). While the oven preheats, heat a nonstick skillet over medium-high heat and cook the reserved tablespoon of meatball mixture as a little test patty to check for seasoning.

Line a half sheet pan with parchment or a silicone baking mat. Using a 2¼-inch cookie scoop, scoop mounds of meatball mixture onto the prepared sheet pan, three to a row, five rows total.

Bake the meatballs for 35 to 40 minutes, or until the internal temperature reads 160°F (71°C) with a digital thermometer. Serve with Fresh Tomato Pomodoro Sauce (page 261).

White Wine–Braised Short Ribs

SERVES 6

Short ribs have been the bastion of schmancy chefs, but they are an economical and easy cut to play with; you just need time. I use white wine instead of red, to offset the richness inherent in the meat, and I don't worry too much if the meat gets so tender that it starts shredding off the bone. Instead of fretting, I go with the flow and treat it like pulled pork, shoving it in a fluffy steamed bun (see page 250). Get yourself some of the root veggies you've stored for the winter and plop them in, and you've got a Michelin-worthy meal or just a superfancy pulled-meat sandwich.

2 thyme sprigs
1 tablespoon whole juniper berries
3 cups dry white wine
1 cup dry vermouth
2 cups chicken stock
3 tablespoons unsalted butter
1 tablespoon neutral oil, such as canola or vegetable
1 large sweet onion, roughly chopped
Kosher salt and ground white pepper
1 tablespoon Dijon mustard
3 tablespoons unbleached all-purpose flour
2 large carrots, peeled and cut into ½-inch rounds
2 large leeks, rinsed and cut into ½-inch rounds
5 pounds bone-in English-cut short ribs
1 garlic head, sliced in half

Preheat the oven to 325°F (165°C).

Wrap the thyme and juniper berries in a small piece of cheesecloth, secured with some baker's twine to make a little sachet. Combine the wine, vermouth, chicken stock, and herb sachet in a large saucepan. Cook over medium heat until reduced by half.

Melt 1 tablespoon of the butter with the oil in a Dutch oven over medium heat. Add the onion, season lightly with salt and white pepper, and sauté until translucent and lightly golden, about 10 minutes. Stir in the Dijon and then sprinkle with the flour. Stir until the mixture thickens and is starting to brown, about 1 minute.

Add the reduced wine mixture, increase the heat to high, and bring to a hearty simmer. Continue to simmer until the mixture thickens a bit, about 5 minutes. Add the carrots and leeks. Season the ribs with salt and white pepper and then nestle the ribs and the garlic head into the pot.

Transfer the pot to the oven and cook, uncovered, for 1½ hours. Remove from the oven, flip the ribs, then cook for 1 to 1½ hours more, until the meat easily pulls from the bone and is fork-tender. Remove from the oven and bring to room temperature. Cover with aluminum foil, then refrigerate for at least 2 hours to overnight.

Preheat the oven to 325°F (165°C).

Once the ribs have rested, the fat will have solidified and risen to the top. Peel off the fat and reserve for another dish, such as steamed buns. Transfer the ribs to a sheet pan lined with foil and cover with additional foil. Heat the ribs in the oven for about 20 minutes.

In the meantime, remove the head of garlic and squeeze out the tender cloves into a blender, discarding the skin, then transfer the remaining vegetables and their juices to the blender and process until smooth. Pour the sauce through a sieve and into a saucepan, then bring to a simmer over medium-high heat until reduced by half, about 5 minutes. Whisk the remaining 2 tablespoons of butter into the sauce and season with salt and white pepper to taste. Serve the ribs smothered in sauce and paired with Creamed Savoy Cabbage (page 112). Alternatively, shred the meat, stir in the sauce, and serve in steamed buns.

Fish Tacos

SERVES 4

When I harvest jalapeño, tomato, and cabbage, I immediately start salivating and thinking of fish tacos. If you've ever spent any amount of time in Southern California/Baja California, you've had this style of fish taco. When I was in law school, on Fridays, we'd pile into whoever's car had enough gas to get us to and from Malibu and spill out onto the beach like the sleep-deprived clowns we were, rushing to the beachside taco stand to order as many fish tacos as we could stuff down our gullets. It was glorious and fresh. The light fry satisfied our more-childish food urges; the toppings woke us with their bright flavors and provided much-needed nutrients. With my garden here on the other side of the country, I can replicate the comforting food of my schooldays.

FOR THE SLAW

3 tablespoons mayonnaise

1 tablespoon pickled jalapeño brine

1 tablespoon diced pickled jalapeño

½ teaspoon pure maple syrup

1 cup finely sliced cabbage

½ small yellow onion, finely diced

FOR THE FISH

½ cup white wine vinegar

Kosher salt

1 pound firm, fresh white fish,* cut into 2-inch chunks

2 quarts neutral frying oil, such as peanut, canola, or vegetable

FOR THE FRYING BATTER

1 cup unbleached all-purpose flour

¼ cup fine cornmeal

1 tablespoon scape powder (see page 45; optional)

1 tablespoon sugar

2 teaspoons baking powder

1 teaspoon prepared yellow mustard

2 cups beer or plain seltzer water

1 large egg

FOR THE SAUCE

¼ cup mayonnaise

2 tablespoons sriracha

1 batch Corn Tortillas (page 254) or 12 store-bought corn tortillas

1 batch Ida Mae's Red Salsa (page 265)

1 ripe avocado, peeled, pitted, and cut into small cubes

1 lime, sliced

MAKE THE SLAW

Whisk together the mayonnaise, jalapeño brine, jalapeños, and maple syrup in a medium bowl. Add the cabbage and onion and toss to coat. Refrigerate until needed.

MAKE THE FISH

Combine the white wine vinegar and a generous pinch of kosher salt in a large nonreactive bowl. Add the fish chunks and toss to coat. Allow to sit for 5 to 10 minutes to season the fish, then immediately transfer to a parchment-lined sheet pan.

MAKE THE FRYING BATTER

Whisk together the flour, cornmeal, scape powder (if using), sugar, and baking powder in a separate large bowl. Then, whisk in the beer or seltzer, mustard, and egg until smooth. The mixture should be thinner than pancake batter but still able to coat the fish. Dip a rubber spatula into the bowl to make sure it clings to the paddle, coating it completely, like a thickened crème anglaise.

MAKE THE SAUCE

Whisk together the mayonnaise and sriracha in a small bowl. Transfer the sauce to a squeeze bottle, if desired.

FRY AND ASSEMBLE

Heat the frying oil in a large Dutch oven to just over 350°F (180°C). You want to maintain a constant temperature between 350 and 375°F (190°C). By starting *above* 350°F, you'll be able to more readily adjust the temperature when it is lowered from adding the cooler fish. If the oil is too hot, it will burn the outer coating and leave the fish raw. Too low, and the batter will start absorbing oil and be soggy and greasy, so continue checking the oil temperature and keep it steady.

Add the fish chunks to the batter mixture and toss to coat evenly. Using your fingers or tongs, add the fish chunks to the hot oil one at a time, "waving" the chunk in the oil to get an initial crisp on the batter so that when it's let go, there's no wet batter on the fish, causing it to stick to the bottom of the Dutch oven. (I call this the "fry hi!"—you are gently waving the little fish nugget to introduce it formally to the oil and then letting go.) Fry until the fish is golden brown, 3 to 4 minutes.

Layer a few chunks of fish into a tortilla. Top with the slaw, salsa, avocado, and a drizzle of the sauce. Serve immediately with a slice of lime.

***NOTE** I'm partial to flounder, but you can use cod, haddock, or tilapia. Use a pale lager, like Corona, for the batter.

MY HARVEST KITCHEN

Roast Chicken with Ají Amarillo Verde Green Sauce

SERVES 6

If you've got a great sauce, you've got a meal. I will have no argument! How many times has a gravy, a hollandaise, a jus, a tzatziki (not a sauce, technically, but I treat it like one), a ranch or green goddess dressing (also not technically sauces but aren't they really?) made everything better when you've dipped that dry meat, underseasoned potato, or limp broccoli into it? Ají verde sauce is right up there in the sauce-as-meal-saver sweepstakes. There is a lot of cilantro in it, part of what makes this sauce green, and while I've heard this refrain again and again, "I hate cilantro," you'll regret not using it. You'll be saying, "Wasn't going to even try it. So glad I did." But it's also a revelation, when you think about it: This is something fresh and green and *in season* that you can make when a snowstorm momentarily pumps the brakes on spring because things like peppers and herbs are so easily grown indoors under grow lights. Whether you buy a hydroponic tabletop unit, a floor to ceiling garden of eatin', or convert a shelf in the kitchen with some cheap strip grow lights for your greens, access to freshness is never far away. Oh, and the chicken doesn't even *need* the sauce. It's that good. But together, chef's kiss.

FOR THE MARINADE

5 garlic cloves, grated to a paste with a Microplane grater
¼ cup dry white wine
2 tablespoons soy sauce or Maggi brand liquid seasoning
2 tablespoons cider vinegar
1 tablespoon freshly squeezed lime juice
1 tablespoon pure maple syrup
1 tablespoon ají amarillo pepper paste*
1 teaspoon ground cumin
1 teaspoon dried oregano
1 teaspoon kosher salt

One 4-pound whole young chicken
Kosher salt
1 pound new potatoes, skins left on and scrubbed clean

FOR THE SAUCE

2 large jalapeño peppers, seeded and roughly chopped
2 large fresh ají amarillo peppers,* seeded and finely chopped
1 cup fresh cilantro leaves, roughly chopped
¾ cup mayonnaise
¼ cup aged sharp Cheddar, finely grated (don't use preshredded)
1 tablespoon extra-virgin olive oil
1 tablespoon cider vinegar
1 tablespoon freshly squeezed lime juice
1 large garlic clove, grated to a paste with a Microplane grater
Kosher salt

TO SERVE

1 lime, cut into wedges

recipe continues . . .

MARINATE THE CHICKEN

Whisk together all the marinade ingredients in a very large bowl or an extra-large resealable plastic bag. Set aside.

Spatchcock the chicken by placing the chicken, breast side down, on a cutting board. Using poultry shears, cut along the sides of the backbone. Remove the backbone and set aside for homemade stock. Turn the chicken breast side up and press down to flatten the chicken; you may hear a crunch. Pat the chicken dry with paper towels and place in the bowl of marinade, rub with the marinade, and cover with plastic wrap *or* place in the jumbo bag of marinade, seal the bag, and turn over to coat the chicken. Refrigerate for 2 hours to overnight.

Preheat your oven to 425°F (220°C). Line a half sheet pan with aluminum foil and then top with an ovenproof cooling rack. Arrange the spatchcocked chicken, breast side up, on the cooling rack, season with salt, and cook for 35 to 40 minutes, until a digital thermometer reads 165°F (73°C) when inserted into the thickest part of the meat. If, after 20 minutes, the skin is already nicely browned from the marinade, tent the chicken with foil to keep it from overbrowning.

While the chicken is cooking, add the potatoes to a liberally salted stockpot of water and bring to a simmer. Cook until the potatoes are just tender, 10 to 14 minutes, and add to the sheet pan with the chicken for the last 10 minutes of cooking, gently tossing in the juices to coat. Once fully cooked, remove from the oven and allow to rest for 10 minutes before serving.

MAKE THE SAUCE

While the chicken roasts, place the jalapeños, ají amarillo peppers, cilantro, mayonnaise, Cheddar, olive oil, vinegar, lime juice, and garlic in a blender and puree until smooth. Alternatively, you can place the sauce ingredients in a bowl and use an immersion blender for this or, a little less successfully, into a food processor (a mini food processor would do a better job at making a very fine and smooth sauce). Season with salt to taste.

Serve the chicken with the sauce, potatoes, and the lime wedges.

*NOTE You can substitute 2 tablespoons Sibarita brand Amarillin ají amarillo paste for the ají amarillo pepper paste.

Chicken Schnitzel

SERVES 4

In Austrian cuisine, there is a very specific culinary term that refers to schnitzel, whether *Wienerschnitzel* (veal), *Hähnchenschnitzel* (chicken), or *Schweineschnitzel* (pork), and that is *Soufflieren*. In Germany, it would refer to the action of a soufflé, that is, the egg soufflé reaching a lofty height. But in Austria, it's all about the schnitzel; specifically, the breading of the schnitzel. For the *perfect* schnitzel, you want the breading to gently steam between the meat and the breading and to lift off, separating itself from the meat. This creates a crisper crust and an overall more attractive schnitzel. By gently brushing the cutlet with lemon juice (or vodka) before dredging in the remaining ingredients, you create a barrier that will steam and gently coax the breading to higher, crispier, heights. The lemon also adds flavor, so it's a win-win in the schnitzel department.

4 boneless chicken breasts, about 8 ounces each
2 cups panko breadcrumbs,* processed in a food processor to make a finer crumb
1 cup unbleached all-purpose flour
4 large eggs
2 cups plus 1 tablespoon neutral oil, such as peanut or canola
¼ cup freshly squeezed lemon juice
Herbamare herbed sea salt or sea salt

TO FINISH
1 lemon, quartered
Chopped fresh flat-leaf parsley, for garnish

Preheat the oven to 300°F (150°C). Place an oven-safe cooling rack on a sheet pan and line a second sheet pan with parchment. Set aside.

Insert one chicken breast into a resealable plastic bag and place on a cutting board. Using a meat tenderizer or rolling pin, pound the chicken breast to ¼ inch thick throughout. The chicken breast should be uniformly thin. Flatten each remaining chicken breast in the same way. Pat each dry with a paper towel.

Line up three rimmed dishes that are wide enough to easily fit an entire chicken breast. Spread the flour in the first dish; in the second, whisk together the eggs and the tablespoon of oil; and in the third, spread the panko.

Using a pastry brush, brush each cutlet on both sides with the lemon juice. Season with Herbamare. Dredge the cutlet in the flour, pressing down on both sides so that it adheres to every nook and cranny. Gently shake off the excess flour. Dredge the cutlet in the egg mixture, using a spoon to gently press the

recipe continues...

cutlet into the egg to coat completely. Next, dredge in the panko on both sides, pressing with the back of a spoon to really adhere the crumbs to both sides of the chicken breast. Transfer to the cooling rack while you bread the remaining breasts.

Add the remaining 2 cups of oil in a large rondeau or high-walled skillet. Make sure that it's about 1 inch deep, but also that it only reaches halfway up the pan. You don't want the oil to spill over and start a grease fire! Alternatively, you can use a deep, wide-bottomed Dutch oven, but it makes lowering and lifting the chicken breast out of the oil a little harder, and the awkward angle might damage the crispy coating. Heat the oil over medium-high heat to between 350 and 375°F (180 to 190°C). Carefully place a cutlet into the oil, laying it down *away* from you into the oil. Shimmy the pan gently but constantly, to make sure the schnitzel doesn't stick to the bottom of the pan and browns evenly. Fry for 2 minutes on each side and flip if needed (sometimes the oil, while shimmying, coats and cooks the top side as well) until the exterior coating is golden brown and has "puffed." Place the fried cutlet on the parchment-lined sheet pan and keep in the warm oven while you continue to fry the remaining cutlets, one at a time. Serve with wedges of lemon and garnish with parsley. The perfect side dishes are cucumber salad and Käse Spätzle (page 105).

*NOTE I use panko because regular canned breadcrumbs don't provide the crispness that fine panko does.

FEASTS

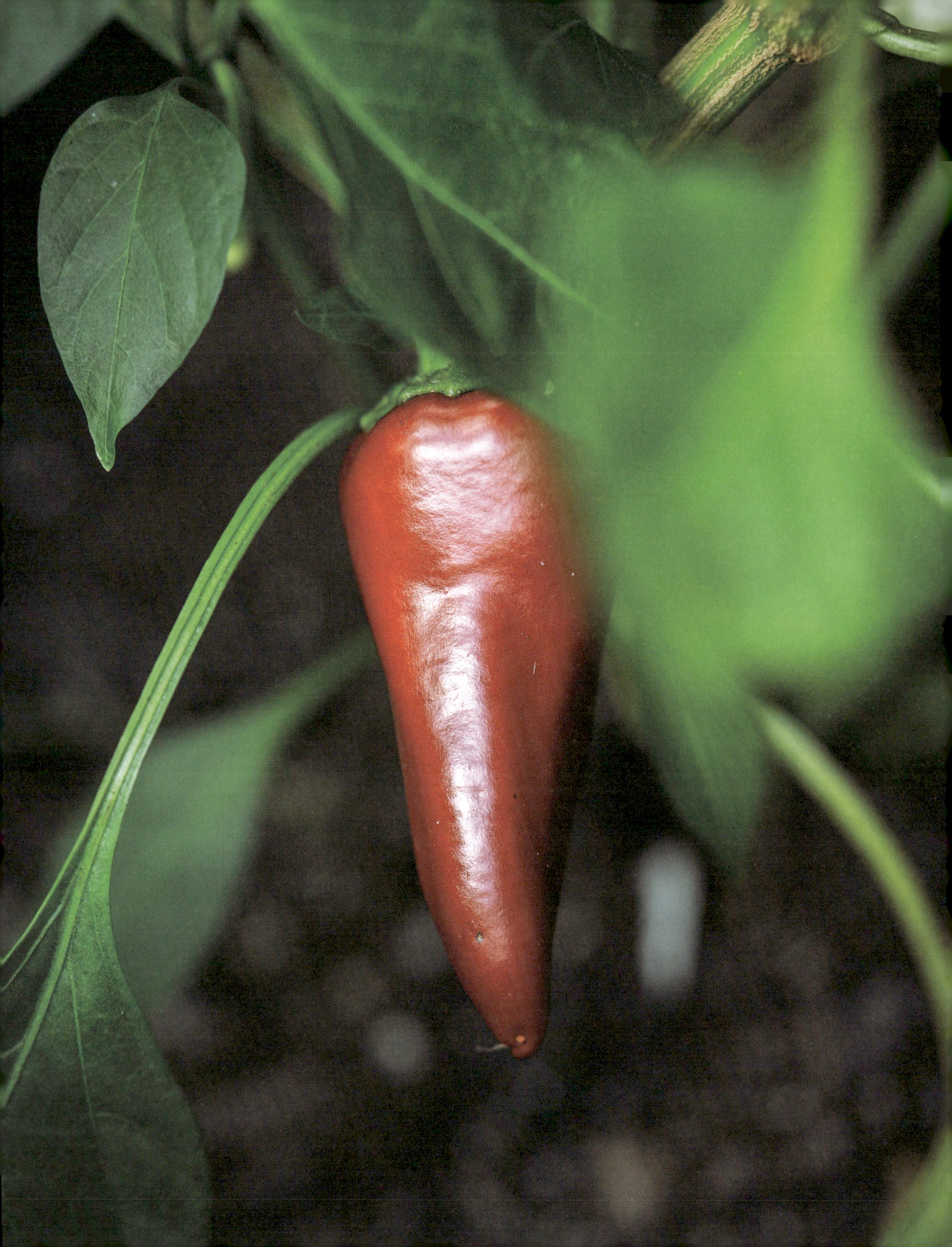

A NOTE FROM MY KITCHEN GARDEN

Peppergate

YEARS AGO, I WAS IN NEW YORK CITY and had an unquenchable craving for Peruvian roast chicken smothered in green sauce. To Pio Pio I went, and I was happy. But that happiness was short-lived, because the craving came back. And I was in Vermont, my home state. And Peruvian chicken is hard to come by here in Vermont unless I make it myself. But the pepper to make the sauce, ají amarillo, isn't something you can buy at the grocery store. I sourced ají pepper paste online. It comes in a convenient pouch that I keep in the fridge once opened and there's enough in one pouch for multiple recipes. But that wasn't enough, because it's *me* we're talking about, and I wouldn't be happy until I tasted the sauce made with *fresh* ají, and that requires a source. Again, in Vermont, I had to be the source. My first step was finding seeds for the pepper in question. I found them. When I received them, the long, jaunty orange pepper pictured on the seed page on the internet was nowhere to be seen. They came in a nondescript, miniature manila envelope with a sticker indicating the varietal of pepper, "ají amarillo," and that's it.

I immediately plopped two seeds in my indoor hydroponic grower. In a few weeks, they began to sprout. In a few months, they began to flower. With a little hand pollination on my part, using a tiny paintbrush and a spicy song in my heart, I went about fertilizing the flowers. In a few weeks, little fruits began to appear. And within a month, I took a picture of the green and then red hat-shaped pepper that had grown. I sent it to the seed company with the accompanying message, "I don't think this was the pepper seed I ordered."

Welcome to "Peppergate." In 2023, gardeners throughout the United States were planting seeds, waiting months, and harvesting peppers they hadn't intended on growing (most, strangely, ended up getting banana pepper seeds). It was blamed on cross-pollination or simply the mislabeling of seeds. In my case, cross-pollination was an absolute impossibility. I was the literal pollinator. Online, many a gardener lamented that though they thought they planted a dark green, deeply spicy jalapeño, they got a light yellow, barely sparky banana pepper instead. Of course, there can be confusion on the grower's part. For instance, jalapeños start dark green and, when left to ripen, turn a delightful red. Someone who wasn't familiar with the growth cycle of a jalapeño might see that red and think they'd been duped. In my case, the pepper I'd grown from seed, waiting for months on end to get a harvest, to be able to make a green sauce from a long orange pepper (the other ingredients in the sauce turn it green), was called the "Mad Hatter." It's a spicy red pepper shaped like a hat. It's adorable. Just not what I wanted or needed. And now, I wait for replacement seeds to sprout and the cycle begins again. This time, hopefully, the right pepper will appear. In the meantime, the internet will provide.

Cali (Turkey) Meatballs

SERVES 4

When I first moved to Los Angeles to go to law school, I lived in a house that had an avocado tree in the backyard. We'd strung up a hammock, using the avocado tree as the main source of shade, and in June, I'd rock back and forth studying for my finals in constitutional law and torts and musing about what to make with all the fruit dangling from the tree, in equal measure. You get creative once you've had enough of guacamole, and I started to venture into using avocado in dressings, such as green goddess, and as a beautiful source of silken fat and texture, as in these meatballs. Avocado also acts as a binder, along with cottage cheese, quinoa, and egg, and brings a load of creaminess to these delightful orbs. And unlike more traditional meatballs that use breadcrumbs as a binder, these are gluten-free and full of protein-rich fiber. Not that you'd know this from how luxurious they are. Serve over even more quinoa and drizzle with bright tahini dressing for the perfect California-inspired early summer meal. Hammock optional.

Extra-virgin olive oil, for brushing
1 small, ripe avocado, peeled and pitted
1 cup small-curd, full-fat cottage cheese
1 small yellow onion, finely chopped
1 large egg
Grated zest and juice of 1 lemon
1 teaspoon Maggi brand liquid seasoning
1 teaspoon dried thyme
1 cup cooked and cooled quinoa (see page 257)
1 pound ground turkey*
Kosher salt and ground white pepper

TO SERVE
Arugula
Tahini Dressing (page 263)

Preheat the oven to 400ºF (200ºC). Line a half sheet pan with parchment and coat with olive oil. Set aside.

Mash the avocado in a large bowl. Add the cottage cheese, onion, egg, lemon zest and juice, Maggi, and thyme. Mix to combine. Add the quinoa and stir into the mixture. Break up the turkey and add to the bowl. Season generously with kosher salt and white pepper. Using your hands, gently combine the ingredients and then shape the mixture into 2-inch balls. Don't compress too tightly. Space the meatballs about an inch apart on the prepared pan. Carefully brush the tops with olive oil and bake until the meatballs are golden brown and the internal temperature reads 165ºF (73ºC) on a digital thermometer. Serve on a bed of arugula and smothered in Tahini Dressing (page 263).

*NOTE I use a higher-fat content ground turkey.

FEASTS

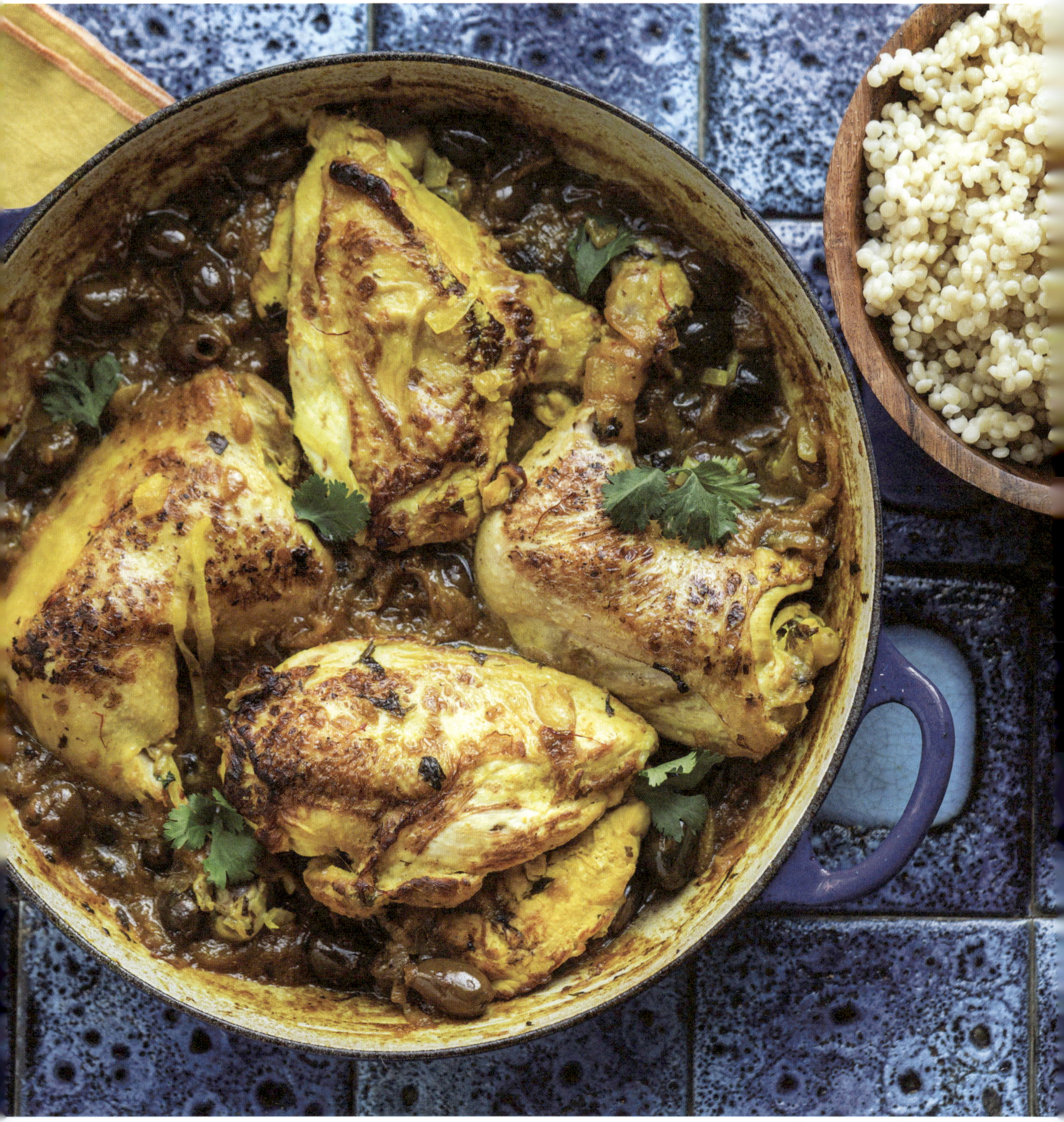

Preserved Lemon and Saffron Chicken Tagine

SERVES 4

When Ray and I went to Morocco on our honeymoon, we got lost in the maze of walled streets in Fez. We were utterly entranced by the amazing food. The use of aromatic spice blends and bright preserved lemons celebrate Moroccan cuisine and bring back the adventures and flavors we shared on our honeymoon.

FOR THE MARINADE

1 cup low-sodium chicken stock

¼ cup freshly squeezed lemon juice

3 tablespoons extra-virgin olive oil

1 preserved lemon, flesh removed, seeded, and rind roughly chopped (see page 269)

4 garlic cloves, grated to a paste with a Microplane grater

2 teaspoons ground turmeric

2 teaspoons grated fresh ginger

1 teaspoon kosher salt

2 skin-on chicken breasts

2 skin-on chicken thighs

FOR THE TAGINE

3 tablespoons extra-virgin olive oil

2 large yellow onions, sliced into half-moons

4 garlic cloves, grated to a paste with a Microplane grater

⅓ cup finely chopped fresh cilantro

Generous pinch of saffron

1 cup low-sodium chicken stock

Kosher salt and freshly ground black pepper

1 cup Kalamata olives, plus 2 tablespoons olive brine

MAKE THE MARINADE

Whisk all the marinade ingredients together in a large bowl and add the chicken, turning over to coat. Cover and refrigerate overnight.

MAKE THE TAGINE

Heat the olive oil in a 3½-quart enameled braiser over medium heat and add the sliced onions. Sauté, stirring occasionally, until softened but not browned, about 10 minutes. Add the garlic, cilantro, and saffron, and then add the marinade mixture (reserving the chicken pieces) and stock, stirring to combine. Season with salt and pepper. Nestle in the chicken pieces, increase the heat to high, and simmer for 1 minute. Lower the heat to low, cover, and gently simmer until the chicken is fully cooked and registers 165°F (73°C) on a thermometer, about 1 hour. Transfer the chicken pieces to a large plate and cover with aluminum foil. Set aside.

To the sauce in the braiser, add the olives and olive brine. Simmer over low heat, stirring occasionally, until the mixture thickens and the oil just begins to separate, 30 to 35 minutes. Season with salt to taste and nestle the chicken back into the mixture, allowing the chicken to simmer in the sauce about 5 minutes more to reheat. Serve with couscous (see page 258).

A NOTE FROM MY KITCHEN GARDEN

Saffron

SAFFRON THREADS ARE JUST THE DRIED STIGMA AND STYLES AT THE CENTER of a crocus. But not just any crocus, which you probably guessed if you've ever dropped a fair few dollars on some saffron. It's the *Crocus sativus*, or "saffron crocus." Don't expect to bop around the garden in the early spring, harvesting these beauties. Those aren't the crocuses you want. The saffron crocus is a fall-blooming crocus, showing up in the late autumn when all other flowers have left the garden. The growing conditions are pretty specific, too. Their native landscape in Iran is slightly replicated in my home state of Vermont, and I harvest from 100-plus plants every year. That's right, you can buy saffron crocus corms online, and if you get them in the ground the second they arrive, you'll likely be able to harvest that very same fall, assuming you live in the right conditions. They don't like shade, so find a sunny slope for them to burst forth and make sure you protect your back while you work, because harvesting those vibrant deep orange threads can do a number on your back. Dry them in a protected sunny spot for 24 hours until they are crisp, then store in an airtight container. Oh the flavors you'll conjure from a single thread and, even better, all that money you'll save!

Butter Chicken

SERVES 6

When I start harvesting my Brandywine tomatoes, those heirloom, big slicers that are so sweet and juicy that they deserve their best life, I ache to make butter chicken, but it's usually way too hot for something so deeply warming. But this reminds me to freeze a large crop of the best of those beauties for when the air turns brisk.

There's a reason that this dish has caused a legal feud in India, two restaurants claiming to have invented the glorious stuff, because, if made right, it manages to fuse savory and sweet. Velvety textures with bright *and* creamy flavors. I make butter chicken even when I have to buy anemic tomatoes at the grocery store in the winter, because it's that good, but I feel remiss if I don't use the sweetest tomatoes from my garden, the juiciest onions and garlic that I've left to cure in my barn, to create a dish that will stand as an all-time favorite in the Prado household. The other reason it's so fun to make is that, in the dead of winter, I can run my summer-frozen tomatoes under warm water and the skin just peels right off, as if by magic. Then you just give them a rough chop, simmer, blend, voilà!

2 pounds skinless, boneless chicken breasts, cut into 1-inch strips

1 tablespoon ginger paste*

1 tablespoon garlic paste*

1 teaspoon Kashmiri red pepper powder or other red chili powder

Salt and freshly ground black pepper

1 tablespoon ghee or clarified butter

1 tablespoon neutral oil, such as canola

FOR THE SAUCE

1 tablespoon ghee or clarified butter

1 large yellow onion, roughly chopped

Salt

2 tablespoons cider vinegar

1 pound superripe, fresh or frozen, Brandywine beefsteak tomatoes, roughly chopped

3 garlic cloves, minced

½ cup cashew pieces

1 cup low-sodium chicken stock

1 tablespoon pure maple syrup

1 teaspoon garam masala

1 teaspoon Kashmiri red pepper powder or other red chili powder (optional)

TO FINISH

½ cup heavy cream

8 tablespoons unsalted butter, cut into tablespoon-size pieces

1 teaspoon fenugreek leaves

Salt and freshly ground black pepper

Place the chicken in a large bowl. Massage the chicken pieces with the ginger paste, garlic paste, and chili powder, then season with a generous pinch of salt and the black pepper. Cover and refrigerate for 30 minutes to an hour.

Melt the tablespoon of ghee along with the

recipe continues . . .

FEASTS

neutral oil in a large skillet over high heat. Add the chicken pieces, shimmy the pan to keep the meat from sticking, and cook until golden, 2 to 3 minutes. Then, turn and cook for 2 to 3 minutes more. Transfer the chicken to a large plate.

MAKE THE SAUCE

Lower the heat to medium, add a tablespoon more of ghee, then add the onion. Season the onion lightly with salt. Sauté until the onion is translucent, about 5 minutes. Add the cider vinegar to the pan to deglaze, and use a wooden spoon to scrape up the fond (the lovely, flavorful brown bits). Add the tomatoes, garlic, and cashews. Sauté over medium heat, stirring occasionally, until the tomatoes are supersoft and falling apart, 10 to 15 minutes. Add the chicken stock, maple syrup, and garam masala. Taste for heat and add the chili powder, if using. Stir to combine.

Transfer the mixture to a blender and blend until smooth. Pour through a sieve and press to get every last bit of goodness out. The sauce should be silken smooth. Alternatively, you can transfer to a large bowl and use an immersion blender to blend the mixture. Transfer the sauce back to the pan, then add the cream, butter, fenugreek, and the chicken pieces. Simmer for 5 minutes, or until the chicken is completely cooked through. Check for seasoning, adding more salt, black pepper, maple syrup, vinegar, and spice as needed. Serve over Jasmine Rice (page 258).

*NOTE I use a Microplane grater to finely grate the ginger and garlic.

FEASTS

MY HARVEST KITCHEN

Chicken, Leek, and Mushroom Pie

SERVES 8

Winter is meat pie time. It's also time to deploy those ingredients that you've invested time in preserving to use in the hibernation times—ingredients that, when fresh, have a beautifully long shelf life, such as leeks. Mushrooms, whether fresh ones that you grow yourself in your own little mushroom container or buy from the grocery store, or ones you've harvested and dried for winter use, shine in this delicious meal that utilizes mushrooms to their greatest advantage.

1 batch G's Zippy, Flaky Pie Dough (page 239)

FOR THE FILLING

½ cup low-sodium chicken stock

1 cup dried mixed forest mushrooms or 8 ounces fresh mushrooms such as shiitake, maitake, and chanterelle

1 tablespoon olive oil

1 tablespoon unsalted butter

1 small onion, finely chopped

1 large leek, washed, dried, and cut into ¼-inch rounds

Kosher salt

1 pound boneless, skinless chicken breasts, cut into 1-inch-thick strips

1 pound boneless, skinless chicken thighs, cut into 1-inch-thick strips

¼ cup dry white wine

2 tablespoons unbleached all-purpose flour

¼ cup heavy cream

2 tablespoons Dijon mustard

1 teaspoon dried thyme

¼ cup grated Parmigiano-Reggiano

Egg wash (1 large egg whisked together with 1 tablespoon water)

Preheat the oven to 350°F (180°C).

Divide the pie dough in half and roll out each half into a rough 12-inch round. Transfer to a parchment-lined sheet pan, cover with plastic wrap, and refrigerate. This allows the dough to rest and cool while you make the filling, so that once you do line the pie tin, the dough will hold its shape.

MAKE THE FILLING

Pour the chicken stock into a small, microwave-safe bowl, then microwave in 30-second bursts to warm. Add the dried mushrooms and stir to coat and soften for 5 minutes then roughly chop. For fresh mushrooms, roughly chop and eliminate the stock. Set aside.

Heat the oil and butter in a Dutch oven over medium heat. Add the onion and leek and season generously with salt. Cook until the onion and leek start to soften, about 5 minutes. Add the chicken pieces and cook over medium-high heat until golden brown, about 3 minutes on each side. Add the mushrooms and continue to cook, stirring occasionally, for about 10 minutes. Add the wine and, using a flat-bottomed wooden spoon, scrape up the fond (browned

recipe continues . . .

bits). Sprinkle the flour over the mixture. Continue to cook over medium heat until the flour is completely incorporated and you can no longer see any dry flour bits, about 1 minute. Add the cream and mustard and cook until the mixture is thickened and the chicken is cooked through, reading 165ºF (73ºC) on a digital thermometer, about 10 minutes. Remove from the heat, stir in the thyme, and allow to cool to room temperature.

Line a 9-inch deep-dish pie tin with one round of dough. Sprinkle the Parmigiano-Reggiano over the dough and then add the filling. Brush the egg wash along the edge of the bottom round of dough and top with the second round of dough, gently pressing along the edge to seal. Using a sharp pair of kitchen shears or a sharp paring knife, trim the dough just at the edge of the tin. Brush the dough with remaining egg wash, making sure the egg wash does not drip over the cut edge of the pie, otherwise the dough won't puff. Bake for 45 to 55 minutes, until deeply golden brown. Serve immediately.

Schweinebraten (German Pork Roast)

SERVES 8

Schweinebraten is succulent and crisp. Juicy and tender. Flavorful and more flavorful. And this is what often flummoxes those who make the assumption that German food is just brown, beige, and flavorless. Well, it is often brown and sometimes beige, but there is always flavor. Paprika and caraway and cumin are spices on heavy rotation in German cooking, as they are here. Choose a pork shoulder (sometimes called "butt" but not because it's describing the origin of the meat; it is named after the barrels or "butts" that colonial New England butchers used to transport inexpensive cuts of meat) with an even fat cap that brings loads of flavor and, if it's not *too* thick, brings a cracklin' crisp to the party. Surrounding the pork with a moat of root veggies toward the end of cooking makes this a one-dish meal full of flavor.

1 teaspoon cumin seeds

1 teaspoon caraway seeds

1 teaspoon yellow mustard seeds

2 teaspoons smoked paprika

2 tablespoons kosher salt

2 teaspoons ground white pepper

One 4-pound boneless pork shoulder

3 tablespoons German mustard

1 pound fingerling potatoes or baby Yukon Gold potatoes

2 medium yellow onions (1 pound total), quartered

1 pound red radishes, halved

2 large carrots, peeled and cut into 1-inch strips

12 ounces German dark (*dunkel*) beer

1½ cups chicken stock

3 tablespoons unsalted butter

2 tablespoons unbleached all-purpose flour

Preheat the oven to 350°F (180°C). Combine the cumin, caraway, and mustard seeds in a small skillet and heat over low heat until fragrant. Remove from the heat and allow to cool completely before transferring to a spice grinder or mortar and pestle. Grind to a powder. Transfer to a small bowl and stir in the paprika, salt, and white pepper.

With a sharp paring knife, score the pork fat cap in a crosshatch. Rub the entire pork shoulder with the German mustard and then season on all sides with the spice mixture. Place the pork on an ovenproof cooling rack set over a half sheet pan, or on a roasting rack placed in a roasting pan. Roast for 1 hour.

Remove the pork from the oven and place on a cutting board. Scrape up any fond, leave in the pan, then add the potatoes, onions, radishes, and carrots. Pour the beer and chicken stock into the pan with the veggies. Nestle the pork

recipe continues . . .

directly on the veggie bed and roast for up to 2 hours more, basting the veggies and pork every 20 minutes, until the internal temperature of the pork reads 165°F (73°C) and the veggies are tender and golden.

Transfer the pork to a cutting board and cover with aluminum foil to rest. Transfer the veggies to a large bowl.

Pour the pan juices into a measuring cup, scraping up any bits of fond on the pan. Allow to sit for a few minutes to allow the fat to rise to the top. Skim off excess fat with a spoon. Melt the butter in a medium saucepan over medium heat, then sprinkle in the flour and whisk to make a roux. Continue to whisk until the mixture thickens and just begins to brown. Pour in the pan juices and continue whisking until the mixture comes to a hearty simmer. Lower the heat and continue whisking until the mixture reduces and thickens, about 10 minutes. Taste for seasoning.

Arrange the pork on a bed of the roasted veggies on a platter. Serve with the sauce on the side or poured over the roast.

Potato Gnocchi with Butternut Squash and Sage Bake

SERVES 8

My mother, after she'd been diagnosed with cancer but before she was terminal, decided that she was going to do some serious culinary exploration, eating things she'd never allowed herself before. As we used to say in the day, she was a "health nut." She ate only organic, all vegan, and exercised constantly. And then, in her late 50s, was diagnosed with colon cancer. And she was pissed. She made it her mission to play in the kitchen and to snag some schmancy reservations (looking at you, Inn at Little Washington) while she still felt well enough to enjoy it all. Her nemesis during this time were gnocchi. She was determined to make them well. It felt like, every visit back home to Virginia, I'd find my mother in the kitchen, cursing at a stockpot of floating potato bits. Every time she'd add the little dumplings to the water, they'd disintegrate. And then one day, boom! she nailed it. We ate those delicious potato pillows, and she moved on to her next challenge. My mom's determination is the backbone of this recipe, because it takes patience and grit to make something this tender and delicate. Not unlike the patience it takes to grow winter squash. That said, feel free to just fry up the gnocchi with some butter and a bit of sage to celebrate your accomplishments. And toast my mom, Helga, while you're at it.

FOR THE GNOCCHI

3 pounds russet potatoes*

2 large egg yolks

1 teaspoon kosher salt

1 cup unbleached all-purpose flour

FOR THE SAUCE

Nonstick baking spray

1 garlic head

2 tablespoons extra-virgin olive oil

1 large butternut squash, peeled, seeded, and cut into 1-inch cubes (1 pound total)

4 fresh sage leaves, roughly chopped

Kosher salt

½ cup heavy cream

½ cup full-fat sour cream

2 cups chicken or vegetable stock

4 pork sausages* (1 pound), removed from their casing, torn into small pieces, and fully cooked over low heat in a skillet (optional)

TO FINISH

2 tablespoons unsalted butter

2 cups shredded provolone

1 cup panko breadcrumbs

MAKE THE GNOCCHI

Preheat the oven to 450°F (230°C). Poke the potatoes with a fork and then place them directly on the oven racks. Bake until fork-tender, 40 to 45 minutes. Reduce the oven temperature to 375°F (190°C).

recipe continues . . .

Cut the potatoes in half while still warm and place, flesh side down, in a potato ricer, one potato half at a time. Press the potato back onto the sheet pan, spreading out the riced potato as you go. After pressing the potato half, remove the skin from the inside of the ricer before processing the next potato half, until all are riced.

Whisk together the egg yolks with the salt in a small bowl. Pour the yolk over the hot potatoes on the sheet pan and then sprinkle ½ cup of the flour over the potatoes. Use a bench knife or bowl scraper to quickly slice through and turn over the potato to incorporate the yolks and flour. (Do this too slowly and you run the risk of cooking the yolks!) Press the mixture together into a rough 4-by-8-inch rectangle, but don't compact too much. Use a rolling pin to gently roll out to double the size. Fold in half. Turn the dough 90 degrees, roll out to double in size again, and sprinkle with ¼ cup of the remaining flour. Fold in half, turn 90 degrees, press to double in size, and then fold in half again. Dust the dough with a bit more flour, then wrap in plastic wrap so the dough doesn't form a dry skin and it retains some warmth.

Using the bench scraper, scrape the work surface to clean off any stuck dough. Dust the work surface with some of the remaining flour. Cut off one-third of the dough and roll that portion with the palm of your hand to create a long, even, ½-inch-thick rope. Use the bench scraper to cut the rope into 1-inch pieces and then transfer the gnocchi to a parchment-lined sheet pan. Cover with plastic wrap to keep a skin from forming while you make the sauce.

MAKE THE SAUCE

Note: Have the squash and garlic ready to go into the oven right after the potatoes are out to save time.

Line a sheet pan with a silicone baking mat or spray a sheet pan with nonstick baking spray. Cut the top of the garlic head, exposing the tips of the cloves. Brush with a bit of the olive oil and then wrap in aluminum foil. Set aside. Add the squash cubes to the prepared sheet pan and toss with the remaining olive oil and the sage. Spread out evenly on the pan and season with kosher salt, leaving a small space; into that space place the foil-wrapped garlic. Roast until the squash is tender, about 45 minutes, then remove from the oven. Leave the oven on.

Remove the garlic from the foil and let cool. Transfer the squash to a food processor or blender. Squeeze the roasted garlic from the skins—it will be pastelike—and add to the squash. Puree until smooth. Add the cream, sour cream, and ½ cup of the stock and process slowly until smooth. Then, slowly add a bit of stock at a time to thin out the sauce to the consistency of a loose batter. Season with salt to taste. Set aside.

COOK THE GNOCCHI

Bring lightly salted water to a boil in a large pot. Once boiling, place a deep, ovenproof cast-iron skillet over medium-high heat on another burner and melt the butter. Using a slotted spoon, carefully lower the gnocchi into the boiling water, cook until they have risen to the top, and then allow them to cook about 30 seconds more. Skim off the gnocchi from the water using the slotted spoon, and immediately transfer to the butter in the skillet. Cook the gnocchi until slightly golden.

TO FINISH

Add 1½ cups of the provolone into the sauce in the processor and pulse once or twice to incorporate. Add the sauce to the skillet, gently folding the sauce and gnocchi together until just coated. Fold in the sausage pieces, if using. Sprinkle the remaining ½ cup of provolone on top and then sprinkle with the panko. Bake in the 450°F (230°C) oven for 20 minutes or until the panko is golden brown.

*NOTE Russets are key because they are dry and starchy and make for a fluffier gnocchi. You can also skip making the gnocchi and use 2 packages (1,000 grams total) premade DeCecco Potato Gnocchi. Boil and crisp as per the recipe. I use Vermont Salumi Fiddlehead IPA Bratwurst.

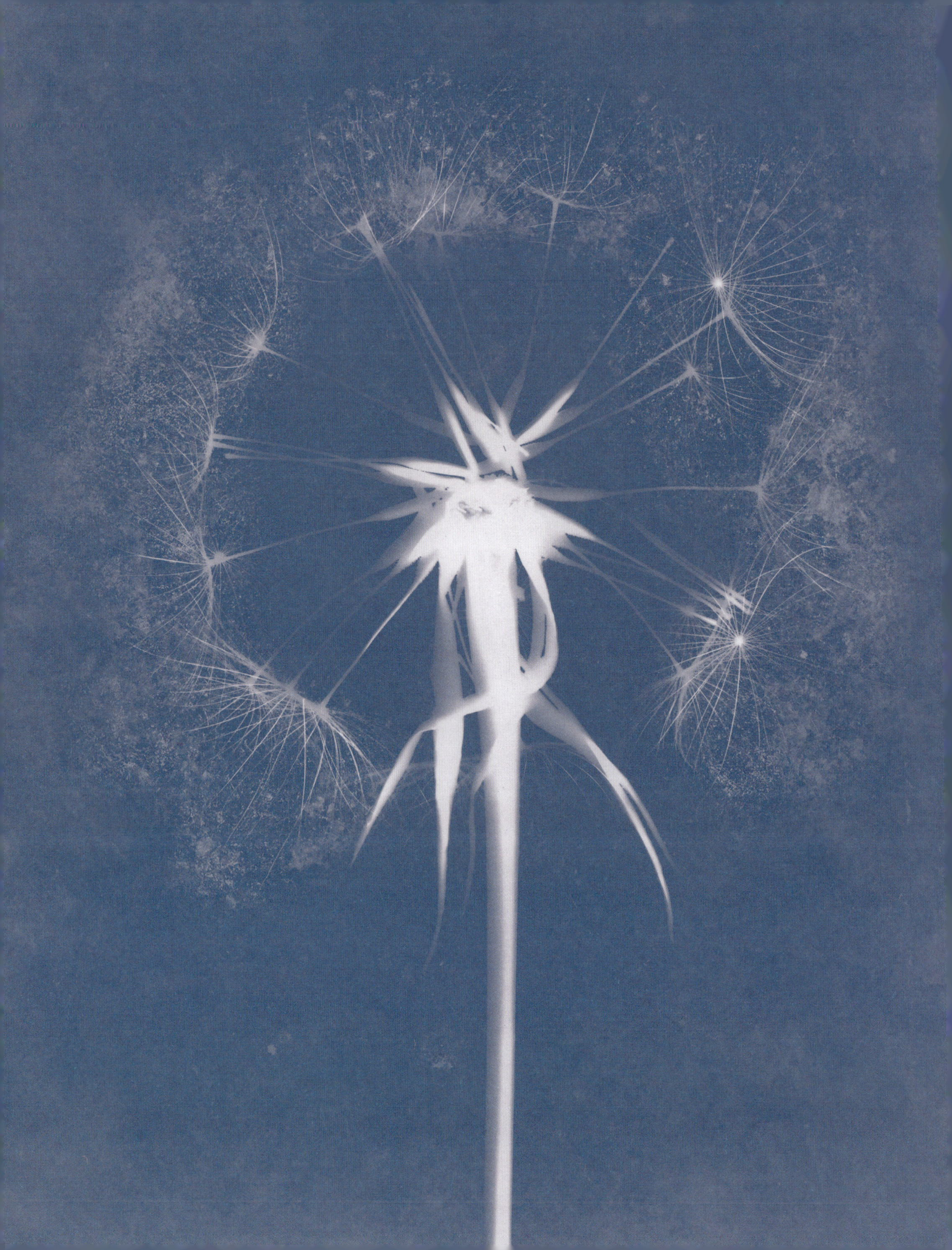

SWEETS

Blueberry-Lemon Bundt

SERVES 8

Brioche dough has many applications, but people tend to stick to just a few: loaves, buns, and doughnuts. But one day, with a batch of brioche dough on the rise and some mischief in my heart, I considered the possibility of making a sweet treat that was a little bit pull-apart "monkey bread" with a dash of Charlotte Royale in its beauty. The flavors? Lemon and blueberry, putting to use an ingredient in season (lemons) and an ingredient I'd harvested and dried for a day just like this. A bit of sunshine on a chilly early spring day.

Nonstick baking spray
1 batch Brioche dough (page 241), bulk fermented
¾ cup (150 grams) granulated sugar
Grated zest of 2 lemons
½ teaspoon citric acid*
Unbleached all-purpose flour, for dusting
4 tablespoons (56 grams) unsalted butter, melted and slightly cooled
1 cup freeze-dried blueberries

Line a sheet pan with parchment and spray with nonstick baking spray. Turn out the brioche dough onto the prepared sheet pan and flatten with your hands to deflate the dough and to spread it out into a rough rectangle. Spray the top of the dough with nonstick baking spray, cover with plastic wrap, and refrigerate until thoroughly chilled, 1 to 2 hours.

Spray a 16-cup Bundt or angel food cake pan with nonstick baking spray. Set aside.

Whisk together the sugar and lemon zest in a small bowl. Rub the zest and sugar together so that the sugar begins to absorb the oils of the zest. Stir in the citric acid and set aside.

Dust a work surface with flour. Remove the dough from the refrigerator and transfer to your work surface. Roll out the dough into a 24-by-8-inch inch rectangle. Using a pastry brush, brush the melted butter over the surface of the dough and then sprinkle with the sugar mixture. Dot the dough evenly with the blueberries, gently pressing them into the dough. Roll the dough as tightly as you can from the long end, like a jelly roll. Cut the roll into twenty-four 1-inch slices. Line the outside wall of the Bundt pan with a layer of the slices, making sure not to overlap. Line the bottom of the pan with a layer, then add a second layer on top of that with the remaining pieces. Cover the pan with plastic wrap and allow to rest at room temperature until doubled in size, 1½ to 2 hours.

Preheat your oven to 350°F (180°C). Bake for 45 to 50 minutes, until the interior of the cake registers between 190 and 200°F (88 and 95°C). If the dough starts to brown in the exposed area and you have a good deal of time left in the bake, tent with aluminum foil to keep the top from overbrowning. Once baked, immediately turn out onto a cooling rack.

*NOTE Citric acid gives the very rich cake an extra-lemony brightness and can be found online at King Arthur Baking Company and at baking stores.

SWEETS

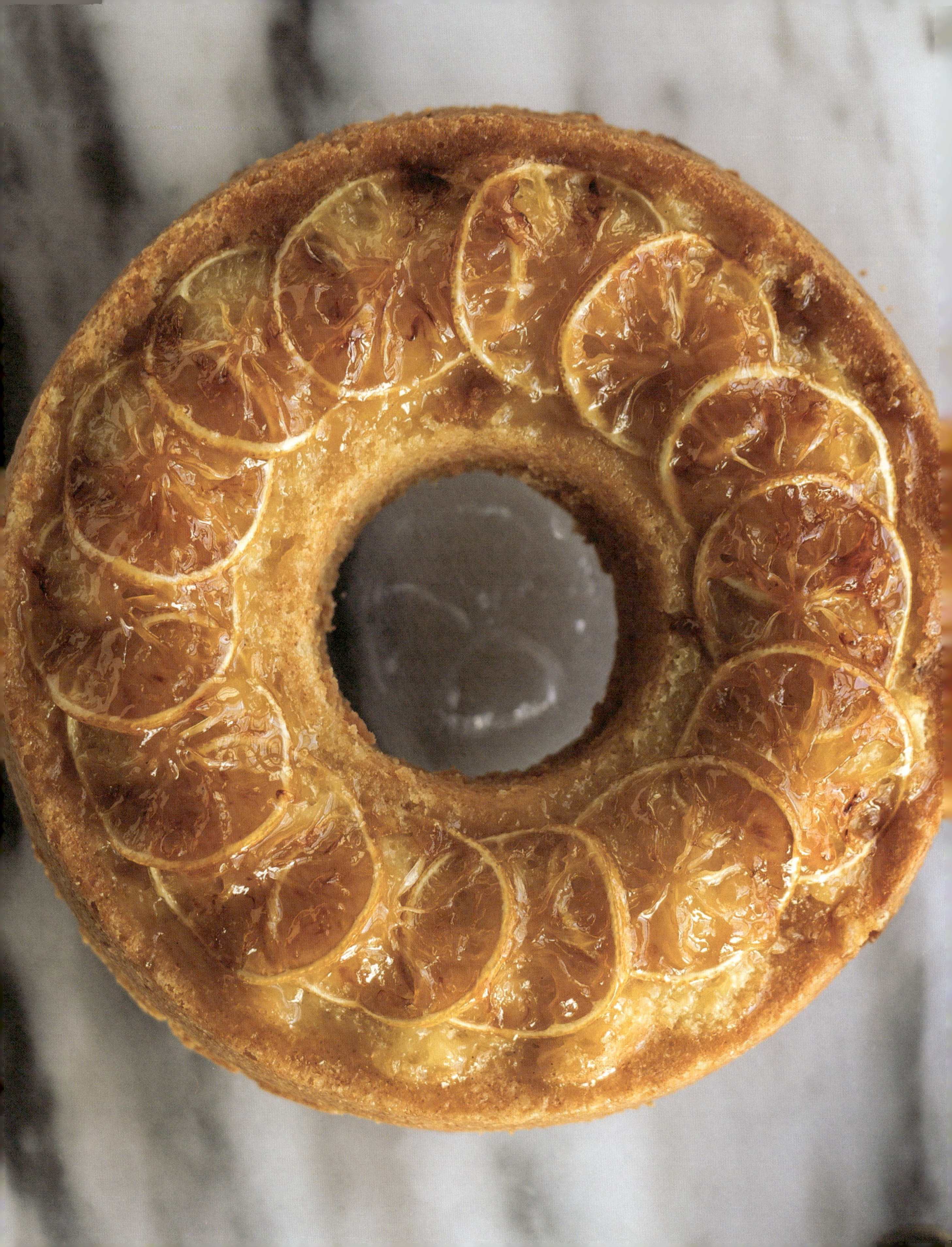

Ellen's Sunshine Cake

SERVES 12

My friend Ellen was in dire need of a burst of citrus and found a recipe that looked to pack the punch she required. But instead of satisfying that midwinter craving, it left her bitter. Literally. So, I made it my mission to create a recipe that ticked all the boxes for her: supertart and lemony? Check. Sweet and delicate? Check. Pretty without being fussy? Check. This is the cake that will lift you straight out of the winter doldrums and carry you happily into spring.

Look for lemons with smoother, thin skin rather than heavy, knobby-skinned lemons. You'll get more juice from them, they'll be easier to cut, and they'll have far less white, bitter pith. Juniper is a spice sympathetic to lemon zest, enhancing the aromatics present in citrus skin. It's not an overwhelming flavor. Instead, it complements the existing aromatics and oils present in the zest, deepening the flavor of the cake as a whole.

FOR THE CAKE

4 large lemons
½ cup (125 grams) whole-milk plain Greek yogurt
1⅔ cups (330 grams) granulated sugar
1 teaspoon ground juniper berries (optional)
2½ cups (300 grams) unbleached all-purpose flour, plus ¼ cup for the pan
2 teaspoons baking powder
½ teaspoon baking soda
1 teaspoon fine sea salt
Nonstick baking spray
1 stick plus 5 tablespoons (185 grams) unsalted butter, at room temperature
4 large eggs, at room temperature
1 teaspoon vanilla bean paste or vanilla extract
1 teaspoon lemon extract (optional)

FOR THE LEMON TOPPING

2 large lemons
½ cup granulated sugar

FOR THE SYRUP

Scant ½ cup reserved lemon juice
½ cup granulated sugar
1 tablespoon whole juniper berries

MAKE THE CAKE

Zest (use a Microplane grater) and juice the four lemons. Measure out ½ cup of the juice for the batter and transfer to a small bowl along with the yogurt. Stir to combine. Pour the rest of the juice (about a scant ½ cup) into a small saucepan and reserve for the cake syrup.

Combine the sugar, lemon zest, and ground juniper berries (if using) in a small mixing bowl. Massage the zest into the sugar. Sugar is hygroscopic: it leeches the moisture from ingredients around it and will absorb the moisture and oils from the zest. Allow to sit for about 10 minutes.

Combine the 2½ cups of flour, baking powder, baking soda, and salt in a large bowl. Whisk

recipe continues . . .

for 30 seconds to distribute the leavening. Set aside.

Preheat the oven to 350°F (180°C). Spray a 9-10 cup Bundt pan with nonstick baking spray, sprinkle with the extra flour, and turn the pan so that there's a coating of flour clinging to the spray. Tap out the excess.

Combine the butter and the sugar mixture in a stand mixer fitted with the paddle attachment. Cream on medium-high speed until light and fluffy. The mixture should become much airier and lighter in both color and texture. Scrape down the bottom and sides of the bowl a few times during the creaming process. This can take up to 15 minutes.

With the mixer on high speed, add the eggs, one at a time, making sure that each egg is completely incorporated before adding the next and scraping down the bottom and sides of the bowl between each addition. After the last egg has been added, mix for 1 minute on high speed to emulsify the batter. Add the vanilla and lemon extract, if using, and mix briefly.

With the mixer running on low speed, add one-third of the flour mixture, then half of the yogurt mixture, then one-third of the flour, the remaining yogurt mixture, ending with the remaining flour mixture. Stop the mixer, scrape down the bottom and sides of the bowl, and continue to mix on low speed until the flour is incorporated, just a few seconds.

MAKE THE LEMON TOPPING

Cut the two lemons into paper-thin slices, using a very sharp chef's knife or a mandoline, removing the seeds as you go along. You'll need 13 or 14 slices total. Dip each slice in the sugar, coating both sides, and line the bottom of the Bundt pan with the lemon slices, overlapping so every slice fits evenly (they will shrink in the baking, so overlapping is crucial). Spoon the batter over the lemon slices. Use the back of a spoon to level the batter and then gently tap the pan on the countertop to settle the batter and to pop any large bubbles. Bake on the middle rack for 45 to 50 minutes, until the cake springs back when gently poked.

MAKE THE SYRUP

Meanwhile, combine the scant ½ cup of reserved lemon juice with the sugar and juniper berries in a small saucepan. Heat over low heat, stirring occasionally, until the sugar has completely dissolved.

The moment the cake is removed from the oven, set a timer for 10 minutes and keep the cake in the Bundt pan. Cakes are at their most fragile when just out of the oven and the crumb is still setting. Using a skewer, poke holes in the top of the cake (which will become its underside when you remove the pan) as it rests in the pan. Using a pastry brush, brush the cake with the syrup (don't use it all). Once the 10 minutes have elapsed, turn the cake out of the pan onto a parchment-lined cooling rack and immediately brush the top and sides of the cake with the remaining syrup. Allow to cool completely before serving.

A NOTE FROM MY KITCHEN GARDEN

Annual, Biennial, Perennial

EVEN IF YOU NEVER INTEND TO GROW a fruit or vegetable, I think it's important to get to know a little bit about how they work. Most vegetables live for only one year, cycling from seed to seedling to flowering plant to fruiting plant to . . . death. That's called an annual. It's a big bummer, but that's life. The good news is if you don't like what the plant produced, you don't have to feel guilty that you no longer have to care for it. There's a benefit to this arrangement where pests and soil health are concerned as well: rotation of where the plant grows helps keep plant-specific pests guessing and allows the soil to take a break from that specific type of plant needs.

Then there are biennials, plants that take two years to go through their life cycle. Elephant garlic and foxgloves are common biennials. They grow a little the first year, go dormant during winter, and then show their stuff the second year. In the case of foxgloves, they send up stalks of resplendent flowers that simply tower above everything else, whereas the year before, they just managed some low-growing, albeit lush, foliage. Elephant garlic sends up some bladelike leaves the first year, forming not a bulb but what's called a "round." You can eat the round, but it's much better to leave it in the ground because, the next year, that little orb will transform into the elephant-cloved bulb that it's meant to become. Just so you know, elephant garlic isn't a proper garlic but a close cousin as a member of the allium family. It's larger, of course, but also milder than garlic.

Then there are perennials, plants that live year after year. Shrubs, canes, or brambles (e.g., raspberries), and trees are perennials. Most herbs are also perennials, which make them the perfect plant to keep indoors, bursts of freshness when nothing is popping up outside. Very few vegetables are perennials, but there are a few. Rhubarb is a prime example (although used as a fruit, it is considered a vegetable), as is asparagus. Both are spring-producing plants as well. Pepper plants, if well tended, can be treated as perennials, and I keep a few inside to reap their spicy benefits year-round.

And there are some perennials that are treated as annuals in colder climes like mine, when the mercury gets too low for them to survive our winters, but farther south, they'll pop back up in the spring. This is where knowing your growing zone comes in very handy when selecting plants. But don't think you can't grow typically southern specimens in the north and vice versa. With some planning, you can harvest okra up north, as I do. You just need to have some room inside to get everything started.

SWEETS

Mandarin-Poppy Tea Cake

SERVES 10

The combination of slightly crunchy poppy seeds with refreshing mandarin oranges is delightful. Combine them with a dense, buttery cake, and you've harnessed a bit of springtime magic. Although mandarin orange skin is very thin, making it a bit fussier to zest, a good-quality Microplane grater will make the job easier. Serve with some homemade jam or jelly, Peony Jelly (page 271) being a favorite, and enjoy the soft sunlight as it streams through the newly green trees.

Nonstick baking spray
2 cups (240 grams) unbleached cake flour
1 teaspoon baking powder
1 teaspoon fine sea salt
½ pound (226 grams) unsalted European-style high-fat butter, at room temperature
1½ cups (300 grams) granulated sugar
5 large eggs, at room temperature
1 teaspoon vanilla bean paste
Grated zest of 2 mandarin oranges
½ cup (118 ml) heavy cream, whisked to soft peaks
2 tablespoons (18 grams) poppy seeds

FOR THE SYRUP

Juice of 2 mandarin oranges
2 tablespoons granulated sugar

Preheat the oven to 350°F (180°C). Spray a 9-by-4-inch loaf pan with nonstick baking spray and line with pieces of parchment long enough to extend a few inches beyond the long sides so you can lift the cake out of the pan. Set aside.

Whisk together the cake flour, baking powder, and salt in a large bowl. Set aside.

Cream the butter in the bowl of a stand mixer fitted with the paddle attachment until very soft and smooth, 4 to 5 minutes. Scrape the bottom and sides of the bowl. Add the 1½ cups sugar and cream until light and fluffy, 5 to 10 minutes. The mixture should be light in color, almost white, and the mixture should start to look "dry" and pillowy, not like compacted wet sand.

Add the eggs, one at a time, scraping between each addition. Add the vanilla bean paste and the mandarin zest and mix until just combined.

With the mixer on low speed, add the flour mixture and mix until just incorporated. Remove the bowl from the mixer and fold in the whipped cream and poppy seeds. Transfer the batter to the prepared pan.

Bake for 55 to 60 minutes, until the cake is golden brown and springs back when gently poked in the middle.

MAKE THE SYRUP

Combine the mandarin orange juice and 2 tablespoons sugar in a microwave-safe bowl or in a small saucepan. Microwave or heat gently to melt the sugar.

Allow the cake to rest in the pan for 10 minutes before using the parchment to lift it from the pan. Use a pastry brush to brush the syrup over the top and sides of the cake while it's still warm.

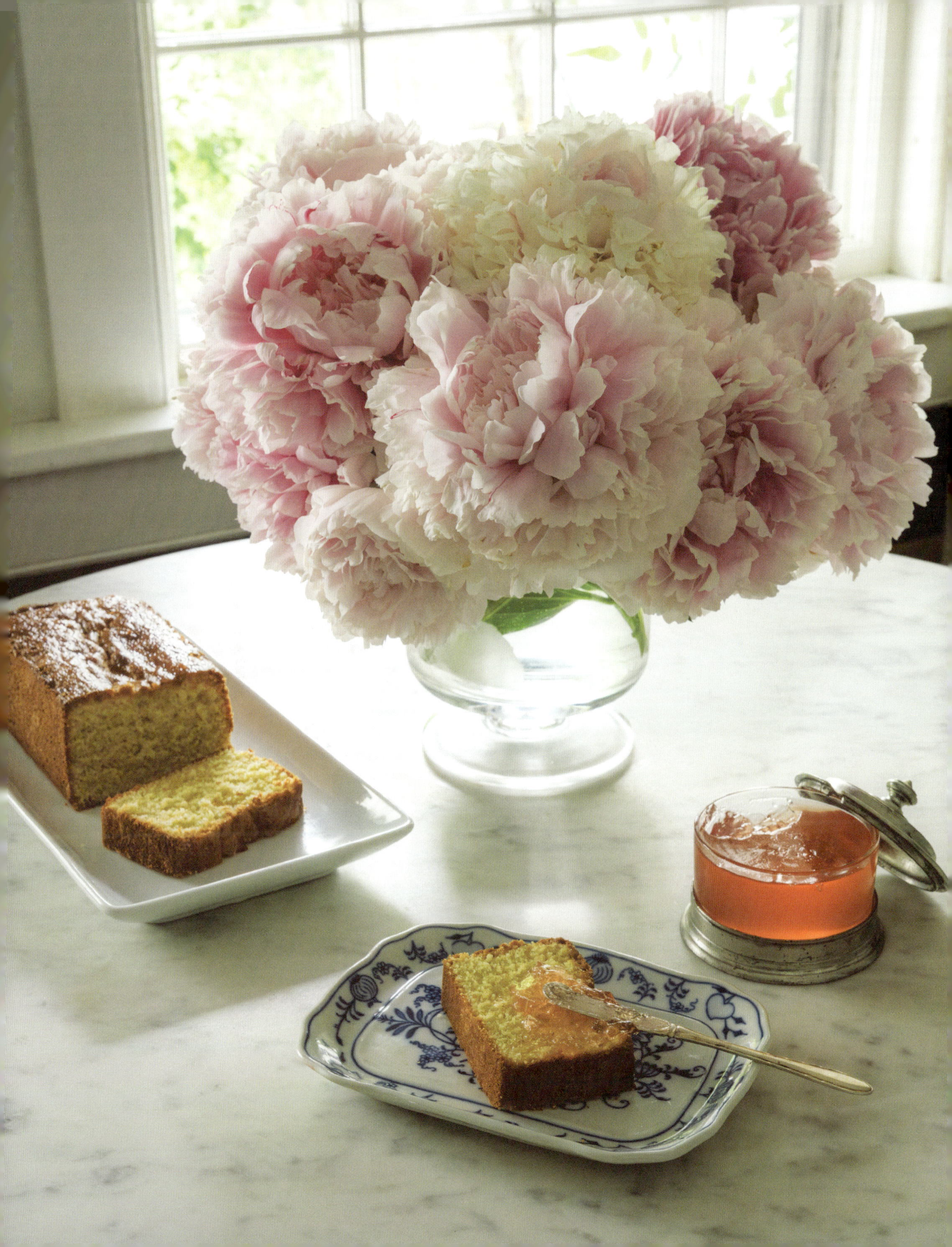

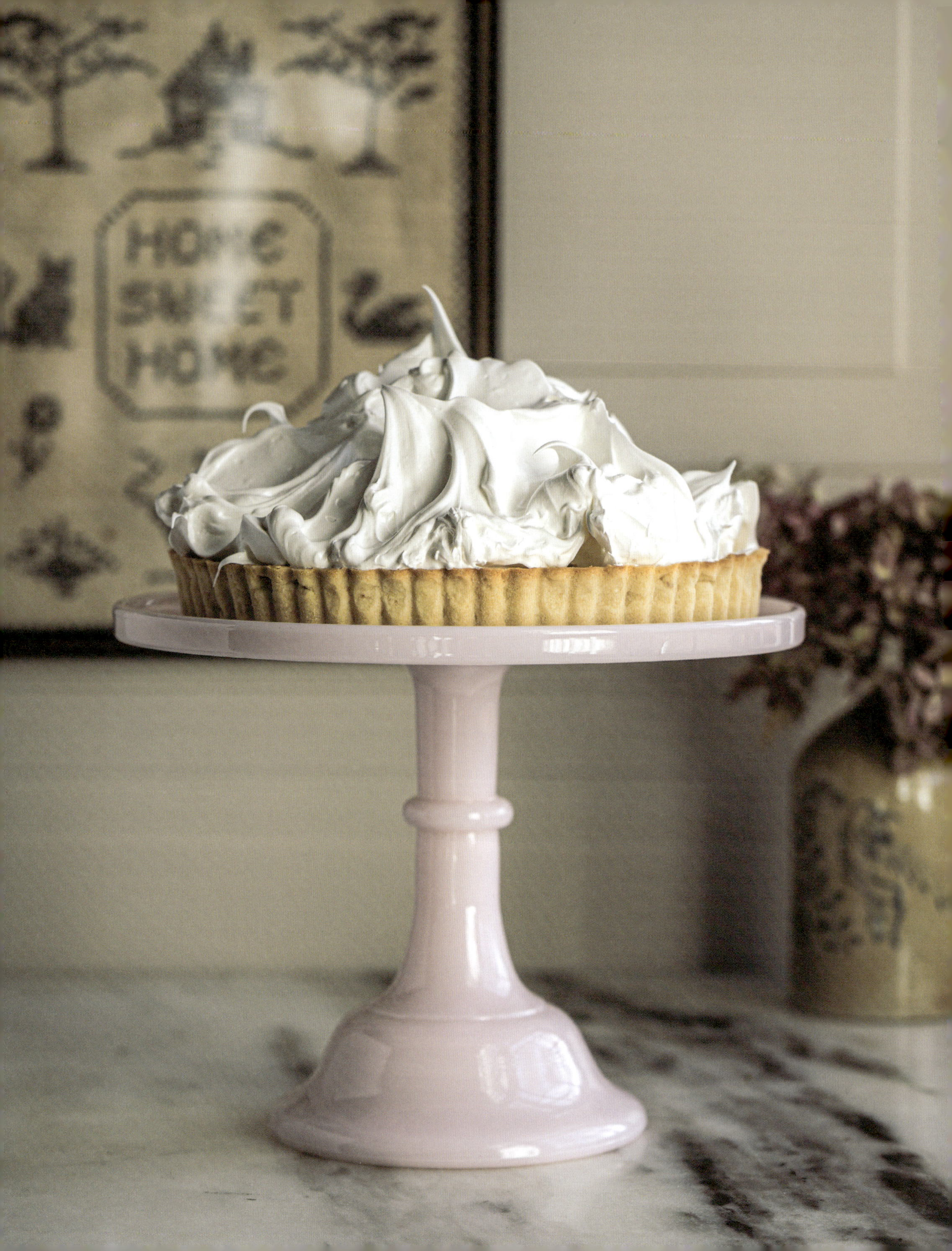
HOME
SWEET
HOME

Key Lime Tart

MAKES 2 TARTS

Key limes are in season throughout the summer and early fall in Florida. But the limes that grow in Florida are no longer the ones you can buy commercially. Instead, most limes, both Persian and Key limes, are exported from Mexico and Central America. Unlike Persian limes, Key limes are smaller and, when fully ripe, slightly yellow. Look for a balance of a bit of green and a bit of yellow. All yellow and the Key lime can bring too much bitterness to the table. When Key limes are in season, and if you can find them, use them in this tart (and the Key Lime Ice Dream, page 198).

You can also grow your own Key limes, no matter where you live (see page 197). Harvest the moment the Key lime has a nice, leathery skin and is both slightly green and slightly yellow. At this stage it will be the most juicy and flavorful. You can also use bottled or frozen Key lime juice, as the natural creaminess of this filling will enhance the slightly less vibrant flavor profile from bottling.

FOR THE PÂTE SUCRÉE

1 cup (120 grams) unbleached all-purpose flour
¼ cup (24 grams) almond flour
½ teaspoon fine sea salt
5 tablespoons (70 grams) unsalted butter, at room temperature
½ cup (56 grams) confectioners' sugar
1 large egg yolk, at room temperature

FOR THE KEY LIME CRÉMEUX

4 leaves gold gelatin
1½ cups (354 ml) Key lime juice
5 large egg yolks
2 large eggs
1 cup (200 grams) granulated sugar
Pinch of salt
12 tablespoons (170 grams) unsalted butter, slightly cooler than room temperature

FOR THE SWISS MERINGUE

5 large egg whites
1 cup (200 grams) granulated sugar
1 teaspoon vanilla bean paste
Pinch of salt

MAKE THE PÂTE SUCRÉE

Whisk together the flour, almond flour, and salt in a medium bowl. Set aside.

Combine the butter and confectioners' sugar in the bowl of a stand mixer fitted with the paddle attachment. Mix until smooth. Add the egg yolk, mixing until incorporated. Scrape down the sides of the bowl. The mixture will look curdled. That's okay.

Add the flour mixture slowly, with the mixer running on low speed, until the dough *just* comes together. Turn off the mixer and gently turn the dough over a few times by hand to make sure all dry bits are incorporated. Form

recipe continues . . .

the dough into a disk. Allow to rest in the refrigerator, wrapped in plastic wrap, for at least 20 minutes or up to overnight.

Preheat the oven to 350°F (180°C). Roll the dough disk into a roughly 12-inch round. Carefully transfer to a 9-inch fluted tart pan. Dock the dough with a fork and bake for 10 to 12 minutes. Remove from the oven and allow to cool completely.

MAKE THE KEY LIME CRÉMEUX
Place the gelatin leaves in a small bowl and cover with cold water. Set aside.

Combine the Key lime juice, egg yolks, eggs, granulated sugar, and salt in a medium saucepan. Cook over medium heat, whisking constantly, until the mixture reaches 170°F (77°C). Remove from the heat. Squeeze the excess water from the gelatin leaves and whisk them into the Key lime mixture until smooth. Run the mixture through a sieve into a bowl. Cover and leave at room temperature until the mixture cools to 140°F (60°C). Using an immersion blender or traditional blender, add the butter a tablespoon at a time, blending completely between each addition. Pour the crémeux into the cooled tart shell. Smooth with a small offset spatula. Refrigerate to set, about 2 hours to overnight.

MAKE THE SWISS MERINGUE
Combine all the Swiss meringue ingredients in the bowl of a stand mixer. Whisk over simmering water until the mixture reaches 170°F (77°C). Transfer the bowl to the stand mixer and whisk until the mixture reaches stiff peaks. Pipe or slather the meringue over the set crémeux. Serve immediately or refrigerate for up to 2 days. You can also freeze the tart without the meringue topping.

A NOTE FROM MY KITCHEN GARDEN

Citrus in Vermont

IN MY HOME STATE OF VERMONT, APPLE TREES GROW WILD, LEAVING JUICY APPLES rolling around roadways in the late fall. Our warmer, tropical-leaning states have their own kind of fruity abundance in the way of citrus, except the overload happens in the spring instead of the fall. Because citrus is a hot climate plant, you'd be correct in assuming that it's impossible to grow a lemon or lime tree outside on my property. But because I'm stubborn and suffer from citrus FOMO, I grow my favorite citrus anyway, just indoors. It's not as simple as putting a tree in a pot and setting it near a window. There simply isn't enough light to keep the plant healthy. What I do is stake a long grow light in the soil and set it on a timer. And every few days, I mist the plant to trick it into thinking there's humidity in the air. I also keep the trees in a smaller room, so when the doors are closed, the ancient radiant heat keeps the room a bit more sultry than the rest of the house. I've just realized that I treat my citrus plants much better than I treat myself.

Key Lime Ice Dream

MAKES 8 CUPS

I had made a large batch of Key Lime Crémeux (page 195) for a class I was teaching and had a few cups left. I woke with a craving for a summer treat from my childhood, lemon gelato. Tart and creamy. Not sorbet, and yet not ice cream either. I thought about what was chilling in my baking school fridge: a batch of crémeux. Hmmm. Would a spoonful of that alone do the trick? I took it out and gave it a stir. It was creamy and luscious, just as its French moniker would suggest, but it wasn't quite scratching that childhood itch. I took out my ice-cream maker and thought about what was present in the crémeux that would lend itself to a great ice cream and what might be lacking. First, it was thick. I thought about the usual custard base that I poured into the churning vat and realized I'd have to loosen the mixture just a bit, but would that hurt the flavor? And would the butter make it . . . weird? I'd only find out in the churning. Then, I turned my musings to what worked in favor of the crémeux. It had plenty of sugar to help prevent crystallization and the gelatin present would go even further in protecting the structure, guaranteeing something luxurious and smooth. I couldn't help but think that everything combined was just primed for the perfect tart yet creamy bite. I plugged in my machine, I whisked in 1 cup of cold heavy cream, and I processed the mixture until it was just set and then piped it into a cone, like soft serve. If I'd had this as a child, it would have been the thing I'd wake up craving decades later, instead of lemon gelato. No notes.

1 batch Key Lime Crémeux (page 195)
1 cup heavy cream, cold

Cover the bowl of crémeux with plastic wrap and refrigerate to completely chill, at least 2 hours to overnight. Whisk in the cream and process according to your ice-cream maker manufacturer's specifications.

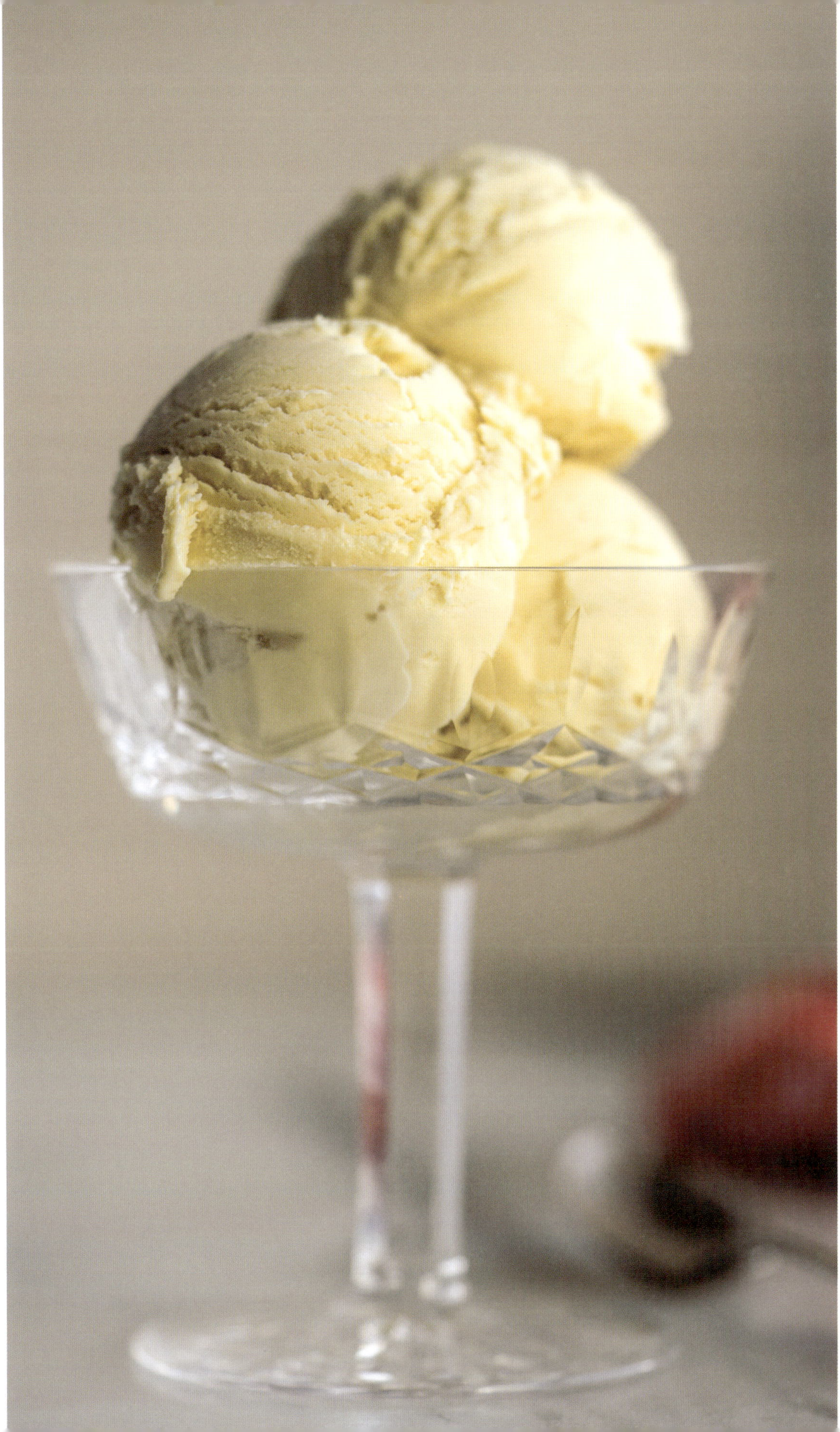

MY HARVEST KITCHEN

Rhubarb–Olive Oil Cake

SERVES 8

Rhubarb is a perennial in the buckwheat family. You read that right. The edible type is only one of many species. Its name comes from its native home, Siberia, where it grew along the Rha river (now called the Volga), which gives you a good hint of where it grows well today—in climates with cool winters. And while *Rheum rhabarbarum* (the Latin horticultural name for the plant we grow in the garden) is now harvested and eaten as a spring delicacy in cakes and pies, its original uses were in medicine, used by the Chinese and Russians in teas for bellyaches and fevers. It was the English who started using rhubarb culinarily rather than medicinally, plucking the stalk and leaf, intending to use it in its entirety because it looked so much like chard. Unfortunately, the broad leaf contains a toxin called oxalic acid that, when not fatal, leads to great intestinal distress. But some brave soul decided to try again (I really want to know who these accidental heroes were), this time just eating the stalk and finding it pleasantly tart and herbaceous.

To complement its natural flavors, bakers have traditionally paired it with large doses of sugar and bright fruits, such as strawberries, that counterbalance the natural earthiness that rhubarb offers. I, on the other hand, like to lean into rhubarb's charms and pair it with another earthy beauty: olive oil. The two together bring a luxurious sophistication to a really simple cake that's moist and singing with spring flavors.

Nonstick baking spray

FOR THE RHUBARB TOPPING

4 to 5 large rhubarb stalks, cut into 8-inch-long pieces

2 tablespoons granulated sugar

FOR THE CAKE BATTER

2 large egg whites

¼ teaspoon cream of tartar

¾ cup (150 grams) granulated sugar

4 large eggs

½ teaspoon fine sea salt

⅓ cup (78 ml) extra-virgin olive oil

1 teaspoon vanilla bean paste

1¼ cups (150 grams) unbleached all-purpose flour

Preheat the oven to 350°F (180°C). Spray an 8-inch square cake pan with nonstick baking spray and line with parchment. Spray the surface of the parchment with nonstick baking spray.

MAKE THE RHUBARB TOPPING

Fit the rhubarb pieces into the prepared pan so that they fit snuggly and you can line them up all in one direction without any gaps. Remove the rhubarb, sprinkle the bottom of the pan with the 2 tablespoons of sugar, and then line the pan again with the rhubarb. Set aside.

recipe continues . . .

MAKE THE CAKE BATTER

Place the egg whites in the bowl of a stand mixer fitted with the whisk attachment. Whisk on medium-high speed until a slight foam appears on the surface, then add the cream of tartar. Continue whisking on medium-high speed as you slowly sprinkle in ¼ cup (50 grams) of the sugar. Whisk until the meringue is smooth and shiny and holds medium-stiff peaks, being careful not to over-mix and dry out the meringue. Transfer the meringue to a clean bowl.

In the same mixer bowl in which you whisked the whites (you don't have to clean it), add the eggs, the remaining ½ cup (100 grams) of sugar, and the salt. Whisk on high speed until the mixture triples in volume, is very light in color, and falls in thick ribbons from the whisk. With the mixer running, add the olive oil and vanilla bean paste and continue to whisk until combined.

Remove the bowl from the stand mixer, sift the flour into it, then fold in the flour until no pockets of flour remain. Gently fold the meringue into the flour mixture until no white streaks remain. Scrape the batter into the cake pan, over the rhubarb.

Bake for 35 to 40 minutes, until the cake springs back when gently poked in the middle. Remove from the oven, allow the cake to rest in the pan for 10 minutes, and then run a paring knife along the sides to gently release the cake and turn over onto a cooling rack. Allow to cool completely before serving.

Sour Cherry Pie

SERVES 8

I planted two Montmorency cherry trees years ago. The first year, no cherries. The second year, three cherries. That's three cherries on two trees. The general rule is that with fruit trees, during the first few years of fruiting, you remove the fruit to allow the tree to concentrate its resources on plant growth, which leads to a greater yield in the years to come. It also keeps the fruit from breaking tender limbs. Three tiny cherries were hardly going to harm my tree. I left them to ripen. They were so red, almost neon, that even though they were tucked inside the foliage, those three tiny orbs shone through. The next year, we got a few more cherries. Six! But this past year, I managed an entire pint and then some. The hard part was harvesting, not because reaching the fruit on the dwarf varietal was difficult but because the sheer charm of those red-orange orbs dangling from the branches made me smile every time I walked past them. I got smart once I saw how much the neighboring house wrens were enjoying the tart juice and collected them all for the only tart cherry pie of the season.

1 batch G's Zippy, Flaky Pie Dough (page 239)
1 cup (200 grams) granulated sugar
¼ cup (32 grams) King Arthur Baking Company Instant ClearJel starch or tapioca starch
Pinch of salt
Pinch of ground cinnamon
6 cups fresh or frozen sour cherries, washed and pitted
1 teaspoon vanilla bean paste or vanilla extract
2 teaspoons crust dust*
2 tablespoons unsalted butter, cold

Preheat the oven to 350°F (180°C). Cut the dough in half. Roll one portion into a rough 12-inch round and line a 9-inch metal pie tin with the dough. Dock the dough using a fork (this means to poke holes in the bottom of the dough for better heat distribution), then refrigerate while you roll out the lattice.

Roll the second piece of dough into a 9-by-16-inch rectangle. Using a sharp chef's knife or a bench scraper, cut fourteen ½-inch-wide, 9-inch-long strips and four 1-inch-wide strips.

Stir together the sugar, Instant ClearJel starch, salt, and cinnamon in a small bowl. Place the cherries in a separate bowl, add the vanilla, and toss to combine. Sprinkle the sugar mixture over the cherries and toss to coat.

Sprinkle the crust dust over the prepared bottom crust, then transfer the cherry filling to the crust. Dot the filling with pieces of the

recipe continues...

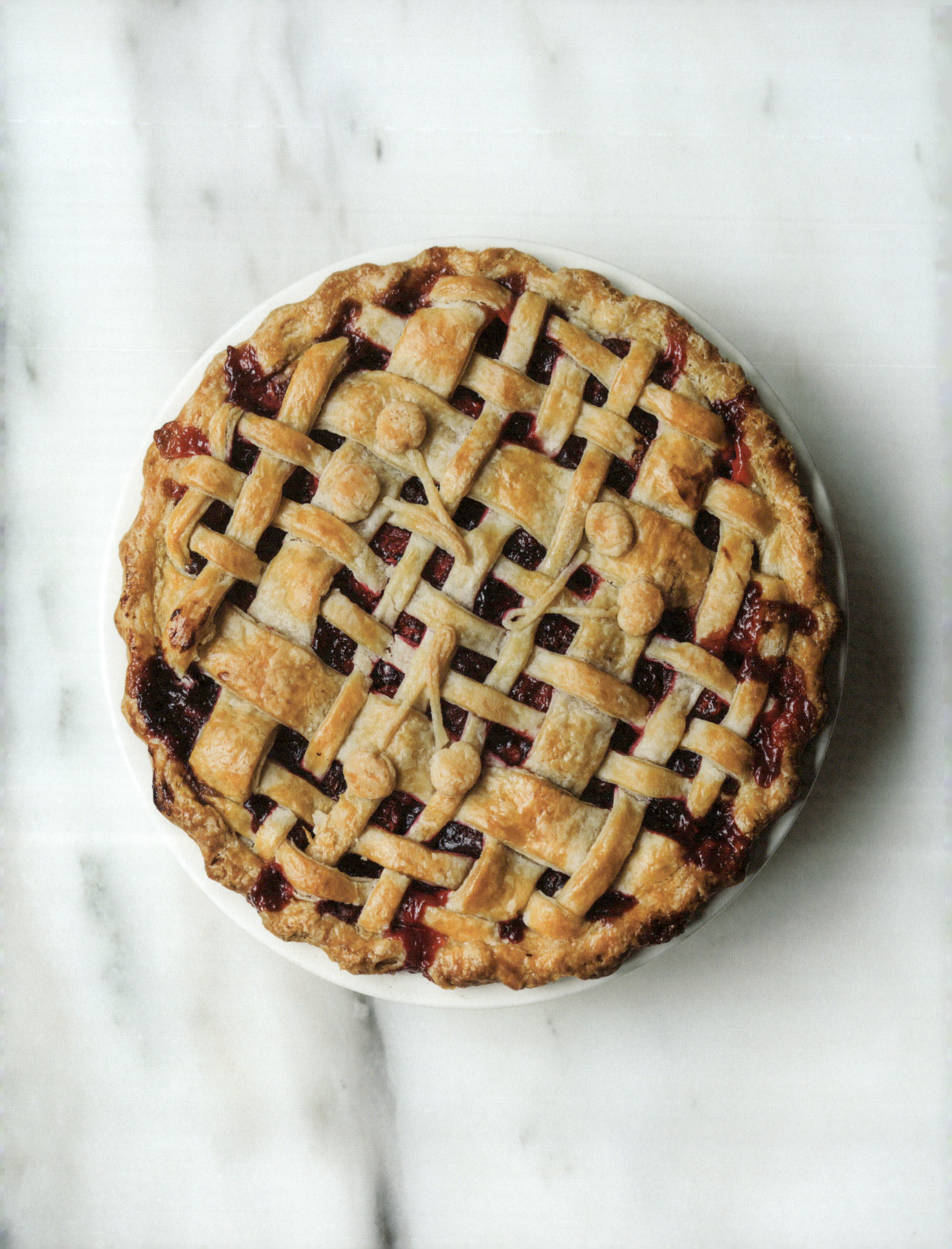

butter. Lay out nine parallel dough strips on top of the filling, alternating the thick and thin accordingly: two ½-inch strips, then one 1-inch strip, then three ½-inch strips, and then two ½-inch strips. Fold back every other strip. Place a ½-inch strip perpendicular to the parallel strips right down the middle. Put the original folded strips back. Next, pull every other strip back that *wasn't* pulled back previously on one side of the perpendicular strip. Lay down a second ½-inch strip and return the folded dough back in place. Pull back every other parallel strip that wasn't pulled back before and lay down a 1-inch strip. Continue pulling back alternating strips and laying down two more ½-inch strips. Turn the pie and continue in the same manner in this pattern with the remaining strips. Trim the strips and the bottom crust with a sharp scissor flush to the edge of the underlying pie dish. Fold the underlying bottom dough about ½ inch over the lattice edge and crimp. Bake for 45 to 50 minutes, until the crust is golden brown and the filling is bubbling. If the edge of the crust is taking on too much color in the first 20 minutes, use aluminum foil to create a ring around the edge to keep the edge of the crust from overbrowning. Remove from the oven and allow the pie to cool completely before serving.

*NOTE To make crust dust: Combine ¼ cup (50 grams) of granulated sugar and ¼ cup (30 grams) of flour in a jar and shake to combine. Store in the pantry and use to line the bottom of a pie crust to create a barrier between the pie juices and the bottom crust.

Strawberry-Rhubarb Sherbet

SERVES 8

Sherbet is creamy and fruity. It's colorful and elegant. That is, if you use the best fruits at the peak of their season. I'm no dummy, I know that most people think of sherbet and think "rainbow!" but this one is simply a single-colored jewel, one that is so beautiful and delicious that you don't need the full ROYGBIV to enjoy this gem of a creamy treat. What's also fabulous about this particular combo is that you can make a huge batch of it when both rhubarb and strawberry are at their zenith of flavor and keep it in the freezer for months (assuming you've got a stable freezer) to enjoy during the days when rhubarb and strawberries are a distant memory.

- 2 cups (265 grams) diced rhubarb
- 2 cups (310 grams) fresh or frozen strawberries, washed, hulled, and cut in half
- 1 cup (215 grams) light brown sugar
- ½ cup (115 grams) whole-milk plain Greek yogurt
- 1 tablespoon vanilla bean paste or vanilla extract
- 1½ cups (340 ml) whole milk
- 1 cup (230 ml) heavy cream
- ¾ cup (150 grams) granulated sugar
- ½ cup (100 grams) honey
- 2 teaspoons Suncore brand dragon fruit natural dye (optional)
- Pinch of salt
- 2 teaspoons tapioca starch
- 2 tablespoons water

Combine the rhubarb, strawberries, and brown sugar in a large saucepan. Cook, stirring, over medium heat until the fruits are soft and the sugar has dissolved, about 10 minutes. Puree the mixture with an immersion blender, traditional blender, food mill, or food processor. You can leave it a bit chunky or run through a sieve for a smoother sherbet. Measure out 1¾ to 2 cups of puree and place in a bowl. Allow to cool.

Once the puree is cool, stir in the yogurt and vanilla. Refrigerate.

Fill a large bowl with ice. Set aside.

To make the sherbet base, combine the milk, cream, granulated sugar, honey, dragon fruit dye, if using, and salt in a saucepan. Bring to a simmer over low heat, stirring occasionally, until the sugar dissolves. In the meantime, in a small bowl, stir the tapioca starch into the water to make a slurry. Once the milk mixture comes to a simmer, remove from the heat and add the tapioca starch slurry. Set the saucepan on the bowl of ice to bring to room temperature quickly and then transfer the mixture to a bowl, cover, and refrigerate overnight.

Stir together the puree and sherbet base. Process in your ice-cream machine per the manufacturer's directions. Transfer the set mixture to a freezer-safe container to set completely, 2 hours to overnight.

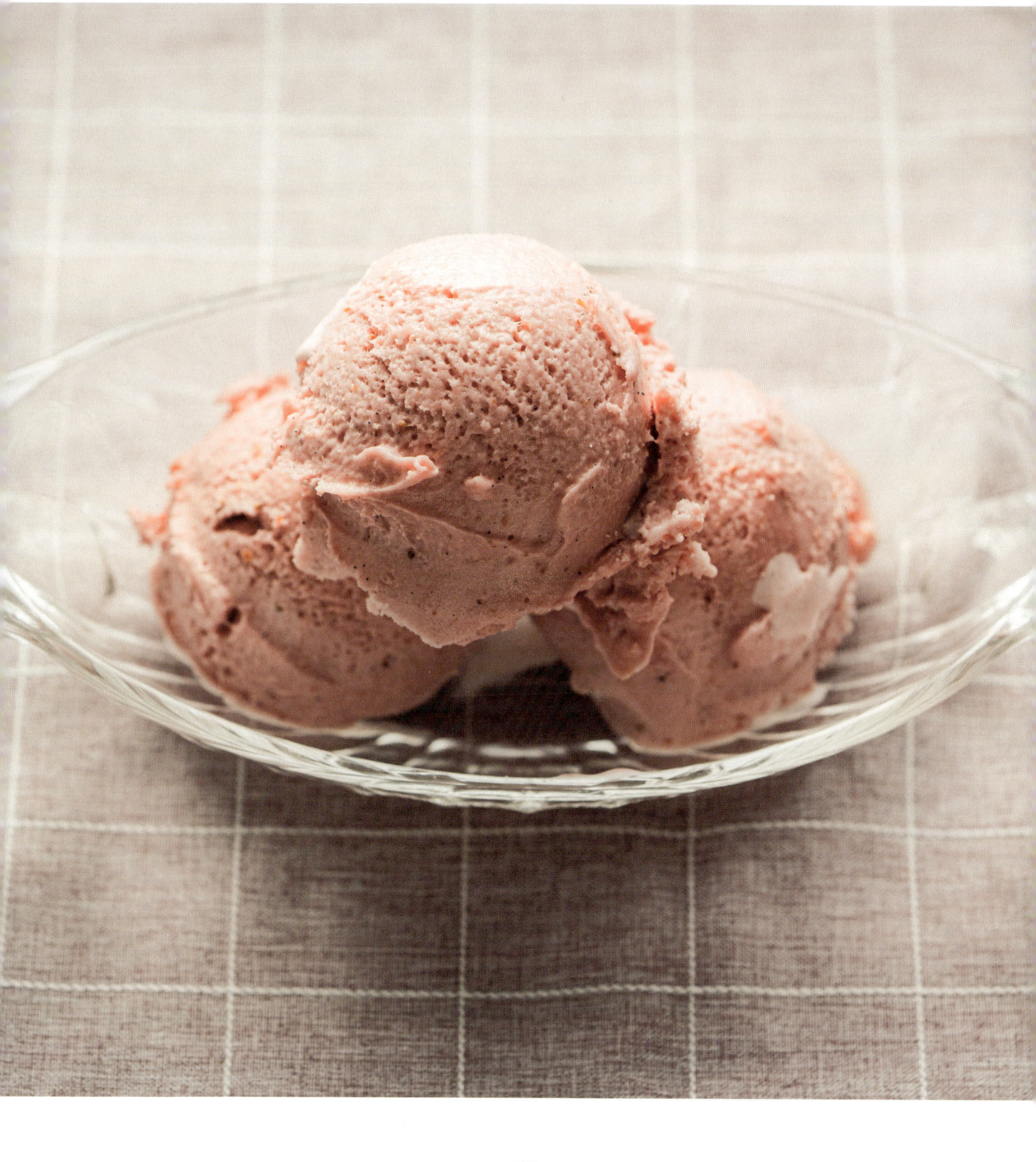

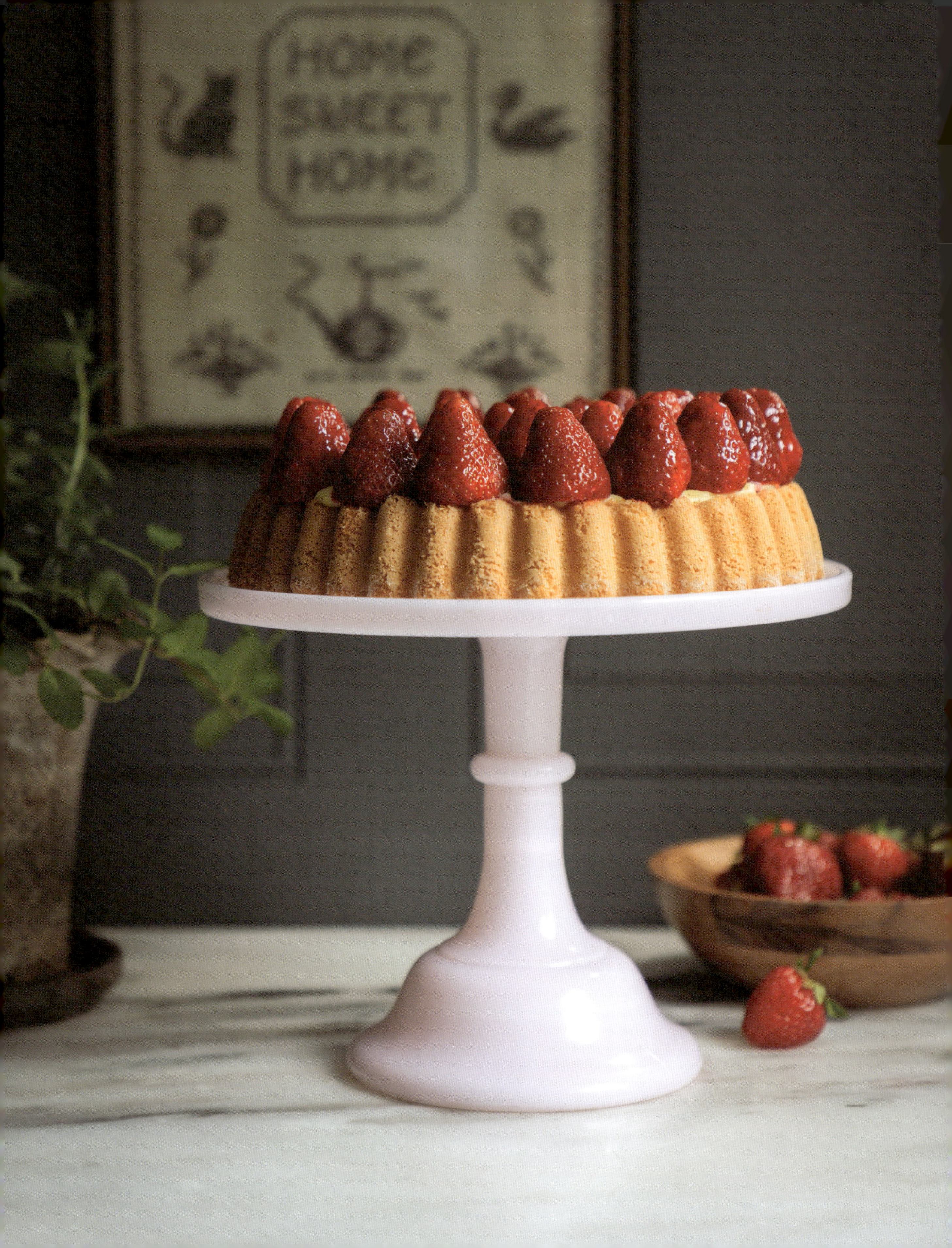
HOME
SWEET
HOME

German Strawberry Cake

SERVES 8

In Germany, my Tante Christel would buy ready-made sponge cakes, called *Obsttortenboden*, for fruit cakes. She'd keep them handy for cake-and-coffee hour and would whip up some cream and have fruits fresh from the garden ready to arrange on top. At least, she thought she did, because if I was in the house, I'd break into that wrapper and scarf the spongy cake layer faster than you can say "Obsttortenboden," leaving her without the cake layer. You can buy something similar in grocery stores during strawberry season in America, but there's a chemical taste to it (that explains why it can sit around for weeks at room temperature) that just doesn't work for me. I make my own Obsttortenboden, using a large tart pan so I get the traditional fluted edges of my childhood favorite. When you flip it over, it looks just like the official thing and the center will drop just a bit to give you room for the pastry cream filling. P.S. Sorry, Tante Christel, for being such a sugar-obsessed monster.

FOR THE CAKE

Unsalted butter, for the pan
½ cup (100 grams) granulated sugar, plus more for the pan
4 large eggs, separated
¼ teaspoon cream of tartar
½ teaspoon fine sea salt
2 tablespoons hot water
2 tablespoons freshly squeezed orange juice
1 teaspoon grated orange zest
1 teaspoon vanilla extract
2 tablespoons (28 grams) unsalted butter, melted
⅓ cup (40 grams) unbleached all-purpose flour
½ cup (58 grams) cornstarch

FOR THE PASTRY CREAM

¼ cup (50 grams) granulated sugar
2 tablespoons (14 grams) cornstarch
Pinch of salt
2 large egg yolks
½ cup whole milk
½ cup heavy cream
2 tablespoons (28 grams) unsalted butter
1 teaspoon vanilla bean paste

TO FINISH

2 pints fresh strawberries
2 tablespoons granulated sugar
1 teaspoon freshly squeezed lemon juice
2 tablespoons Strawberry Jam (page 270)

MAKE THE CAKE

Preheat the oven to 350°F (180°C). Butter a 10-by-2-inch fluted tart pan or a 10-inch cake pan and then coat with sugar. Line the bottom with a round of parchment. Set aside.

Place the egg whites in the bowl of a stand mixer fitted with the whisk attachment. Whisk on medium speed until the top of the whites are foamy. Add the cream of tartar and the salt. Increase the speed to medium high (but never any higher). Slowly sprinkle in 80 grams (roughly 6 tablespoons) of the sugar. Continue

recipe continues . . .

SWEETS

to whisk until the meringue holds medium stiff peaks.

Transfer the meringue to a clean metal bowl. Place the yolks and the remaining 20 grams (roughly 1½ tablespoons) of sugar in the emptied stand mixer bowl. Whisk on high speed until the mixture thickens and lightens to a light butter yellow; this is the ribbon stage. With the mixer on medium speed, add the hot water and orange juice, then the orange zest, vanilla, melted butter, flour, and cornstarch. Whisk until combined. Using a large rubber spatula, fold the meringue into the batter until you no longer see obvious streaks of white or yellow. Transfer the batter to the prepared pan and bake for 25 to 30 minutes, until the top is golden brown, slightly puffy, and the cake springs back when gently poked in the middle. Remove from the oven, immediately unmold the cake, and transfer to a cake platter. Allow to cool completely.

MAKE THE PASTRY CREAM

Whisk together the sugar, cornstarch, and salt in a small bowl. Combine the egg yolks, the sugar mixture, and the milk and heavy cream in a medium saucepan. Whisk over medium heat until the mixture thickens to the consistency of mayonnaise and starts to "burp." Continue to whisk for about 1 minute more (this neutralizes the amylase in the egg that could otherwise reverse the thickening if it's not properly heated, but any more than 1 minute and you can ruin the efficacy of the cornstarch). Remove from the heat and immediately whisk in the butter and vanilla bean paste. Transfer to a clean bowl and cover with plastic wrap. Cool completely in the fridge, about 1 hour.

ASSEMBLE THE CAKE

Cut four of the least conical and symmetrical berries into small squares, transfer to a small bowl and sprinkle with the sugar and lemon juice, then stir. Allow to macerate for 10 minutes until the strawberries juice out and the sugar dissolves.

Add 1 teaspoon of the strawberry juice to the jam, to loosen the jam a bit. Set aside.

Add the strawberry pieces, along with the remaining juice, to the cake base. Stir the pastry cream to loosen, then spoon in an even layer onto the strawberry-topped cake base. You may not need all of the pastry cream, so don't feel the need to add it all.

Hull 36 to 44 of the most conical strawberries and arrange in concentric circles on the pastry cream. Brush them with the jam glaze. Serve immediately or refrigerate for up to a few hours before serving.

Peach Cobbler

SERVES 8

After I taught a baking class at King Arthur's baking education center in Norwich, Vermont, a student told me she had a present for me back in her truck. I followed her to the parking lot and stopped at the cab, thinking she'd brought something easily transportable. Instead, she kept walking to the bed to reveal a tree. A peach tree. That tree has been producing baskets of peaches for a decade now. Come late summer, every other year, there are so many peaches, the branches bow so heavily that I have to prop them up. The next year, the tree offers far fewer peaches. That was, until I planted two more peach trees and now . . . now . . . there are peaches enough for my whole town every late summer. That means cobbler is on the menu most late-August nights.

FOR THE FILLING

2 pounds ripe fresh peaches

1 tablespoon freshly squeezed lemon juice

1 tablespoon vanilla bean paste

½ cup (110) grams light brown sugar

1 teaspoon King Arthur Baking Company Instant ClearJel starch

Pinch of fine sea salt

Pinch of ground cardamom

Pinch of ground ginger

FOR THE BISCUIT TOPPING

1¼ cups (150 grams) unbleached all-purpose flour

½ cup (100 grams) granulated sugar

1 teaspoon baking powder

½ teaspoon baking soda

½ teaspoon fine sea salt

8 tablespoons (113 grams) unsalted butter, cold

½ cup (118 ml) buttermilk

MAKE THE FILLING

Preheat the oven to 400°F (200°C). Halve and pit the peaches. Cut them into quarters and then into ½-inch cubes. Place in an 8-inch square casserole dish and toss with the lemon juice and vanilla bean paste to coat. Set aside.

Combine the brown sugar, Instant ClearJel starch, sea salt, cardamom, and ginger in a small bowl. Stir well (the ClearJel starch must be mixed in with the sugar; otherwise, it will clump). Sprinkle the brown sugar mixture over the peaches and toss to coat. Bake for 10 minutes.

MAKE THE BISCUIT TOPPING

Stir together the flour, sugar, baking powder, baking soda, and salt in a large bowl. Grate the butter, straight from the refrigerator, using the largest holes on a box grater. Add the butter to the flour mixture and toss to break up the pieces and to coat. Use the tips of your fingers to gently massage the butter into the flour mixture, creating a dry, coarse mixture. Pour the buttermilk

recipe continues . . .

over the mixture and use a flexible rubber spatula to toss and distribute the moisture. Use the spatula to slice through any large clumps, then use your fingertips to pull apart the mixture to create smaller clumps. Continue to mix, gently, until a slightly sticky dough comes together.

Using a tablespoon, spoon the biscuit dough over the peaches, distributing it as evenly as possible. Bake for 30 to 35 minutes, until the biscuit topping is golden brown. Serve with Philadelphia-Style Vanilla and Honey Ice Cream (page 213).

Philadelphia-Style Vanilla and Honey Ice Cream

MAKES ABOUT 4 CUPS

This ice cream is fast. Truly. You just need to be ready to whisk whisk whisk to get that sugar dissolved. Getting your hands on superfine really helps move the dissolving process along more quickly. But the lack of heating allows you to go straight from the mixing bowl to the ice-cream maker. Honey helps keep ice crystals from forming and will bring a beautiful flavor to the finished product, and the Instant ClearJel starch is a thickening agent to enhance creaminess.

½ cup (100 grams) superfine or caster sugar
1 tablespoon King Arthur Baking Company Instant ClearJel starch
Pinch of salt
1 cup (236 ml) whole milk, slightly warmed
2 cups (472 ml) heavy cream, cold
¼ cup (84 grams) honey
1 tablespoon vanilla bean paste

Whisk together the sugar, Instant ClearJel starch, and salt in a medium bowl (make sure to whisk together well; otherwise, the ClearJel starch will clump). Continue to whisk while you slowly pour in the milk and then the heavy cream. Add the honey and vanilla bean paste, then whisk until the mixture is a bit fluffy and the sugar has completely dissolved.

Transfer the mixture to your ice-cream machine by pouring through a sieve into the machine bowl, then process per your manufacturer's instructions. Once the ice cream is the consistency of soft serve, immediately transfer to a freezable (preferably insulated) storage vessel and place in the freezer to continue firming up. Store in the freezer for up to a month.

A NOTE FROM MY KITCHEN GARDEN

Bees

I KEPT BEES FOR A FEW YEARS. THE nuc I started with, a small little pod of bees with a queen, multiplied so quickly that, within a few weeks of transferring them to the big hive on my property, I found swarm cells at the bottom of the frames. I diligently scraped them off, but still they swarmed. My beekeeping mentor, who also happens to be my great friend, baking colleague, and famed bread guru Jeffrey Hamelman, was shocked at the rate at which the colony grew and then reproduced (think of the whole hive as a single entity; swarming and creating a second colony is how they reproduce). I became adept at swarm catching, trying to keep up with each hive's activity and keeping extra hives on standby to which to move the newly created colony. In one summer, I had four hives. No matter how well I tended them, how many frames I added to expand their home, how many swarm cells I removed, the bees kept multiplying. And then the bears came. My protective fencing grew as well: a solar-powered electric perimeter festooned with pie tins slathered with peanut butter (bears are, allegedly, only deterred if their snouts get a shock and the pie tin is supposed to take care of that). But bears will be bears, and they knocked the hives to smithereens. We cobbled together what we could but, in the end, my beekeeping career ended a little over a year after I started, when I realized that my very active bees were luring very hungry bears and there were young families in the area that could do without a honey-hungry Yogi trundling through their yards. The hives went to safer pastures and, I'm sure, are keeping their new beekeeper on their toes. That said, the honey that came from that year of bees was so specific to our little spot of heaven. It was ever so slightly minty from the meadow of mint that I called "Mojito Alley." And it was buttery. The same is true of the maple we tap from our trees—it's simply more buttery than any other syrup we've ever tasted. Now, students bring me their honey when they come for classes. I get to experience the tastes of the little slices of heaven my students have created through the bounty of their bees and, while I miss my own, I consider it an honor to share in the sweetness of other hives.

Apple Crumble Tart

SERVES 8

We have four apple trees on our little farm. Two are ancient, the gnarly lower branches looking straight out of a haunted Grimm fairy tale. And way up high, heirloom apples of a forgotten Russet variety hang just out of reach . . . until I grab my apple ladder and snatch them from their teasing branches. But the other two trees are dwarf varieties, staying small enough that, at the most, I have to get on my tippy toes to gather fruit. Gravenstein is the one I gather for this tart, an apple that is full of sweetness, with a slight backbone of tartness, and has a milky flesh that keeps its integrity in a hot oven, mounded with butter crumb. Unlike a traditional apple pie, this tart has a substantial base, a cookielike foundation that give the apples a run for their money.

FOR THE BASE

Nonstick baking or cooking spray

½ cup (106 grams) light brown sugar

12 tablespoons (169 grams) unsalted butter, at room temperature

1 large egg, at room temperature

1 large egg yolk

1½ cups (180 grams) unbleached all-purpose flour

1½ teaspoons baking powder

½ teaspoon fine sea salt

FOR THE APPLES

Juice of 1 lemon

4 tart baking apples

FOR THE CRUMBLE

1¼ cups (150 grams) all-purpose flour

¼ cup (50 grams) granulated sugar

¼ cup (53 grams) dark brown sugar

½ teaspoon fine sea salt

Grated zest of 1 lemon

8 tablespoons (113 grams) unsalted butter, melted

Preheat the oven to 350°F (180°C). Line a sheet pan with parchment or a silicone baking mat. Place a 12-inch cake pan or 12-inch cake ring on the prepared sheet pan. Spray the pan with nonstick spray. Set aside.

MAKE THE BASE

Combine the brown sugar and butter in a bowl. Stir with a wooden spoon until smooth. Add the whole egg and egg yolk, then stir until incorporated.

Whisk together the flour, baking powder, and salt in a small bowl. Add to the butter mixture and stir until combined and smooth. Spoon the batter into the cake pan and smooth with an offset spatula. Set aside.

MAKE THE APPLES

Combine the lemon juice and 4 cups of water in a large bowl. Add the apples as you finish peeling, coring, and cutting each of them into eighths. Place an oven-safe cooling rack on a half sheet

recipe continues . . .

pan. Place the apples on the rack in an even layer and bake for 10 minutes. Line the batter in the cake pan with the apples. Pack the apples tightly next to each other, but don't overlap.

MAKE THE CRUMBLE
Stir together the flour, granulated sugar, brown sugar, salt, and lemon zest in a large bowl. Add the melted butter and stir until the mixture just comes together in clumps. Use your fingers to break apart the mixture, if needed. Sprinkle the crumble over the apples. Bake for 40 to 45 minutes, until the crumble on top is golden brown.

Serve with Brown Butter Butterscotch Ice Cream (page 217).

Brown Butter Butterscotch Ice Cream

MAKES 4 CUPS

Boy oh boy, is this a rich and deeply flavorful ice cream. You'd think that browning butter wouldn't work in ice cream, being butter, but it just boosts the deeply butterscotch flavor of the brown sugar. The addition of sea salt and vanilla just pile on to the butterscotch symphony. Eat this alone or scoop a generous amount onto an Apple Crumble Tart (page 215).

8 tablespoons (113 grams) unsalted butter

2 cups (473 ml) heavy cream, at room temperature

1 cup (227 ml) whole milk, at room temperature

¾ cup (160 grams) dark brown sugar

6 large egg yolks

2 teaspoons tapioca starch

2 tablespoons water

1 tablespoon vanilla bean paste or vanilla extract

¼ teaspoon fine sea salt

Fill a large bowl with ice. Set aside.

Melt the butter in a large saucepan over medium-low heat and continue to cook until the butter stops "popping" and the milk solids begin to brown and the butter smells nutty. Add the cream and milk, slowly. While whisking constantly, add the brown sugar and then the egg yolks. Continue to whisk over low heat until the mixture reaches 170 to 180°F (76 to 82°C). Stir together the tapioca starch and water in a small bowl. Remove the ice cream mixture from the heat and add the tapioca starch mixture, vanilla, and salt. Transfer to a bowl and cover with plastic wrap, then set on the bowl of ice to cool down the mixture quickly, stirring it every now and again with a clean spoon. Once the mixture has reached room temperature, transfer to the refrigerator to chill overnight.

Run the mixture through a sieve, then process in an ice-cream machine per the manufacturer's instructions. Transfer the finished ice cream to a freezer-safe container.

I Have Too Much Fruit Cake

SERVES 10

This isn't a fruit cake in the "doorstop" tradition. This is a light, tender cake that is a vessel to transport end-of-season harvests. Specifically, I use leftover plums or pears. Sometimes peaches. Even apples. I've been known to throw in a grape. You see where I'm going here. When summer is waving bye-bye and you're finding ways to responsibly (and tastefully) use fruits that you were *so* excited about growing or picking (apple pickers, this is for you) and then realize you don't know what the heck to do with your windfall, this delicious and simple cake is what you need. It also calls for honey, which is an ingredient harvested at the same time and happens to be more than a sweetener; it's also a humectant, which means it keeps the cake shelf-stable longer. What I'm telling you is that you can make a few cakes, even freeze a few, and you'll have your fruit beautifully used in no time. And it keeps . . . for a long time!

Nonstick baking spray, or 1 tablespoon unsalted butter plus a sprinkling of flour for the pan

1½ cups (180 grams) unbleached cake flour

1½ teaspoons baking powder

1 teaspoon fine sea salt

½ pound (226 grams) unsalted butter, at room temperature

½ cup (100 grams) granulated sugar

¼ cup (85 grams) honey

3 large eggs, at room temperature

1 teaspoon vanilla bean paste

2 to 3 small to medium pears or apples, cored and cut into ¼-inch wedges, or 2 to 3 peaches, pitted and cut into ¼-inch wedges, or 10 to 12 plums, halved and pitted

2 tablespoons apricot jam

1 tablespoon water

Preheat the oven to 350ºF (180ºC). Spray an 8-inch cake pan or springform pan with nonstick baking spray or smear with 1 tablespoon of butter and coat with flour. Line the bottom with parchment. Set aside.

Whisk together the cake flour, baking powder, and salt in a small bowl. Set aside.

Combine the butter, sugar, and honey in the bowl of a stand mixer fitted with the paddle attachment. Mix on medium-high speed until light and fluffy, 5 to 10 minutes depending on the temperature of the room. Scrape down the bottom and sides of the bowl and, with the mixer on medium speed, add the eggs, one at a time, scraping the bowl between additions, and then add the vanilla bean paste and mix. Add the flour mixture all at once and mix on low speed until the mixture just comes together. Using a rubber spatula, gently fold the mixture to make sure all the dry ingredients are incorporated.

Pour the mixture into the prepared pan and smooth the top with a small offset spatula. Arrange your fruit of choice on top of the cake. Bake for 45 minutes, or until the cake gently springs back when poked or a digital thermometer reads between 205 and 210°F (96 and 99°C).

Combine the apricot jam and water in a small saucepan and warm over low heat until the mixture is thin. Using a pastry brush, brush the top of the cake with the apricot glaze.

ODE TO HIBERNATION

OUR first frost usually comes mid-October. The day before, my tomatoes and peppers, squash vines, and dahlias are perky with healthy green foliage and vibrant blooms. The next morning, there's an icy sheen covering our fields and everything once green and perky is all droopy and black. The fruits, flowers, and foliage are destroyed. So, I harvest the pumpkins from their newly dead vines and I announce full hibernation mode to all the world (or our sleepy road in Vermont) by grabbing Ray and pronouncing, "Take out Skelly!"

Skelly is our 12-foot Halloween skeleton. During the rest of the year, he lives inside the barn, scaring the pants off anyone who happens to stray inside for the first time and comes face to face with his giant bones. But the moment the first frost hits in early October, we carry Skelly out front, to the delight of me (I need cheering after that frost) and the local kids. We stake him down to keep him from blowing over, and the harvested carving pumpkins help weigh his scary butt down. I gather the remaining eating squash and bring them inside to store, but I always keep out a plump butternut to make a creamy sauce for my Potato Gnocchi with Butternut Squash and Sage Bake (page 181). Comfort food, here I come!

As I clear out the beds, I plant garlic bulbs, so their roots can take hold a bit before the first snow and then they'll be raring to go come the last frost in late spring. I put a bit of straw onto my strawberry plants, protecting their shallow roots, and I pluck the last of the fruit that's barely hanging on but still sweet and juicy, even if the leaves are frosted over.

This is the time to take advantage of cold-hearty greens and make a comforting winter salad with crisp sorrel, chewy barley, and warm bacon dressing. It's also when, at the moment I think all is lost from the cover of frost, I spy a friendly saffron crocus opening to the sun with its poppy red stigma flopping over like silly string. I grab my handy culinary tweezers (see—they come in handy in so many situations!) and gently pry the tendrils from their purchase next to the pollen heavy stamens, gently arrange them on a paper towel, and leave them on a sunny perch in my kitchen to dry out for 24 hours before I store the treasured strands in a small jar to make Preserved Lemon and Saffron Chicken Tagine (page 171). It's also when I look to chocolate and all things festive, such as a show-stopping Gâteau Concorde (page 226), things I cannot grow but that bring me joy in the darkest days of winter.

The momentary heartbreak of waking to see my beautiful garden full of limp and blackened plants is soothed when I remember all that I did to preserve and store during harvest so that our time of hibernation would be delicious and abundant.

Pumpkin-Mandarin Tart

SERVES 12

There is a time and a place for pumpkin pie and that's Thanksgiving. I cannot think of an occasion where serving the pie outside of turkey day would be acceptable. It just feels wrong. This tart, on the other hand, is a welcome addition to Thanksgiving but won't make you feel weird if you make it in September or October. In fact, please make it in September and October. Pumpkin is delicious and deserves her flowers.

FOR THE PÂTE SUCRÉE

2 cups (240 grams) unbleached all-purpose flour, plus more for dusting

½ cup (48 grams) almond flour

½ teaspoon fine sea salt

10 tablespoons (141 grams) unsalted butter, at room temperature

¾ cup (84 grams) confectioners' sugar

1 large egg, at room temperature

FOR THE FILLING

3 leaves gold gelatin

1 cup (213 grams) packed light brown sugar

2 teaspoons ground cinnamon

1 teaspoon ground ginger

½ teaspoon grated nutmeg

¼ teaspoon ground allspice

¼ teaspoon ground cloves

Zest of 3 mandarin oranges

¾ cup (177 ml) freshly squeezed mandarin orange juice (from about 5 mandarin oranges)

1 cup (245 grams) pumpkin puree

5 large eggs, lightly beaten

Pinch salt

10 ounces (283 grams) unsalted butter, slightly cooler than room temperature

MAKE THE PÂTE SUCRÉE

In a mixing bowl, combine the flour, the almond flour, and salt. Whisk to combine. Set aside.

In the bowl of a stand mixer fitted with the paddle attachment, combine the butter and confectioners' sugar. Mix until smooth. Add the egg, mixing until incorporated. Scrape down the sides and bottom of the bowl. The mixture will look curdled. That's perfectly okay.

Add the flour mixture all at once. With the mixer running on low speed, mix until the dough just comes together. Turn out the dough onto a large (doubled) piece of plastic wrap. Gently turn the dough over a few times by hand, using the plastic wrap to make sure all the dry bits are incorporated. Allow to rest in the refrigerator, wrapped in plastic wrap, at least 20 minutes or overnight before rolling out.

Preheat the oven to 350°F (176°C).

Lightly dust your work surface and the top of the tart dough with flour. Roll the dough into a rough 13-inch round. Line a high-walled 10-inch tart tin with the dough. Use a paring knife to trim the edges. Gently gather the leftover dough, cover and refrigerate. Crumple a piece of parchment and then rub it to soften the

recipe continues . . .

sharp edges. Line the tart tin with the softened piece of parchment and fill with baking beans. Bake for 10 to 15 minutes or until the sides of the tart dough have set and the edges are barely beginning to brown. Remove the beans and parchment and continue baking until the tart shell is fully baked through, 5 to 7 minutes more.

Roll out the leftover dough and cut into leaf shapes. Place on a sheet pan and bake for 5 to 8 minutes or until the edges of the dough just begin to brown. Allow to cool completely and then store in a resealable plastic bag or airtight container until you're ready to serve the tart.

MAKE THE FILLING

Submerge the gelatin, one leaf at a time, into a tall glass of ice cold water. Make sure the gelatin is completely submerged. Set aside.

Combine the brown sugar, cinnamon, ginger, nutmeg, allspice, cloves, and mandarin orange zest in a large saucepan. Rub the zest into the sugar-spice mixture and allow to sit for 10 minutes so the sugar absorbs the oils of the zest.

Add the orange juice, pumpkin puree, eggs, and salt to the saucepan. Cook, whisking, over medium heat until the mixture thickens and the temperature reads 180°F (82°C) on a digital thermometer. Remove from the heat and immediately squeeze out excess water from the gelatin and then add the gelatin to the saucepan. Whisk to combine.

Pour the mixture through a sieve and into a bowl or a blender. Allow the mixture to cool to 140°F (60°C), then run the blender or use an immersion blender if the mixture is in a bowl. Add the butter a tablespoon at a time, processing with the blender, until all the butter is added. Pour the filling into the prepared tart shell. Refrigerate to set, overnight. Once set and ready to serve, arrange the "leaves" decoratively on the tart. Store in the refrigerator for up to 2 days. Alternatively, make the tart ahead of time and freeze, well wrapped in plastic wrap, up to a month, storing the leaves separately in a resealable plastic bag in the freezer.

SWEETS

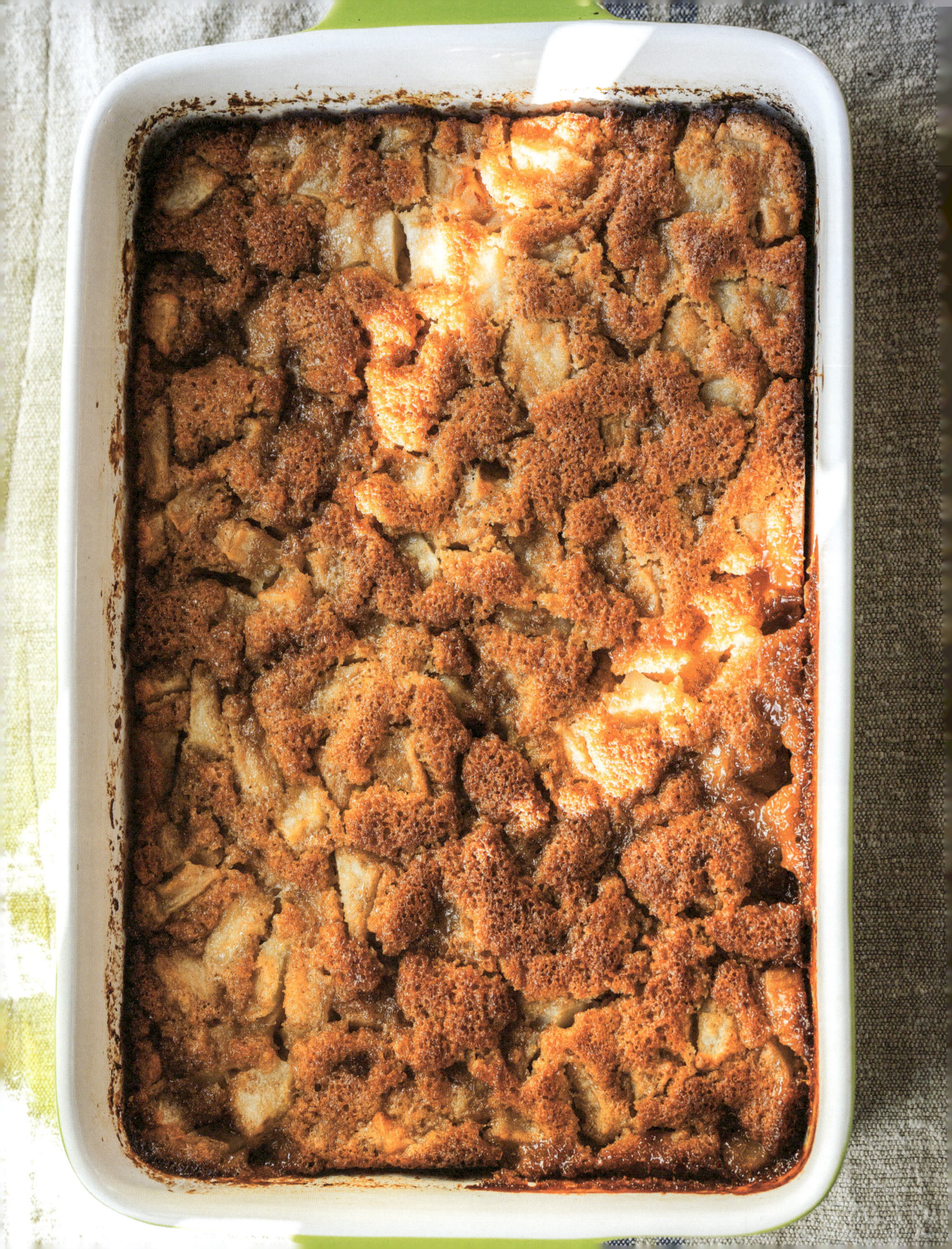

Caramel Apple Pudding

SERVES 12

Oh, goodness. What can I say? I have held apple crisp in such high regard all my life. Sweet crumbles over lightly tart apples? Yes, please! Just make sure there are not oats in my crumble. I'll get my fiber elsewhere. But then I thought, what would be better than apple crisp? Something with all the texture and flavor but with more of *everything*? Well, this is the result of my dreaming. You get apple, you get a crisp, you get caramel notes, and you get SAUCE! Please and THANK YOU! You can make this with just apples or you can also use firm pears. Feel free to use a mix of both as well.

Unsalted butter or nonstick baking spray, for baking dish
2 cups (240 grams) unbleached all-purpose flour
1 cup (215 grams) light brown sugar
1 tablespoon baking powder
1 teaspoon fine sea salt
1 teaspoon ground cinnamon
¼ teaspoon freshly grated nutmeg
¼ teaspoon ground cloves
1 cup full-fat buttermilk
1 teaspoon vanilla bean paste
5 cups peeled, cored, and chopped apples (½-inch pieces)

FOR THE CARAMEL

4 tablespoons (56 grams) unsalted butter
½ cup boiling water
¼ cup boiled cider (see page 16)
½ cup packed dark brown sugar
Pinch of fine sea salt

Preheat the oven to 400°F (200°C). Smear a 9-by-13-inch baking dish with butter or spray with nonstick baking spray.

Whisk together the flour, brown sugar, baking powder, salt, cinnamon, nutmeg, and cloves in a large bowl. Create a well in the middle of the mixture and pour in the buttermilk and vanilla bean paste. Whisk until smooth. Fold in the apples and, once everything is incorporated, transfer to the prepared baking dish. Set aside.

MAKE THE CARAMEL

Melt the butter in a small saucepan, then add the boiling water, boiled cider, brown sugar, and salt. Cook over medium heat, stirring, until the sugar has dissolved. Immediately drizzle over the apple mixture and bake until golden brown and crisp, 45 to 50 minutes, covering with aluminum foil after 30 minutes to prevent overbrowning.

Serve warm with Philadelphia-Style Vanilla and Honey Ice Cream (page 213).

Gâteau Concorde

SERVES 10

Back in the day, the Concorde was *the* elite manner in which to travel internationally, not private planes. The supersonic jet could get you from New York City to London in 3½ hours, cruising at twice the speed of sound. Its in-flight meal service had to rival the luxury of the flight itself, so preeminent Parisian pastry chef Gaston Lenôtre was tasked with creating the perfect dessert. And that he did, combining chocolate meringue and chocolate mousse into a resplendent gâteau that is still celebrated and eaten with delight to this very day, even when the Concorde itself no longer flies the friendly skies. During the longest nights of winter, I make this cake for friends, to speed up the darkest season.

FOR THE MERINGUE

Scant ½ teaspoon (1.7 grams) cream of tartar

4 large egg whites (132 grams), at room temperature

Generous pinch of salt

1¼ cups (250 grams) granulated sugar

1⅓ cups (150 grams) confectioners' sugar

½ cup (42 grams) Dutch-processed cocoa powder

FOR THE MOUSSE

1¾ cups (415 grams) heavy cream, cold (portion A)

8½ ounces (240 grams) bittersweet chocolate

3½ ounces (100 grams) heavy cream (portion B)

5 large egg yolks

1 large egg

½ cup plus 1 tablespoon (110 grams) granulated sugar

Pinch of salt

Preheat the oven to 280°F (137°C). Trace three 6-inch circles onto a half sheet of parchment, turn over, and use the parchment to line a sheet pan. Line a second half sheet pan with parchment as well. Set aside.

MAKE THE MERINGUE

Combine the cream of tartar, egg whites, and salt in the bowl of a stand mixer fitted with the whisk attachment. Whisk on medium speed and slowly rain in the granulated sugar. Continue to mix on medium to medium-high speed until the meringue holds medium peaks. Remove the bowl from the stand mixer.

Sift the confectioners' sugar and cocoa powder together into a small bowl and then spoon one-third of the mixture back into the sieve and sieve over the meringue. Using a large rubber spatula, gently fold the cocoa mixture into the meringue. Do the same with the remaining cocoa mixture, sifting one-third over the meringue at a time and then folding it in.

Fit a piping bag with an Ateco 805 tip (7/16 inch open tip) and fill with the meringue mixture. Pipe a coil of meringue onto each of the 6-inch circles on the first prepared sheet pan. On the second prepared pan, pipe long strips of the remaining meringue. Bake the strips for 1 hour and the coils for 1½ hours.

recipe continues . . .

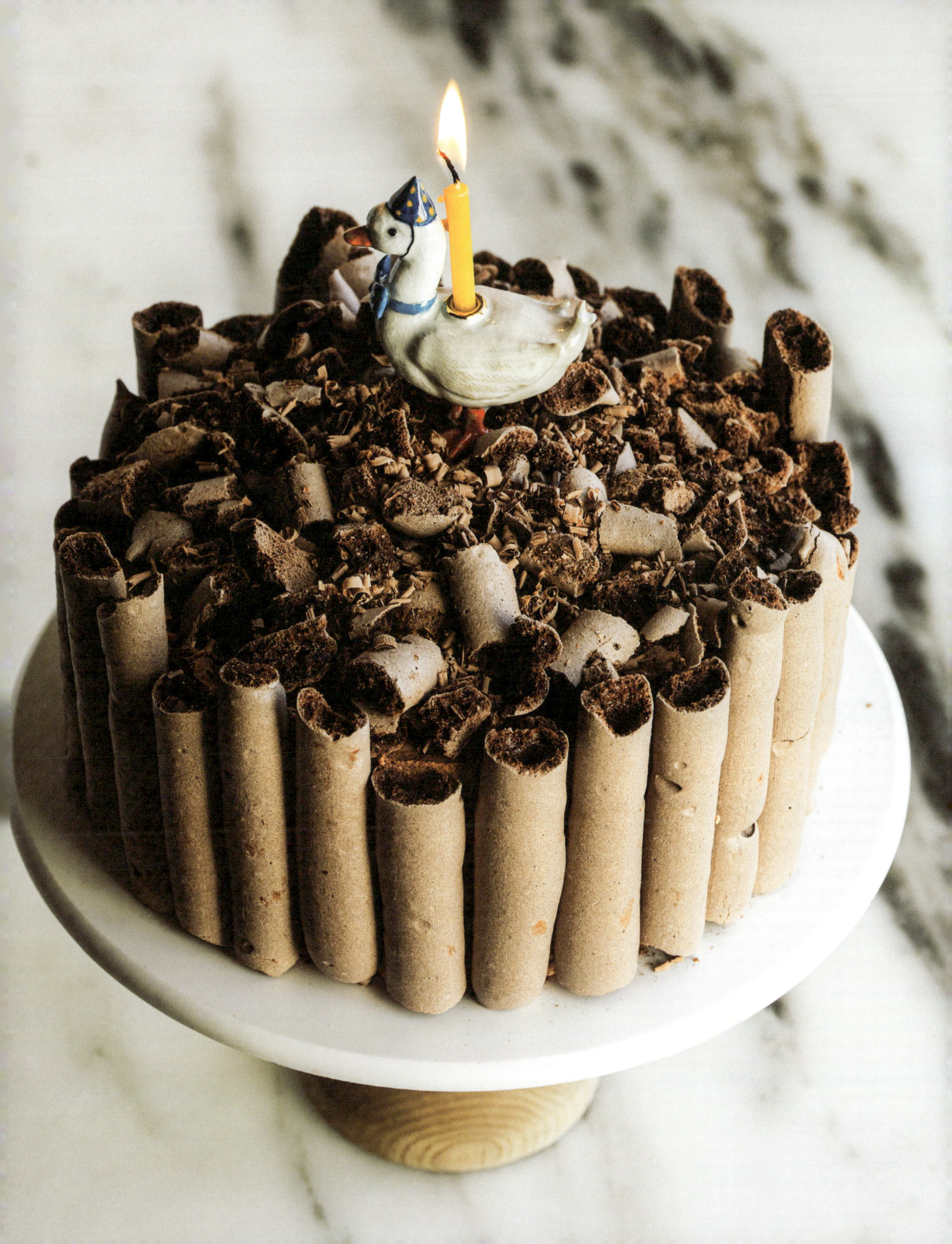

Remove from the oven and allow to cool completely. Break the strips into 2-inch shards and place in a resealable plastic bag or airtight container until you're ready to serve the cake.

MAKE THE MOUSSE

Whisk portion A (415 grams) of the heavy cream in the bowl of a stand mixer fitted with the whisk attachment until it reaches medium-stiff peaks. Transfer to a bowl and refrigerate.

Melt the chocolate in a metal bowl over simmering water until two-thirds of the chocolate has melted. Heat portion B (100 grams) of the cream separately, remove the chocolate from the heat, and pour the warm cream into the melted chocolate. Whisk until combined and emulsified. Make sure not to overheat the chocolate before adding the cream, otherwise the mixture could split.

Combine the egg yolks, egg, sugar, and salt in the clean bowl of a stand mixer. Whisk over simmering water until the mixture reaches between 160 and 170°F (71 and 77°C) on a digital thermometer. Transfer the bowl to the mixer and whisk on high speed until the mixture thickens and turns pale yellow, almost white. This mixture is called a pâte à bombe. Check the temperature of the melted chocolate. It should still be fluid, but shouldn't be hotter than 86 to 90°F (30 to 35°C). Fold the pâte à bombe into the chocolate and then fold in the chilled whipped cream.

TO ASSEMBLE

Place an 8-inch cake ring or the ring portion of a springform pan on a serving platter. Place a dollop of mousse at the center of the platter and place a meringue coil on top. Fill a piping bag with mousse and cut a 1-inch opening at the tip. Pipe about one-third of the mousse onto the sides and on top of the coil. Place a second meringue coil on top of the mousse and pipe one-third more of the mousse on top of the coil and the mousse, to fill the gap between the coil and the sides of the cake ring. Top with the last meringue coil and add the remaining mousse, smoothing the mousse to fill the gaps between the ring and the coil. Refrigerate or freeze to set, 3 hours to overnight.

Release the cake from the ring by warming the sides with a heat gun or blow dryer. Place the meringue strips along the sides and top of the mousse. Refrigerate and serve within 48 hours or, alternatively, wrap the cake in plastic wrap and freeze for up to a month.

S'mores Schoko Crossies

SERVES 8

Schoko Crossies are my childhood obsession, along with Maoam (IYKYK), that I'll always indulge the first chance I get when I land back in Germany and can get to an Edeka (my favorite grocery store). It's a crispy and smooth combo of cornflakes, almond flakes, and dark chocolate. That might not sound like a treat to be obsessed over but, believe me, it's tasty. As I'm both German *and* American, I always have a need to smoosh my two identities together, culling from the one to enhance the other. And while Schoko Crossies are addictive, I'm here to say that I've made them better by s'more-ing them up. (See the photo on page 232.)

1½ cups cornflakes

1½ cups Golden Grahams or similar graham cracker cereal

½ cup slivered almonds

½ cup sliced almonds

2 cups mini marshmallows

12 ounces bittersweet chocolate

4 ounces milk chocolate

Generous pinch of kosher salt

1 tablespoon neutral oil, such as canola

Combine the cornflakes, Golden Grahams, slivered and sliced almonds, and mini marshmallows in a large bowl. Toss gently.

In a metal bowl over simmering water, melt together the bittersweet and milk chocolate. Add the salt and oil. Stir to combine.

Pour the melted chocolate over the cereal mixture and, using a large rubber spatula, toss to coat. Spread the mixture on a parchment-lined sheet pan and refrigerate or freeze until set, 10 to 15 minutes.

Break up into smaller pieces and store in an airtight container in the refrigerator for up to 2 weeks.

SWEETS

Pfeffernüsse (German Spice Cookies)

MAKES 50 COOKIES

I like a bit of kick in my cookies. The spice blend in this traditional German Christmas staple will have you going back for more and more and more. You can feel free to swap out orange or mandarin juice for the lemon juice in the glaze, using the winter fruit that's on hand to give this buttery cookie the citrus lift of your choice. (See the photo on page 232.)

- 3 cups (360 grams) unbleached all-purpose flour
- ½ cup (48 grams) blanched almond flour
- 1 teaspoon baking powder
- 1 teaspoon fine sea salt
- ⅛ teaspoon ground cinnamon
- ⅛ teaspoon ground anise seed
- ⅛ teaspoon freshly grated nutmeg
- ⅛ teaspoon ground white pepper
- ⅛ teaspoon ground ginger
- ⅛ teaspoon ground cloves
- ½ cup (100 grams) granulated sugar
- 8 tablespoons (113 grams) unsalted butter, at room temperature
- ¼ cup plus 1 tablespoon (105 grams) honey
- 1 large egg

FOR THE GLAZE
- 1 cup (113 grams) confectioners' sugar
- 1 tablespoon freshly squeezed lemon juice (or citrus juice of your choice)

Whisk together the flour, almond flour, baking powder, salt, cinnamon, anise, nutmeg, white pepper, ginger, and cloves in a large bowl. Set aside.

Combine the granulated sugar and butter in the bowl of a stand mixer fitted with the paddle attachment. Mix on medium speed until smooth. Add the honey and continue to mix until incorporated, then add the egg and continue to mix until combined. Add the flour mixture all at once and mix on low speed until the mixture just comes together. Transfer the mixture to a piece of plastic wrap and press the dough together, incorporating any dry bits. Cover well and refrigerate for 30 minutes.

Line a sheet pan with parchment. Preheat the oven to 300°F (150°C).

Using a tablespoon-size cookie scoop, scoop rounds of dough and gently roll with your hands to smooth. Place on the prepared pan, spacing the cookies about 1 inch apart. Bake for 15 minutes, or until barely browning at the very edges. Remove from the oven and allow to cool completely.

MAKE THE GLAZE
Whisk together the confectioners' sugar and lemon juice in a small bowl until smooth. Brush the glaze over the cooled cookies. Allow glaze to set before transferring the cookies to an airtight container to store for up to 2 weeks.

Tante Erika's Creamy Chocolate Oatmeal Squares

MAKES 16 SQUARES

My mom's baby sister, my Tante Erika, sends us a much-anticipated package full of goodies every December. As is our family tradition, we celebrate Christmas on December 24, making a simple meal and then assembling a tray of cookies that we place by the Christmas tree. Whereas the presents were once my main focus, it's now all about watching the kids opening their treats. Who am I kidding? I'm all about the cookie platter. And if that cookie platter doesn't contain Tante Erika's Creamy Chocolate Oatmeal Squares, I go full Grinch. Luckily, they are simple to whip up, and I'll never have to go without. (See the photo on page 233.)

FOR THE CRUST

- 2 cups (178 grams) old-fashioned rolled oats (not quick-cooking)
- 2½ cups (300 grams) unbleached all-purpose flour
- 1½ cups (319 grams) firmly packed light brown sugar
- 1 teaspoon baking soda
- ½ teaspoon fine sea salt
- ½ pound (226 grams) unsalted butter, at room temperature

FOR THE FILLING

- 2 cups (340 grams) bittersweet chocolate chips
- 14 ounces (414 ml) sweetened condensed milk
- 2 tablespoons unsalted butter, at room temperature
- ½ teaspoon fine sea salt
- 2 teaspoons vanilla bean paste

Preheat the oven to 350°F (180°C). Line a half sheet pan with parchment. Set aside.

MAKE THE CRUST

Combine the oats, flour, brown sugar, baking soda, and salt in the bowl of a stand mixer fitted with the paddle attachment. Give them a quick mix and then add the butter. Mix on low speed until the mixture starts to get crumbly. Sprinkle 4 cups of the oat mixture into the prepared pan and, using your hands, press into an even layer. Set aside.

MAKE THE FILLING

Combine the chocolate chips, sweetened condensed milk, butter, and salt in a medium saucepan. Cook, stirring, over low heat until the butter and chocolate have completely melted and the mixture is smooth. Remove from the heat and stir in the vanilla bean paste.

Immediately pour the filling mixture over the prepared crust, using a small offset spatula to even out the mixture. Work quickly. Crumble the remaining oat mixture evenly over the filling and bake for 25 to 30 minutes, until the topping is golden brown. Remove from the oven, let cool, then cut into squares. Store in an airtight container for up to a month.

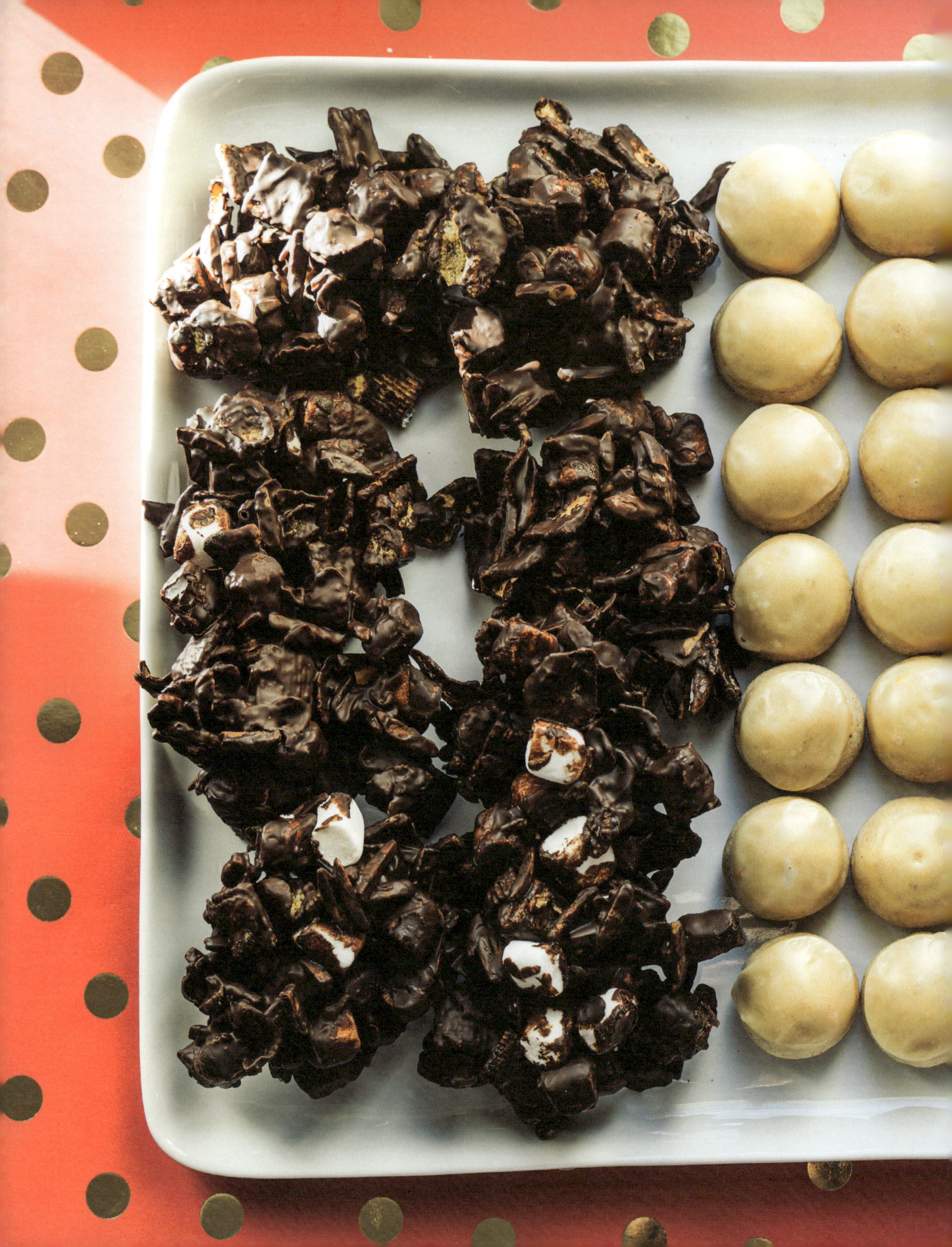

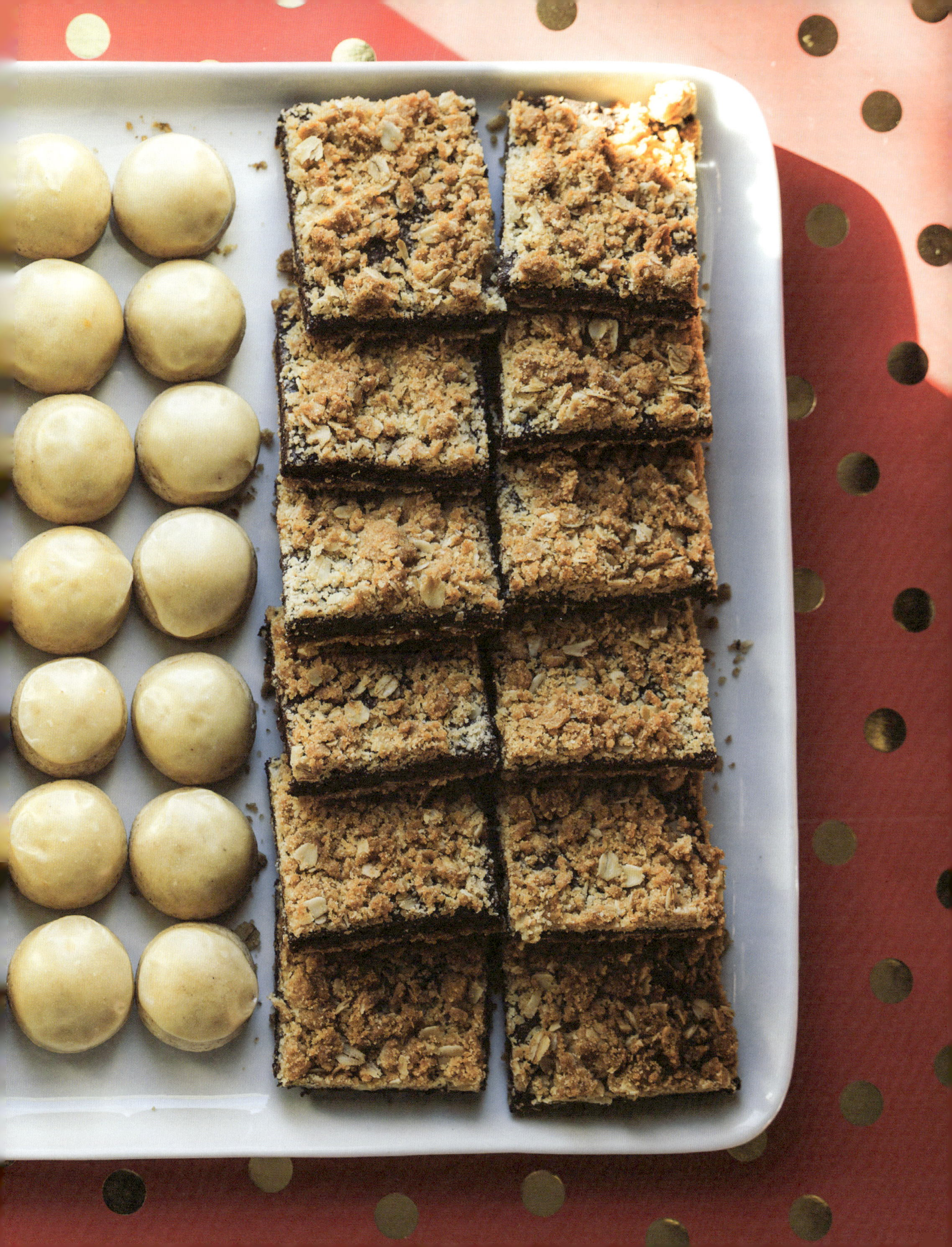

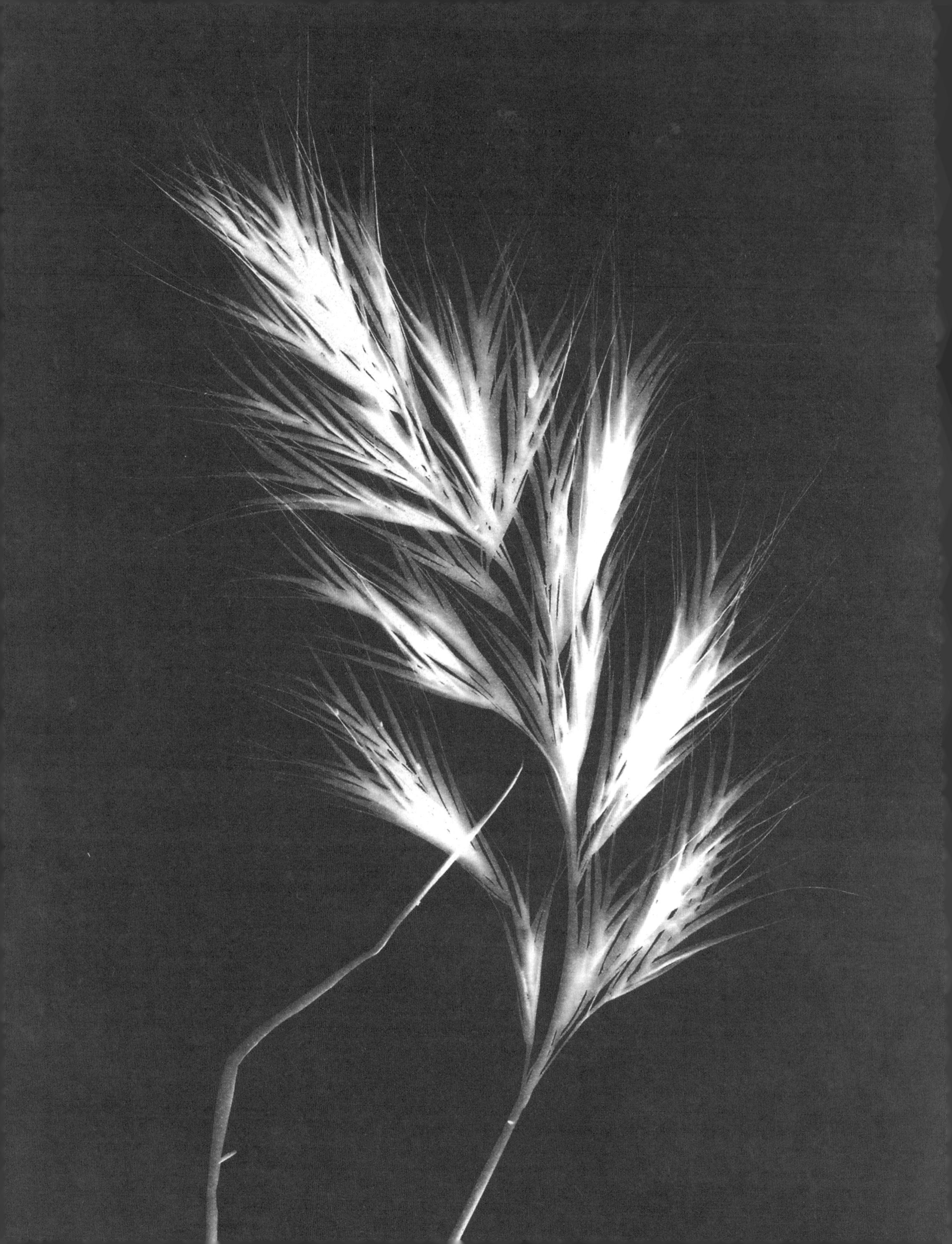

ESSENTIALS

EGGS

Perfect Jammy Eggs

MAKES 6 EGGS

I have given my hens very specific weights and measures for the perfect large egg. It's just a suggestion because they can't really dial in specifics, but I know they try. And any egg that they lay is perfect, in my eyes. It's just that the standard for baking and cooking is the "large" egg and that means the egg *should* weigh, in the shell, 56.8 grams. A medium egg, 49.6 grams. An extra-large, 63.8 grams. Get a carton of large eggs and each one will rarely hit that persnickety "large" weight. It's easy enough to get things *just* right by cracking the eggs open, whisking them up and then measuring for perfection. But when you cook them in the shell, cracking them open isn't an option. What I have found is that, if I choose eggs from my hens that fall in between large and just shy of extra-large, I can nail down the perfect jammy egg, an egg that isn't hard-boiled, but isn't quite soft-boiled, either. The edge of the yolk is just set and the center is ever so slightly . . . jammy. Not runny, but jammy. A few seconds on either side of the perfect timing can result in too soft or too hard, so start those timers and get your ice bath ready. It's time to jam.

6 large eggs, at room temperature

In a large saucepan or saucier, bring water to a healthy simmer over medium-high heat. You want a pan that can hold all six eggs comfortably without their overlapping, and you want the water to be high enough that it covers the eggs entirely (you can, of course, cook fewer eggs).

Carefully lower the eggs into the simmering water, using a large slotted spoon or a spider, and *immediately* set a timer for 6 minutes 20 seconds. In the meantime, fill a large bowl with ice and just cover with cold water. The ice water should be deep enough that the eggs will be fully submerged. Once the timer goes off, immediately transfer the eggs to the ice bath. After 20 seconds, give the eggs a turn. And then, after a minute, another turn, just to make sure they are cooling evenly.

I often eat a jammy egg in an egg cup, slicing off the top with a butter knife, or use as jewel-like jammy garnishes on bread, salads, and soups. In that case, I'll label each egg with a wax marker so I know that they are jammy eggs and not raw eggs. You can also peel them and make delicious Soy-Marinated Eggs (page 238).

Hard-Boiled Eggs

MAKES 6 EGGS

Boiling eggs. So easy, yet hard enough that to illustrate someone's lack of cooking skill, they just have to say, "I can't even boil an egg." The first trick is to be consistent with the size and weight of the eggs you use. If you use medium-size and use the timing for a large egg, you'll overcook it and get that horrifying green ring that just screams, "I CAN'T BOIL AN EGG!" Use an extra-large egg and you'll have a soft-set yolk. So, stick with large eggs and, if you're being persnickety, weigh each egg for certitude.

6 large eggs, at room temperature

Fill a large bowl with 2 cups of ice and 2 cups of cold water. Set aside.

In a large saucepan, bring a quart of water to a vigorous simmer but not a rolling boil. Too "rolling" and your eggs will knock into one another, cracking the shells.

Using a spider or slotted spoon, carefully lower the room-temperature eggs into the water (and try to get them all in at once, or as close together as humanly possible). *Immediately* start a timer for 10 minutes and, when the alarm goes off, transfer the eggs to the ice bath, turning the eggs every 30 seconds to cool them down evenly.

Once cool, drain away most of the cold water but leave just a bit in the bowl with the eggs. Shimmy the bowl so that the eggs crack gently against one another. Take an egg and gently tap on a hard surface, starting at the top and winding your way to the bottom, making small cracks. (If you start by cracking the egg on its side, it tends to crack the egg itself right at the center.) Start peeling at the bottom, or larger end, where the air cell is located.

Soy-Marinated Eggs

MAKES 6 EGGS

If you've ever had a great bowl of ramen, you've had a great soy-marinated egg. I make batches and keep them in a large Weck jar in the fridge. They don't last. They are a perfect quick (and delicious) snack, needing no extra seasoning. Just be careful that you don't spill yolk down your shirt.

- 1 cup water
- 1 garlic clove, grated to a paste with a Microplane grater
- ½ teaspoon peeled and grated fresh ginger
- ½ cup soy sauce (not low-sodium)
- ¼ cup mirin
- 1 tablespoon pure maple syrup
- 6 Perfect Jammy Eggs (page 236), peeled

In a small saucepan, combine ½ cup of the water, the garlic, and the ginger. Bring to a simmer over medium-low heat, then immediately remove from the heat and allow to cool completely.

Transfer the cooled mixture into a small mixing bowl and stir in the soy sauce, mirin, and maple syrup.

Add the eggs, making sure that they fit in the bowl in an even layer (if not, find a vessel that allows the eggs to rest next to each other but not so large that the marinade doesn't reach at least halfway up the eggs). Allow the eggs to sit for 2 hours, then turn them a half rotation to marinate evenly for another 2 hours.

Carefully transfer the eggs to a quart-size jar. Stir the remaining ½ cup water into the marinade mixture and then pour over the eggs in the jar. Cover with the lid and refrigerate for up to 5 days.

> PIE DOUGH, BREADS & TORTILLAS

G's Zippy, Flaky Pie Dough

**MAKES ENOUGH FOR ONE DOUBLE-CRUST PIE
OR TWO SINGLE-CRUST PIES**

If you make this and don't fall in love, you don't have a pulse. And if you make it and have some left over, you can freeze it. And if you freeze it and find yourself with some extra fruit, you can make a little pie. So, why not just make some and freeze some for emergencies?

3 cups (360 grams) unbleached all-purpose flour, plus more for dusting
1 tablespoon granulated sugar
1 teaspoon fine sea salt
3 fluid ounces (90 ml) ice-cold vodka
3 fluid ounces (90 ml) ice-cold water
1 teaspoon freshly squeezed lemon juice
¾ cup (339 grams) unsalted butter, chilled

Stir together the flour, sugar, and salt in a large bowl.

Combine the vodka, water, and lemon juice in a measuring cup and refrigerate.

Cut the sticks of butter in half lengthwise and then cut each half into four equal-width, long strips. Add the butter to the flour mixture and toss to coat the butter in flour. Using your fingers, flatten the butter and flour together. It's important that you aren't kneading the two together, you are pressing the two together so as to coat some of the flour with fat, which will protect some of the flour from producing too much gluten. You're also flattening the butter a bit more to create a very flaky dough. The butter should still feel cold after you've flattened each piece of it. If, at any point, the mixture seems to be getting warm, or if you feel the butter is melting rather than staying cool, immediately transfer the bowl to the freezer to chill for 5 to 10 minutes.

Pour the vodka mixture over the flour mixture and, using a large rubber spatula, toss the dry and wet ingredients to gently distribute. Vodka is used because it acts as a liquid binder without creating too much gluten, since it has a much higher percentage of alcohol (which will evaporate when baked!) and alcohol won't convert the flour's proteins into gluten; only water does that. This ensures you won't have a tough crust. Use the rubber spatula to slice through any large clumps of moisture, then gather the dough into your hands and use your thumbs like windshield

recipe continues . . .

wipers to break up any large clumps that you weren't able to break up using the spatula.

Using your fist or the palm of your hand, gently press and schmear the dough against the side of the bowl. This motion, called *frissage*, compresses the dough and creates layers of butter in the dough.

Turn out the dough onto a floured work surface. It should still look a bit piecey; it should not be a perfectly smooth dough. Use your hands to compress the dough a bit into a rough rectangle, lightly dust the top of the dough with flour, and then, using a rolling pin, roll the dough into a 12-by-16-inch rectangle. Make a "letter fold" by folding the dough into thirds, as you would a business letter. Turn the dough 90 degrees and then roll out again to 12 by 16 inches and perform another letter fold. Roll out once more to 12 by 16 inches and perform a third and last letter fold. Wrap the dough in beeswax wrap or plastic wrap and refrigerate for at least 30 minutes to overnight.

Brioche

MAKES TWO 8-BY-4-INCH LOAVES OR 14 BUNS

What do you think of when you hear the word "brioche"? I'll tell you what I hear: "BUTTER!" There is more, of course, to this stupendous bread, but butter is really up there in what makes it simply superior to just about anything else. It's why, when you get a restaurant burger, they'll *always* mention the brioche bun. It's the signal that it's elevated, luxurious . . . dare I say, fancy. Brioche is a type of bread called "enriched," meaning it has added fats (here, butter and egg yolk), sugars, and proteins (egg) that make a very soft and tender dough. It also requires a specific type of yeast that is osmotolerant, meaning that it can handle the extra fat and sugars that would otherwise interfere with the efficacy of standard yeasts. And when you make it into a loaf, you need to divide it into separate sections that go into the loaf pan, so that it has a better structure, each section acting like a little backbone to keep the loaf structurally stable. Not to worry; it slices up like a champ. And I've got one more trick up my sleeve: I use a small amount of a cooked starch mixture, called tangzhong, which helps with the structure and elevates the texture even more.

FOR THE TANGZHONG

⅓ cup (79 ml) whole milk

⅓ cup (79 ml) water

⅓ cup (40 grams) unbleached all-purpose flour

FOR THE DOUGH

4 large eggs

¼ cup (59 ml) whole milk

2 tablespoons (40 grams) pure maple syrup

2 teaspoons fine sea salt

4 cups (480 grams) unbleached all-purpose flour

1 packet (7 grams) osmotolerant instant yeast

½ pound (226 grams) unsalted European-style high-fat butter, at room temperature

Nonstick cooking spray

MAKE THE TANGZHONG

Pour the milk and water into a small saucepan, then add the flour. Whisk over medium heat until the mixture thickens. Remove from the heat and transfer the mixture to the bowl of a stand mixer. Allow to cool completely before proceeding.

MAKE THE DOUGH

To the tangzhong already in the stand mixer bowl, add the eggs, milk, maple syrup, and salt. Whisk with a fork to break up the eggs and combine the wet ingredients. Add the flour and then sprinkle the yeast over the flour (instant yeast can be added directly to dry ingredients). Using a dough hook, mix the dough on low speed for 5 minutes, to develop a bit of gluten before adding the butter. Gluten provides structure for the bread, but adding too much fat too soon will impede gluten development. Mix until the dough is a rough ball.

With the mixer running on low speed, add the butter, 1 tablespoon at a time, waiting until

recipe continues . . .

the last piece is completely incorporated, about 30 seconds to a minute, before adding the next. Once all the butter is incorporated, continue to mix until the dough is shiny, smooth, starts to pull away from the bottom of the bowl, and begins working its way up the dough hook and then releasing again in a shearing motion. This can take up to 15 minutes. Because this dough is naturally so soft, it's not recommended to work the dough by hand.

    Spray a large bowl with nonstick cooking spray. Transfer the dough to the prepared bowl, spray the top of the dough, then cover with beeswax wrap or plastic wrap. Allow to bulk ferment until doubled in size, about 1 hour, and then refrigerate for 1 hour to overnight.

TO BAKE AS LOAVES

Line two 8-by-4-by-4-inch loaf pans with parchment so that the parchment hangs over the long sides of the pan. Spray with nonstick cooking spray. Divide the dough in half and then divide each half into eight equal pieces. Roll each piece into a tight bun, then place eight buns in each pan, smooshing them next to one another. Cover the pans with plastic wrap and allow the dough to rise until it just reaches the rim of the pan, 2 to 3 hours.

    In the meantime, preheat your oven to 350°F (180°C). Then, remove the plastic wrap and bake the loaves for 30 to 35 minutes, or until the internal temperature reads 190°F (88°C) on a digital thermometer. Remove the loaves from the pan, using the parchment "wings" to lift them out, and allow to cool completely on a cooling rack.

TO BAKE AS BUNS

Divide the dough into sixteen equal-size pieces. Space about 2 inches apart on two sheet pans lined with parchment and cover loosely with plastic wrap to proof until doubled, 1 to 2 hours. In the meantime, preheat your oven to 350°F (180°C). Remove the plastic wrap and bake the buns for 15 to 20 minutes, or until the internal temperature reads 190°F (88°C).

Vollkorn Brot (German Whole Grain Bread)

MAKES ONE 16-BY-4-INCH LOAF

Vollkorn means "whole wheat" in German, and if you've ever seen a loaf of Vollkorn Brot, you can't help but notice that it's dense with nutty grain goodness. Many German recipes call for *Dinkel* (spelt flour); most American recipes call for rye flour. But the name of the bread itself tells you what you need to know: whole meal or *whole grain*. So, if you want to use rye, or spelt, or a whole-grain mix, that's up to you, as long as the entirety of the flour used is unprocessed. This bread has great things going for it: it has tons of fiber and whole-grain flavor and it's usually studded with inclusions, such as sunflower seeds or rye berries. If you grow sunflowers, this is a perfect opportunity to wrestle the birds for a cup of seeds. But one issue with it is that it *is* very dense and can often be dry. But you know I've got some workarounds to make this loftier and moister than any other homemade Vollkorn Brot. The solution is incredibly easy: presoaking. First, you soak the sunflower seeds in a portion of the water. This helps hydrate the seeds and keeps them from leeching moisture from the bread itself. It's literally called a "soaker," and it's something you should do with anything like seeds or oats if you're going to add them to a bread, to keep the bread's texture beautiful. The other trick is to soak the flour itself with the remaining water. This process, called autolyse, is a common practice with many high-hydration (high percentage of water) breads because it is a simple way of producing gluten, the structural powerhouse of bread, without a lot of extra kneading. But in the case of a bread with *this* much whole grain, where there's not a lick of white flour at play, soaking the flour by itself softens the bran in the wheat that makes it whole wheat (salt and yeast compete with the flour for the water, so they're left out of the autolyse). Why is this important? Because, if you start mixing all the ingredients together without the presoak, a.k.a. autolyse, the sharp outer layer of whole grains that make them "whole" wheat cut through the emergent gluten strands that allow the bread to rise and hold its structure, leaving you with a superdense loaf. If you soak the whole wheat, not only do you get gluten formation, but you soften the bran, allowing for a more successful rise and improving the overall texture of the bread. All it takes is just a little time and a bit of water.

recipe continues . . .

MY HARVEST KITCHEN

1 cup (135 grams) unsalted sunflower seeds
1¾ cups (414 ml) lukewarm water (105°F [41°C])
4 cups plus 2 tablespoons (500 grams) whole-grain flour
1 tablespoon honey
1 tablespoon fine sea salt
1 packet (7 grams) instant yeast
Nonstick cooking spray

To make the soaker, combine the sunflower seeds and ½ cup of the warm water in a small bowl. Set aside.

To make the autolyse, place the flour in a large bowl and stir in the remaining 1¼ cups of warm water. Stir and knead by hand until all the flour is absorbed and no dry bits remain. Cover with beeswax wrap or plastic wrap. Allow both the soaker and the autolyse to sit for 1 hour at room temperature.

After the hour has elapsed, add the sunflower soaker to the flour mixture. Add the honey, then sprinkle the salt on one side of the mixture and the yeast on the other. Use your hands in a scissorlike motion to combine the wet soaker and seeds, salt, and yeast. Continue to knead in the bowl by pulling the dough up and over toward the middle and then pressing down. Give the bowl a one-quarter turn and continue to knead in this fashion for 8 to 10 minutes, until the dough is firmer. The dough is paste-like, so don't let the consistency alarm you. Cover the bowl with plastic wrap and allow to rise at room temperature until almost doubled in size (this is called bulk fermentation, or the first proof), which will take 1 to 1½ hours, depending on the temperature of your room. Whole-grain breads tend to take a little longer to proof than do those made with white flours. Be patient!

Spray a Pullman loaf pan (measuring 16 by 4 by 4 inches, or use two 8-by-4-by-4-inch pans) with nonstick cooking spray, then line with parchment, with the parchment extending above the loaf pan on the long sides so you can easily lift the bread out of the pan once baked.

Turn out the dough onto a work surface that's been lightly sprayed with nonstick cooking spray. With your fingertips, gently press the dough into a rough 16-by-8-inch rectangle, if using a long Pullman, or divide the dough in half and press the two pieces into rough 8-inch squares, if using regular loaf pans. Starting from the long side for the Pullman, roll each piece of dough into a tight cylinder, using a bowl scraper that's been sprayed with nonstick cooking spray to help you along. Tuck your hands underneath the dough and carefully place in the prepared pan(s). Once in the pan, gently press the dough with your fingertips to even it out, cover loosely with beeswax wrap or plastic wrap, and allow to rise at room temperature until the dough is risen about ½ inch from the rim of the baking pan, 1 to 1½ hours (the timing will depend on the temperature of the room and could be shorter or longer). Don't overproof the dough; otherwise, it will collapse in the oven.

In the meantime, preheat your oven to 375°F (190°C). Bake for 50 to 60 minutes, or until the internal temperature reads 190°F (88°C) on a digital thermometer.

Ciabatta Rolls

MAKES 8 ROLLS

Ciabatta translates from Italian to "slipper," named for the shape of the bread, but could also refer to how it fits just *perfectly*, like Cinderella's shoe, into its role as a vessel to transport delicious fillings. Its rough crust has a slight crispness, while its open-crumbed interior is chewy and moist. This bread has it all, and its craggy insides just beg to be filled with a garden's overflowing bounty. Shove it full of spicy arugula and juicy tomatoes. Wantonly adorn with creamy burrata. Douse with olive oil and balsamic vinegar. Layer with sweet roasted peppers and salty speck. And don't let words like "biga" and "preferment" scare you off. Those are just ways of saying "yeasty head start." *Biga* is an Italian name for a type of preferment that is a mixture of water, flour, and a small amount of yeast. It's left on its own overnight or up to 24 hours. It brings great flavor to the bread and is incredibly simple. So, dive into that slipper with confidence. It'll be the perfect fit.

FOR THE BIGA (PREFERMENT)

1 cup (120 grams) unbleached bread flour

½ cup (114 grams) room-temperature water (70°F [21°C])

Scant ¼ teaspoon instant yeast

FOR THE DOUGH

2 cups (240 grams) unbleached bread flour, plus more for dusting

¾ cup (177 ml) room-temperature water (70°F [21°C])

1 teaspoon (3 grams) instant yeast

1 teaspoon (7 grams) fine sea salt

Semolina, for dusting

Nonstick cooking spray

8 to 10 ice cubes

Spray bottle of water (optional)

MAKE THE BIGA

Mix together all the biga ingredients in a large bowl until no dry flour remains at all. Cover with beeswax wrap or plastic wrap and keep at room temperature for at least 12 hours and up to 24.

MAKE THE DOUGH

Combine the bread flour and water in a large bowl and mix until there is no dry flour. Cover and allow to rest for at least 30 minutes to 1 hour. This process, called autolyse, allows for gluten development without any real mixing on your part.

Add the yeast and salt to the autolyse by sprinkling them on either side of the little dough ball so they aren't really touching, then add the biga. Start mixing with a wooden spoon or with a Dutch dough whisk until a sticky mass forms. It will feel dry at first, but don't add more water! Continue to mix with your hands until all the flour mixture is incorporated. It's a messy job, but worth it. Use a bowl scraper to help scrape dough from your hands back into the bowl. Once you've mixed the dough, cover the bowl with beeswax wrap or plastic wrap and allow to sit at room temperature for 45 minutes. Once the time is up, wet your hands or a plastic bowl scraper and slightly reach your dominant hand (or a bowl scraper) under the dough mass farthest from you. Draw up the dough and over toward the middle. That's your first fold. Turn the bowl 90 degrees and perform another fold, then turn again, fold, and then turn once more and fold, so that you've performed a total of four folds going all around the dough. Cover the bowl and allow to rest again for 1 hour, and then perform the four folds again. Give it another hour's rest and then do your final four folds. This will make a total of twelve folds.

Allow to rest, covered, for 45 minutes.

While the dough rests, preheat your oven to 450°F (230°C), arranging one oven rack at the very bottom and one in the middle. Place a cast-iron skillet on the bottom rack and allow it to preheat while the dough rests. Line two sheet pans with parchment and sprinkle lightly with semolina.

Scrape out the dough onto a floured work surface. Spray a bench scraper with nonstick cooking spray and use it to divide the dough into eight equal pieces. It's a sticky dough, so you'll likely need to respray the scraper. Wet your hands and gently press each piece of dough into a rough square/rectangle with your fingertips, being careful not to really stretch the dough but simply shaping it just a little to make it more uniform. Transfer the ciabattas to the prepared sheet pans, spacing them a few inches apart.

Lightly dust the tops of the ciabattas with flour and cover very loosely with plastic wrap. Allow to rest for 1 hour, or until they look inflated and jiggly. Remove the plastic wrap.

Bake one sheet pan at a time by quickly opening the oven and carefully placing four or five ice cubes in the preheated skillet, immediately placing one pan of ciabatta on the middle rack, and spraying four or five spritzes of water (if using) just above the dough (don't spray on the dough). Do this quickly so you don't lose steam and the oven doesn't lose too much heat. Bake for 20 to 25 minutes, until the ciabatta is lightly golden brown and its internal temperature reads 200°F (95°C) on a digital thermometer. Remove the pan of ciabatta, allow the oven to come back up to temperature, and repeat to bake the second pan of ciabatta.

Allow the slippers of bread to cool completely on a wire rack.

Crusty Bread

SERVES 12

Life is a bit better when you've got a rustic round loaf of bread waiting for you. I add just a touch of whole wheat flour to the mix to add more flavor and then a skosh of maple to coax the yeast along and to add a hint of Vermont sweetness. The crust shatters just enough and the interior is just pillowy enough that, when you slather it with butter, it soothes you just enough to get on with your day. This is the bread I eat happily on its own but have on hand for things like making the big crouton for my French Onion Soup (page 49), or to grill with a little olive oil and scrape with a knob of home-grown garlic to act as the base of avocado toast. It's simple, reliable, and delicious. By giving the dough an initial autolyse (see page 243), a quick knead, and then a series of gentle folds, you get maximum flavor and lift from a few simple ingredients.

1½ cups (180 grams) whole wheat flour

2½ cups (300 grams) unbleached bread flour, plus more for dusting

1⅔ cup (394 ml) lukewarm water (80 to 90°F [27 to 32°C])

1 packet (7 grams) instant yeast

1½ teaspoons fine sea salt

1 tablespoon pure maple syrup

1 tablespoon extra-virgin olive oil

Rice flour or semolina, for sprinkling

Combine the whole wheat flour, bread flour, and warm water in a large bowl or Cambro container, then stir with a wooden spoon. Mix until the flour is completely saturated with the water. Cover and allow to rest (autolyse) for 45 minutes to 1 hour.

Sprinkle the yeast on one side of the autolysed dough and the salt on the other, and then add the maple syrup. Stir with a wooden spoon until combined, then transfer to a stand mixer fitted with the dough hook. Mix on medium-low speed for 5 minutes, or until the dough is smooth and elastic. Alternatively, you can knead by hand, but it may take a few more minutes for it to develop properly. Transfer to a clean bowl or Cambro and coat the dough on both sides with the olive oil. Cover and allow to rest for 20 minutes.

Wet your dominant hand and gently tuck it under the edge of the dough, pulling and stretching one side of the dough up and over toward the center to make a fold. Turn it 90 degrees and continue to stretch and fold the dough, turning by 90 degrees each time, repeating until you've made a full circuit around the dough. Cover and allow to rest for 20 more minutes, and then perform four more folds as before. Cover the dough again and allow to double in size at room temperature, 1 to 1½ hours.

Flour a lined banneton (proofing basket) or line a medium bowl with a clean kitchen towel (not terrycloth) that's been generously floured. Set aside.

Lightly flour your work surface and tip out the dough right in the middle. Gently knock out any huge bubbles with your fingertips but don't deflate the dough completely, forming a rough square as you go. Take the edge of dough farthest from you and gently stretch and fold it toward the center, as you did when making the earlier folds. Fold in the other three sides toward the center and then flip the dough over onto its seam. Gently place your hands, palms up and slightly cupping, on either side of the dough and turn the dough clockwise while simultaneously drawing the dough toward you to make the dough into a taut ball. Continue rotating, pulling, and tightening until the dough is perfectly round and very tight, being careful not to tear the dough.

Gently place the ball of dough, seam side up, in the prepared banneton and pinch the seam a bit to keep it sealed. Cover with beeswax wrap or plastic wrap and allow to rest at room temperature for about 1 hour, or until doubled in size.

Alternatively, to enhance the flavor of the bread, after you place the dough into the banneton, cover completely and refrigerate overnight, to allow the yeast to slowly develop more yeasty depth.

Preheat your oven to 475ºF (245ºC), placing a round Dutch oven or bread oven (I use the Challenger Breadware's bread pan) inside to preheat.

Gently turn out the dough, seam side down, onto a half sheet of parchment sprinkled with rice flour or semolina. Score the top of the bread with a bread lame, a razor blade, or a very sharp paring knife, creating ½-inch-deep slashes in a crosshatch on top of the bread.

Carefully transfer the dough to the preheated baking vessel and cover. Bake for 35 minutes, covered, and 10 more minutes, uncovered. Remove from the oven and allow to cool completely.

Steamed Buns (Bao)

MAKES 24 BUNS

Steamed buns have the most heavenly texture. They are as close to eating a cloud as you can get. And when combined with very luxurious, fatty fillings like the White Wine–Braised Short Ribs (page 156), they round out both flavor and texture beautifully. Steaming is also a great way to "bake" something if you don't have an oven or if it's too stinkin' hot to turn one on. It requires a bamboo steaming basket, but this is a tool that is both economical and incredibly versatile in the kitchen.

1 cup (236 ml) whole milk
½ cup (118 ml) lukewarm water (100 to 105°F [37 to 40°C])
¼ cup (78 grams) sweetened condensed milk*
⅓ cup (61 grams) duck or pork fat, at room temperature
1 tablespoon pure maple syrup
4 cups (480 grams) unbleached bread flour
1 packet (7 grams) instant yeast
1 tablespoon fine sea salt
½ teaspoon baking powder
½ teaspoon baking soda
Nonstick cooking spray

Combine the milk, water, sweetened condensed milk, fat, and maple syrup in the bowl of a stand mixer fitted with the dough hook attachment.

Stir together the flour, yeast, salt, baking powder, and baking soda in a large bowl. Whisk to combine for 30 seconds. Add the flour mixture to the stand mixer bowl and mix on medium-low speed until the dough is smooth and shiny, 10 to 15 minutes.

Spray a large bowl with nonstick cooking spray and transfer the dough to the bowl. Spray the top of the dough, cover with beeswax wrap or plastic wrap, and allow to bulk ferment at room temperature until doubled in size, 1 to 2 hours.

Cut twenty-four 3-inch squares of parchment and line a sheet pan with them.

Punch down the dough to expel the gas, then divide the dough into three equal pieces. Roll each piece into a rope and divide each rope into eight equal pieces. Roll each piece into a ball and place each ball, seam side down, on a parchment square. Cover the sheet pan loosely with plastic wrap and allow the dough to rest for 30 minutes.

Lightly spray a work surface with nonstick cooking spray. Place a dough ball, seam side up, on the counter and, using your palm, press and stretch the dough into an oval. Fold the dough over and gently press the dough along the edges. Return each piece to its parchment and cover loosely again with plastic wrap. Allow to rest at room temperature until puffy, 30 minutes to 1 hour.

Fill a wok or wok-size saucier with a few inches of water and bring to a simmer. Place six buns, on their parchment, on each level of a multilevel bamboo steamer, and place over the simmering water. Steam for 14 to 15 minutes.

MY HARVEST KITCHEN

Repeat with the remaining buns. Use immediately or store in a freezer-safe container or resealable plastic bag in the freezer for up to a month. To thaw, remove from the freezer and leave at room temperature for about 30 minutes and then resteam for 2 to 3 minutes. Gently pry open at the fold and fill.

*NOTE You can now purchase condensed milk in pouches that allow you to seal and refrigerate what's left over, to store for your next project.

ON CORN

In the gardening world, we quite rightly exult in the presence of our pollinator friends. We grow pollinator gardens, dapple our edible beds with bee-alluring blooms, and stay away from big box stores that sell plants that disrupt our pollinator friends. In the homestead gardening world, I'd say 90 percent of what we grow is reliant on our winged friends, be they honeybees, bumblebees, flies, wasps, moths, butterflies, or mason bees. This, of course, is a very unscientific deduction based on how I grow and what my gardening friends grow. In the industrial food world, however, the majority (65 percent) of crops are wind pollinated. These crops include wheat, corn, and rice, where the air itself is responsible for stirring up the pollen and delivering it to the fertile receptors.

I grow corn every year. Always sweet corn. Sometimes flint corn. It really depends on my crop rotation schedule and which raised bed I'm moving the corn to. If the area is too small, I'll only choose one corn. Why? It's that wind pollination. That means the tassels up top get jostled by wind and the pollen falls down onto the emerging silks of the nascent cobs. Growing corn in tight grids instead of rows allows for better pollination among the stalks. I hand pollinate by pulling off pollen-laden tassels and swatting the silks to cover them with pollen. Each kernel represents a successfully pollinated silk. I pull a tassel from the top of the plant and tap tap tap at the silks, trying to get each silk touched by the tassel's load of pollen. I still don't get a full boat of kernels, but I do get a cob that's delightfully packed *almost* to the top of the cob. If you look at large farms, their corn fields are gigantic, allowing for a ton of pollen dispersal. If you grow corn at home, the likelihood is that you won't have a field's worth growing, but a few dozen. I recommend getting on your toes, grabbing a tassel, and tapping at those silks.

If my plot is too small, growing two varieties, such as sweet corn and flint corn, can be iffy because they can cross pollinate, creating a flinty sweet corn and a sweet flint corn. Not optimal for either. But when I do have enough room, I always marvel at how high flint corn grows, feet above the sweet corn. And my harvesting is different as well. Sweet corn, I harvest as soon as I can feel the kernels fully filled out underneath the husk. But the flint, I let that dry on the stalk. This makes for a sweeter finished product. Back in the day, corn was left to dry on the stalk, increasing the sweetness, and then processed after a final storing and drying. But when industrial production allowed for mechanical processing of cornmeal, the process was curtailed, cobs taken from the stalks before they were able to fully dry out in the field and sweeten, making for a flavorless finished product and angering cornbread makers from the Deep South to the cold North. Because I can put in the effort with my twenty or so cobs, I leave them on the stalk to dry and sweeten. Then I transfer them to my corncrib, a little outbuilding with open air slats, allowing for a continued drying process. And because the cobs can be so beautiful, full of multicolored kernels, I'll hang a few on the front door as decoration.

Once dried, I flick the kernels from the cobs

with my thumb, doing my best to keep them from skittering off the table and cursing as I start to feel blisters forming. Then, the kernels go into my little KitchenAid mill. If the corn isn't dry enough, it can gum up the works, so spending the time on the stalk *and* in the corncrib makes all the difference. When I'm done, maybe I'll get a cup of cornmeal. The *labor* is no joke in this labor of love. Thankfully, there are fabulous products, such as King Arthur Baking Company Organic Masa Harina Flour and Anson Mills Spring Water Masa, that bring the sweetness back into the mix and make for a gorgeous corn tortilla without all the growing, drying, and blisters. But the joy of seeing the stalks sway in the wind and then pulling back the husks to get a peep at the gorgeous kernels is reason enough to try your hand at growing your own corn.

Corn Tortillas

MAKES 12 TORTILLAS

Homemade corn tortillas are simple and so delicious. They are tender. They are great vehicles for fillings. They are outrageously tasty. Whether you mill your own cornmeal or you buy a high-quality brand, the results will be great either way. With just three simple ingredients, you can create a foundational element of so many great dishes. And they freeze beautifully, so you can make a single, double, or triple batch and enjoy your handiwork for months! Having a tortilla press makes the work zippy, and it's relatively inexpensive and small enough to store easily.

2 cups (186 grams) masa harina*
Generous pinch of kosher salt
1¼ cups (300 ml) lukewarm water (100 to 105°F [37 to 40°C])

Stir together the masa harina and salt in a large bowl. While stirring with a rubber spatula, slowly pour in the warm water, stirring until a cohesive dough forms. If you need to, go in with your hands and gently knead together to incorporate any dry bits.

Transfer the dough to a clean work surface and continue to knead with your hands until the mixture is smooth, about 2 minutes. If it still feels sticky, sprinkle with a bit of masa harina and continue to work. (Don't add too much masa harina or the dough will be dry and won't hold together.)

Heat a cast-iron or nonstick skillet over medium-high heat until very hot, about 5 minutes.

Divide the dough into 12 equal pieces. Place them on a parchment-lined sheet pan and place a damp towel over them while you work them one by one. Roll each piece into a tight ball. Place a dough ball on a piece of plastic wrap and then place a second dough ball on top. Using a rolling pin, roll the two layers of dough into a thin round, a little less than ⅛ inch thick. Alternatively, you can use a tortilla press for this, if you have one. It makes the work more efficient. In that case, place a square of plastic wrap underneath and on top of each ball of dough as you use the press, to keep it from sticking. Either way, keep the tortillas layered in plastic as you work to keep them from drying out.

To cook, remove the top piece of plastic wrap. I place the tortilla in my hand, its plastic on the bottom, and then gently flip the tortilla face down onto the skillet (the plastic will now be on top), immediately pulling off the plastic. This keeps the tortilla from tearing.

Cook for 30 to 45 seconds on the first side, flipping with a large rubber spatula once the tortilla releases from the pan. Continue to cook on the second side for a minute or so more, or until the edges just start to get golden. Flip the tortilla again and cook until the tortilla just begins to puff, and then continue to cook for 20 to 30 seconds more, to make sure it is fully cooked through. Transfer the cooked tortilla to a clean kitchen towel and wrap it to keep it from drying out. Repeat with the remaining tortillas.

Use immediately or store in the refrigerator, layered with parchment in between each tortilla, for 3 days, or freeze for up to a month.

*NOTE You can mill your own masa harina from flint corn or use store-bought.

GRAINS

Perfect Japanese Short-Grain Rice

SERVES 2 TO 4

Japanese short-grain rice is often labeled "sushi" rice in the US, but it's used for many other dishes. It is *not* sticky rice; that's another type of rice altogether. The grains of Japanese short-grain rice are short and plump and contain less amylose than long-grain rice, such as basmati and jasmine. Amylose is a starch that that helps separate rice grains, but sushi rice, with its stocky shape, gently clings to the other grains and is moister, absorbing more water than long-grain rice. This makes it easier to pick up rice with chopsticks and gives it a lovely chew. All this makes it imperative to treat the rice differently before and during cooking. But the first job you have is buying the right rice, so look for Japanese short-grain and don't be confused if it's labeled as "sushi" rice, because you can use it for other things as well.

1 cup short-grain Japanese "sushi" rice*
1 cup plus 2 tablespoons water

Place the rice in a large bowl and then barely cover with cold water. Using your hand like a claw, circle in a clockwise motion to agitate. Drain and do this two more times, or until the water is almost clear. Don't use a sieve to do this, as it can damage the rice granules.

Once you've discarded the third water rinse, cover the rice again with cool water and allow to soak for 25 to 30 minutes. This isn't a step you can skip. Because of the shape of the rice, this soaking allows the rice to absorb the right amount of moisture so that, when it's cooked, it will be done all the way through. Skip this step and you'll have an uncooked rice core. Rinsing and soaking are nonnegotiable steps.

Rinse again. It's here that I'll drain in a sieve and bounce the grains a few times to ensure there's not too much extra water.

Combine the 1 cup plus 2 tablespoons of fresh water and the rice in a heavy-bottomed pot (I use a small enameled cast-iron pot) and bring to a boil, partially covered. Once boiling, lower the heat to low and cover completely. Set your timer for 12 minutes. Once the timer goes off, quickly check to make sure all the water's absorbed and, if not, cook for a minute longer, covered.

Remove from the heat and leave covered for 10 minutes. Fluff the rice with a wooden spoon or rice paddle.

***NOTE** Measure the rice by mounding and then carefully leveling off the rice in the cup.

Perfect Quinoa

SERVES 4

Quinoa is a wonderful side dish. It's packed with fiber and protein. It's delicate yet toothsome. It takes on flavor easily. And, boy, does it cook quickly. But sometimes, for all that, it comes out bitter and less than fluffy. I'm here to help. The first thing you have to do with quinoa is rinse it. Why? Because quinoa is naturally coated with a bitter substance called saponin that protects the little seeds from insects and birds but, left on before cooking, it's also a deterrent to humans. Rinsing the quinoa in a fine-mesh sieve will remove the bitterness. But say you live in an arid place and you're thinking, "What a waste of water!" Or even if you don't live in an arid place you probably hate the thought of the aquatic waste. Well, I've got news for you. That water is something you should absolutely harvest and use to water your garden, especially if you are burdened by the infamous jumping worm, a plague on gardens everywhere. Those bitter compounds in saponin are a deterrent to jumping worms. You may have heard of the use of tea meal for the same purpose, an expensive soil amendment that helps with the problem, but why not use some free bitter water, instead, and get a tasty side dish in the meantime.

1 cup quinoa

1¾ cups low-sodium vegetable or chicken stock

Salt

Rinse the quinoa in a fine-mesh sieve, stirring with your fingers to ensure every small grain is rinsed. Transfer the wet quinoa to a deep saucepan and heat over low heat, stirring constantly to dry the seeds and gently toast them. Once the quinoa looks dry and the mixture smells pleasantly aromatic, transfer the quinoa to a bowl.

Add the stock to the empty saucepan and bring to a boil. Add the quinoa, lower the heat to low, stir, and cover (it's at this point on my gas stove that I'll put a burner diffuser under the pot to stop hot spots from burning the quinoa). Cook for 10 to 15 minutes. Remove from the heat, keep covered, and allow to rest for 5 minutes more before fluffing and serving.

Jasmine Rice

SERVES 2 TO 4

1¼ cups water
1 cup jasmine rice
Salt and freshly ground black pepper

Pour the water into a small, heavy-bottomed saucepan, then stir in the rice. Bring to a boil over high heat. Add a burner diffuser beneath the pot if using a gas range, cover the pot, and continue to cook over low heat for 12 minutes. Remove from the heat, keep covered, and allow to sit for 10 minutes. Fluff, then season with salt and pepper.

ON COUSCOUS

THERE are different types of couscous—Moroccan, Israeli pearl, Lebanese, and instant—all made from durum wheat that's ground into semolina flour, but occasionally made with barley or millet. What type to use is really up to you and what you are serving it with or how it's incorporated into a dish.

Moroccan couscous is the smallest—the tiny granules cook in minutes—which makes it incredibly convenient. Its fluffy nature is a nice textural counterpoint to deeply spiced meats.

Pearl couscous is aptly named because it is larger and perfectly round, like a cultured pearl, and comes in about the size of a peppercorn. It's chewier than Moroccan couscous and is great in soups and salads.

Lebanese couscous is the largest and, therefore, takes the longest to cook. It is hearty and often paired with chickpeas and shredded chicken.

The packaging instructions will lead you to the right cooking method for each.

SAUCES & CONDIMENTS

Chermoula

MAKES ½ CUP

Chermoula is an aromatic and flavorful sauce packed with herbs. It's traditionally served with fish but with the amount of aromatics involved, it's lovely with all kinds of meat, lamb included.

- **1½ cups roughly chopped fresh cilantro leaves (about 2 bunches)**
- **1½ cups roughly chopped fresh parsley leaves (about 2 bunches)**
- **Rind of ½ preserved lemon (see page 269), roughly chopped**
- **4 garlic cloves, grated to a paste with a Microplane grater**
- **2 teaspoons paprika**
- **2 teaspoons cumin seeds, lightly toasted and ground in a mortar and pestle or in a spice mill**
- **1 teaspoon coriander seeds, lightly toasted and ground in a mortar and pestle or in a spice mill**
- **Pinch of saffron (optional)**
- **½ cup extra-virgin olive oil**
- **Kosher salt**

Place the cilantro and parsley in a food processor along with the preserved lemon, garlic, paprika, cumin, coriander, and saffron (if using). With the processor running, slowly drizzle in the olive oil to emulsify. Add salt to taste. Use immediately or store in an airtight container in the refrigerator for up to 2 days.

Choron

MAKES 1½ CUPS

I am a saucy gal. If there's hollandaise on offer, I'm on it. If you give me fries, I'm searching for a jug of yummy to dip them in. All sauces are fair game for me, but there are times when a little bit of tang and tomato sweetness are called for and plain ketchup just won't do. That's where Choron sauce (named after its creator) comes in, also known as *béarnaise tomatée*. Béarnaise is the creamy classic that's already a riff on hollandaise. And this is a riff on the riff, putting fresh tomatoes from the garden to good use. And then I'm adding some spice to the mix, so it's a riff on a riff on a riff. My house, my rules.

1 pound ripe paste tomatoes, halved*
½ cup dry white wine
¼ cup white wine vinegar
3 chervil or curly parsley sprigs
3 tarragon sprigs
1 small shallot, roughly chopped
2 large egg yolks
1 teaspoon sriracha
Salt
¾ cup (170 grams) unsalted butter

Cook the tomatoes in a large saucepan over medium heat until very soft, 8 to 10 minutes. Lower the heat to a simmer, stirring occasionally, until the very watery moisture has evaporated, 5 to 10 minutes more.

Transfer the tomatoes to a tamis, fine-mesh sieve, or chinois set over a large bowl and press with a bowl scraper through the sieve or process through the chinois to extract the pulp and juice from the tomatoes, leaving the skin and seeds behind. You should be left with about ½ cup. Set aside.

Combine the wine, white wine vinegar, parsley, tarragon, and shallot in a large saucepan. Simmer over low heat for 10 to 15 minutes, until the mixture is reduced and very syrupy, and you have about 2 tablespoons of reduced syrup after straining out the herbs.

Transfer the reduced wine syrup to a blender whose lid has a small, removable center. Add the egg yolks, sriracha, and a pinch of salt. Blend the mixture (lid fully closed) to combine. Melt the butter in a small saucepan over medium-high heat. With the blender on, remove the center section of its lid and slowly pour the melted butter into the blender through the opening; then add the reduced tomatoes, a tablespoon at a time, through that same small opening, until the mixture is smooth, thick, and emulsified. Turn off the blender and taste, season with salt if needed, and serve immediately over poached eggs, grilled meats, or veggies.

*NOTE I grow both San Marzano and Midnight Roma paste tomatoes. Alternatively, you can use San Marzanos from a 28-ounce can. Drain away the juice before using canned tomatoes in this recipe.

Fresh Tomato Pomodoro Sauce

MAKES ABOUT 3 CUPS

The difference between a fresh tomato sauce made with run-of-the-mill tomatoes from the grocery store and one made with garden-fresh, sweet as can be tomatoes plucked warm from the vine is night and day. And when you grow tomatoes specific to the purpose, such as the San Marzano varietal and Roma tomatoes, tomatoes that are naturally less pulpy and more meaty (that's why they're called paste tomatoes, after all), you can prepare a batch that's big enough to enjoy the day of and more to freeze for winter nights when a burst of sweet, fresh tomato is a reminder that warmer days are to come.

5 pounds fresh, superripe paste tomatoes*
2 large garlic cloves, peeled
1 small onion, finely chopped
¼ cup extra-virgin olive oil
2 small bunches fresh basil, roughly chopped
Salt

Halve the tomatoes and discard the seeds. I just use my thumb to gently press the seed mass out of the tomato and into a bowl. (You can dry the seeds to plant next year, if you like.) Place the tomatoes, whole garlic cloves, and chopped onion in a cast-iron braiser or rondeau. Cook, stirring occasionally, over medium heat until the tomatoes are very soft and juicy, 45 minutes to 1 hour. As you stir, use tongs or a culinary tweezer to pluck out and discard any tomato skins that have detached. The skins curl up naturally and get "pointy" toward the end of cooking and are pretty easy to identify. If you'd rather not spend time plucking out skins, once the sauce is cooked, you can suspend a colander over a deep bowl and press it through with a rubber spatula. This allows the tomato and finely chopped onion to pass through and will leave the skins and whole garlic behind in less than a minute. Transfer the sauce, without the skins, back to the braiser and add back the garlic as well.

Using a fork, gently mash the garlic into the sauce. Add the olive oil and basil and continue to cook until the sauce has thickened and reduced by half. Give your sauce a taste and add salt as needed. Use immediately over pasta and meatballs or allow to cool and store in a freezer-safe container. It will keep, frozen, for up to 3 months.

> *NOTE I use a combination of San Marzano varietal and Midnight Roma tomatoes. that I grow

Tzatziki

MAKES 2½ CUPS

If there's something on the table for dipping or slathering, I'll take double helpings. Tzatziki happens to be one of my all-time favorites. A crispy cucumber (any kind will do, but English are my preferred), fresh garlic, fresh dill, rich yogurt, and a little science will make this your go-to double-dipping obsession.

1 English cucumber, peeled and seeded
Salt
4 garlic cloves
1 teaspoon freshly squeezed lemon juice
2 tablespoons extra-virgin olive oil
2 cups whole-milk plain Greek yogurt
¼ cup chopped fresh dill
Freshly ground black pepper

Use a box grater to grate the cucumber. Place the grated cucumber in a sieve over a bowl and sprinkle with a large pinch of salt. Toss and allow to sit for 10 minutes to draw moisture from the cucumber.

Use a Microplane grater to grate the garlic. Place in a medium bowl along with the lemon juice. Stir to combine and allow to sit for 10 minutes. The acid in the lemon juice works on the enzyme alliinase, which is responsible for the bite in garlic. A weak acid, such as lemon (or vinegar), mellows the alliinase but doesn't take away its flavor. Alliinase is especially pungent when garlic is grated or finely chopped. Add a hearty pinch of salt to the garlic mixture, along with the olive oil. Stir to combine.

Squeeze the cucumber to remove excess moisture. Add the cucumber, yogurt, dill, and pepper to taste to the garlic mixture. Stir to combine. Cover and refrigerate for 30 minutes to allow the mixture to thicken. Serve with dolmas or as a dip with veggies.

Tahini Dressing

MAKES 1 CUP

Tahini had an outsized role in my childhood. It landed in everything from chickpea soup to hummus to, inexplicably, my bag lunch vegan sandwiches. I can't blame my mom for being creative with the stuff. It is delicious but just might not be right on, well, everything. Now grown, I can appreciate what it brings to my table and it's a staple that can live in my pantry for ages, a perfect addition to a summer meal of Cali (Turkey) Meatballs (page 168) and a midwinter hero, when fresh produce isn't at its finest but the garlic harvest is still holding strong and citrus is truly in season. It makes for a lovely sauce on just about anything. Helga would be very pleased.

½ cup smooth tahini (stir before measuring)
¼ cup warm water
¼ cup extra-virgin olive oil
Grated zest and juice of 1 lemon
1 tablespoon sesame oil
1 tablespoon pure maple syrup
1 large garlic clove, grated to a paste with a Microplane grater (about 1 teaspoon)
¼ teaspoon ground cumin
Salt and freshly ground black pepper

Whisk together all the ingredients in a small bowl until smooth. Transfer to a mason jar and refrigerate.

Garlic Aioli

MAKES ½ CUP

½ cup extra-virgin olive oil
4 large garlic cloves, peeled
1 large egg yolk
½ teaspoon freshly squeezed lemon juice
Generous pinch of kosher salt

Combine the olive oil and garlic cloves in a small saucepan and infuse over low heat until the garlic just begins to take on color and soften, about 15 minutes. Remove from the heat and allow to come to room temperature.

Transfer the garlic cloves from the oil to a blender whose lid has a removable center section. Add the egg yolk, lemon juice, and salt to the blender, cover with the lid, and remove the center section. With the blender on, slowly drizzle in the oil through the opening until thick and creamy. Refrigerate in an airtight container for up to 3 days.

PICKLED & PRESERVED

Quick! Let's Pickle!

MAKES 5 TO 6 CUPS

I grow veggies. I love pickles. I love to pickle veggies. My love of a quick pickle is no surprise. I pickle red onions all the time and have them on just about everything from salads to cheese boards to sandwiches. But red onions aren't the only guys that get the treatment: bell peppers mixed with hot peppers, beans, cauliflower, cucumbers (natch), and carrots. Oh, and eggs.

You don't have to stick to my spice medley, choosing to add a kick or a mellow amendment as you please. But I like what I like, and I tend to stick with it.

6 garlic cloves

2 dill sprigs

1 tablespoon yellow mustard seeds

5 to 6 cups* fresh veggies, washed and cut or left whole, *or* 6 hard-boiled eggs, peeled

2 cups distilled white vinegar

2 cups water

¼ cup pure maple syrup

2 tablespoons kosher salt

Sterilize a 2-quart mason jar (see directions, page 227). Add the garlic, dill, and mustard seeds to the jar. Add the veggies or eggs, leaving an inch of headspace to the rim of the jar.

Combine the vinegar, water, maple syrup, and salt in a saucepan and bring to a boil. Pour the hot pickling liquid into the jar, making sure the ingredients are completely covered (you can use the end of a wooden spoon to poke them down a bit). Let the pickles sit at room temperature until the liquid is cool. Seal the jar and refrigerate.

These keep up to 2 weeks in the fridge.

*NOTE The total amount of vegetables should be able to fit into a 2-quart mason jar.

Ida Mae's Red Salsa

MAKES 1 CUP

My friend Terri makes the best salsa. It's quick and fresh. It packs as much heat as you want it to (pick your green chilis wisely). As it turns out, like many great recipes, it originated with her mom, Ida Mae of El Paso, Texas. Each of the Rodriguez kids, Terri and her sister and brother, have added their own twist to the proceedings, but they all follow Ida Mae's brilliant hack of using a food processor to make quick work of the proceedings.

2 large, medium-hot long green chilis (Anaheim for milder heat or Hatch for a kick)

2 large superripe tomatoes (8 ounces total), blanched, peeled, and cut into quarters

1 small jalapeño pepper, stemmed and seeded

2 tablespoons roughly chopped onion

½ garlic clove

¼ cup cilantro leaves, tightly packed

¼ teaspoon dried oregano

1 teaspoon extra-virgin olive oil

1½ teaspoons kosher salt

Place an oven rack in the top position and preheat the broiler. Line a sheet pan with aluminum foil. Place the green chilis on the foil and place under the broiler for 10 minutes, or until the skin just begins to blister. Gather the foil around the chilis and leave to steam for 10 more minutes. Remove the stem end, pull off the skin, and seed. Set aside.

In a food processor, combine the tomatoes, jalapeño, onion, garlic, cilantro, oregano, olive oil, and salt. Pulse three to four times until the mixture is roughly chopped. Add the green chilis and pulse until you achieve your desired chunkiness.

Italian Sweet and Spicy Pickled Pepper Salad

MAKES ABOUT 1 QUART

When you have an abundance of peppers, make pepper salad. Whether it's a bounty of bells and cherries from my garden, jalapeño and Mad Hatters dangling from my indoor pepper plants, or excess after teaching a decorated focaccia class at my baking school, Sugar Glider Kitchen, where I prep for each student by slicing and dicing vegetables, peppers especially, that lend themselves to both tastiness and beautiful food art, I always seem to be in possession of bright peppers with nowhere to go. But then I remember that I have canning jars waiting empty, garlic I've harvested and cured hanging in the kitchen, and carafes of beautiful vinegar, all waiting to get busy making a beautiful pickled pepper salad.

1½ pounds bell peppers, in a variety of colors
½ pound hot cherry peppers or jalapeños
1 quart white wine vinegar
2 tablespoons kosher salt
2 tablespoons black peppercorns
8 garlic cloves, finely chopped
1 tablespoon pure maple syrup

Sterilize a 1-quart mason jar (see page 227).

Core, seed, and cut the bell peppers and hot peppers into ½-inch wide strips.

Combine 2 cups of the white wine vinegar, 2 cups of water, and the salt in a large nonreactive pot or Dutch oven. Bring to a boil over high heat and add both kinds of peppers. Allow to boil for 2 minutes, remove from the heat, cover, and steep for 10 minutes, or until the peppers soften enough that they bend easily but are not mushy.

Drain the peppers in a colander and shake to remove any excess water. Place the pepper slices in the canning jar along with the peppercorns and garlic.

Combine the remaining 2 cups of vinegar and the maple syrup in a small nonreactive pot, bring to a boil, then immediately pour over the peppers in the jar. Close the lid and allow to come to room temperature.

Refrigerate the pickled peppers for up to 2 weeks before eating to develop their flavor.

Giardiniera (Italian Garden Pickles)

MAKES ABOUT 1 QUART

Giardiniera is a gorgeous condiment of pickled mixed veggies that comes from the Italian word *giardino*, which means "garden." That's no wonder when you look at a jar, jam-packed with preserved garden beauties, looking as if someone like me took their odd bits that hadn't made it into a dish and shoved them in a jar because they needed a home immediately. It's also called *sotaceti*, meaning "under vinegar," which also is no wonder because the veggies are swimming in a scrumptious pool of white wine vinegar and olive oil with a touch of salt and sweetness. Your mix of garden delights doesn't need to be mine. You can choose to bring in the heat with fresh hot peppers. You can toss in some green beans that decided to appear on the vine and just don't add up to enough to make a dish all on their own. You can serve it as an accompaniment on an antipasto platter, include it in a cheese board, or, as I love it, on a flavor-packed summer sandwich. You can cut your vegetables bigger or smaller—perhaps little nibs of cauliflower and large rounds of carrot! I enjoy making sure everything is similarly sized and relatively small so that, when added to a sandwich, the mixture sits nestled in the bread just right.

2 cups cauliflower florets, cut into small pieces
1 large carrot, cut into ⅛-inch pieces
1 large yellow onion, cut into ⅛-inch pieces
2 celery ribs, cut into ⅛-inch pieces
4 garlic cloves, crushed
½ cup pimiento-stuffed olives
4 oregano sprigs
1 cup white wine vinegar
¼ cup extra-virgin olive oil
2 tablespoons salt
1 tablespoon pure maple syrup
½ teaspoon red pepper flakes
1 bay leaf
1 tablespoon black peppercorns

Place the cauliflower, carrot, onion, celery, garlic, olives, and oregano in a sterilized 1-quart mason jar (see page 227).

Combine the white wine vinegar, olive oil, salt, maple syrup, red pepper flakes, bay leaf, and peppercorns in a large nonreactive saucepan. Bring the mixture to a simmer and continue to simmer for 5 minutes. Remove the peppercorns, immediately pour the mixture over the vegetables, and allow to steep at room temperature for 2 days before using. Refrigerate once ready.

Pickled Peaches

MAKES ABOUT 1 QUART

Sweet and a little sour. Warm spices with a touch of heat. These peaches may sound strange if you aren't familiar with the idea, but they are such a delight served over a warm biscuit with ice cream or on a cheese platter to accompany a bright blue cheese. Because peach season is so fleeting, and because my tree is so heavy with them, I make sure to make batches and batches of pickled peaches to keep summer alive for months to come.

8 to 10 medium-ripe peaches
Juice of 1 lemon
1 tablespoon allspice berries
1 tablespoon whole cloves
1 cinnamon stick
2 cups granulated sugar
1 cup cider vinegar
1 cup water

Fill a large bowl halfway with ice and just cover with water. Set aside.

Gently score the bottom of each peach with an X. Bring a large pot of water to a boil and, using a spider or slotted spoon, gently drop in the peaches to boil for 30 to 40 seconds each. Immediately transfer to the ice bath and then, using the X as a starting point, peel the skin off the peaches. Transfer the peaches to a large bowl and drizzle with the lemon juice.

Make a sachet of the allspice berries, cloves, and cinnamon stick by placing the spices in the middle of a large, doubled piece of cheesecloth and tying with baker's twine to contain them.

Combine the sugar, cider vinegar, and the water in a stockpot over low heat and stir until the sugar has dissolved. Add the spice bag and bring to a boil over high heat for 5 minutes. Lower the heat to a simmer and add the peaches. Continue to simmer for 5 minutes or until the peaches are tender.

Using a slotted spoon, transfer the peaches to a bowl and then pour the brining liquid over them. Cover and refrigerate overnight.

Process large canning jars to sterilize (see page 227).

Transfer the brining liquid to a clean pot. Cut the peaches into halves or quarters, removing the pits. Add the peaches to the liquid and bring to a boil for 2 minutes. Pack the hot peaches in the sterilized jars and cover with the liquid, leaving ½ inch headspace. Seal and allow to come to room temperature before refrigerating for up to 2 weeks.

Preserved Lemons

MAKES 12 TO 13 PRESERVED LEMONS

My sister in California has a lemon tree that produces that most enormous citrus. I didn't realize lemons could grow so large until one fell on my head. And while it wasn't anything as lethal as a coconut, it did leave a little bruise on my forehead. There were enough lemons that I knew they'd go to waste if I didn't spring into action. So, I sterilized a giant jar and made preserved lemons. The process allows you to store whole lemons to use in everything from tagines to salads. I keep it simple: lemons and salt. That's it. And when the zest muse calls, I rinse it, remove the pulp, and chop up the rind so it can bring its gorgeous zing.

12 to 13 large organic lemons, plus 2 to 3 extra lemons should you need more juice

2 cups kosher salt

Wash and dry the lemons well. Cut the lemons in half, starting at the stem end, stopping just short of the bottom, and do the same in the other direction to cut the lemons into quarters while leaving the bottom attached. Gently pry the sections apart and sprinkle about 1 tablespoon of the kosher salt onto each section of lemon, making sure that the salt is sticking to the flesh of the lemon. Transfer the lemon to a 2-quart sterilized jar (see page 227) and, using a wooden muddler or the end of a rolling pin, smash the lemon to release its juices. I do this with every lemon as I add it to the jar. Continue cutting, salting, and smashing until all the lemons are added. If the juice isn't reaching to the top of the last lemon, squeeze the juice of the remaining lemons into the jar until there's enough juice. Sprinkle a layer of salt on top and seal the jar. Leave at room temperature for 3 to 4 weeks to ripen. The rinds should be very tender at the end of this period. After the ripening period is up, you can start using the rinds in recipes. Just make sure to store in the refrigerator at this point. They will stay fresh for up to 2 weeks.

Strawberry Jam

MAKES ABOUT 4 CUPS

You can count on strawberries to bounce back pretty stinkin' fast every year. Just as the first frost threatens, I pile on straw to protect the vulnerable crowns, and the moment the last frost is past, I remove the straw and marvel at the green leaves stretching out to the sun. Within days, it seems, their flowers start to bloom and hungry pollinators do their work and make sure that the little alpine berries start growing. Once I have a decent amount, if I haven't eaten too many straight off the plant, I make jam.

2 pounds strawberries, washed, hulled, and halved
1½ cups granulated sugar
¼ cup freshly squeezed lemon juice
Grated zest of 1 lemon

Sterilize four half-pint canning jars (see page 227). Place a small plate in the freezer.

Combine all the ingredients in a Dutch oven over medium heat. Bring the mixture to a boil, stirring frequently. Allow to boil for 5 minutes, stirring constantly, and then lower the heat to a simmer over low heat. Continue to cook, stirring frequently, until the mixture has thickened considerably and has reached 220°F (104°C) on a digital thermometer, about 50 minutes.

To check if the jam has thickened properly, smear a dollop of jam on the cold plate and return it to the freezer for 3 to 4 minutes. Run a finger through the jam to create a trough. If the trough stays put, the jam has thickened properly. Otherwise, continue to simmer a few minutes more, testing intermittently to ensure the right set.

Transfer the jam to the prepared jars. Seal and refrigerate overnight before using.

Peony Jelly

MAKES 2 CUPS

I am not a fan of "flower-flavored" things. I remember being at a friend's house on New Year's Eve as a kid and her mom, a French woman, made a little dessert in a beautiful cup that I thought was Jell-O. I didn't get Jell-O at home and was delighted with the prospect of a jiggly, supersweet treat. Well, I was sorely disappointed. The texture was nice, elegant even. But I hadn't counted on getting a mouthful of rosey soap. Not everyone feels this way about rose-flavored things. My host family clearly loved the stuff and couldn't get over my pained reaction. Since then, I've tried rose jam and jelly, rose Turkish delight, rose pudding—I don't like any of it. (However, I love rose hips!) But when I learned peonies could be edible, just like roses, I jumped at the chance to make a jelly. So many of those floppy heads, still vibrant and new, had fallen during a storm that there were only so many I could bring inside for flower arrangements. I didn't want a single petal to go to waste. And I wasn't disappointed. Instead of being soapy, the jelly is slightly perfumed. It's subtle and also slightly tart from the lemon that helps it set and brings out the light pink that makes it so darn pretty. And, if roses are your thing, you can use the same amount of rose petals as peony for a jelly that will scratch that rosy itch.

4 cups peony petals*
1 quart spring water
2 tablespoons freshly squeezed lemon juice
1 packet (1.75 ounces) powdered fruit pectin
4 cups granulated sugar

Sterilize two half-pint jars (see page 227).

Place the peony petals in a glass bowl and pick out any debris or nonpetal flower parts. Bring the water to a boil in a kettle or saucepan and pour over the petals. Let steep for 15 to 20 minutes. Pour the mixture through a strainer into a stainless-steel saucepan, discarding the petals. Add the lemon juice. Whisk in the pectin and bring to a boil. Allow to boil for 1 minute. Immediately add the sugar, stirring to incorporate, and return to a boil. Boil for 1 minute more. Pour the jelly into the prepared jars and store in the refrigerator for up to 2 weeks.

*****NOTE** Choose very fresh, vibrantly colored peonies, organically grown.

Currant Jam
(Red or Black or Champagne)

MAKES 3 TO 4 PINTS

I grow red, black, and Champagne currants. I started with two bushes and then kept adding on, to guarantee I'd get a decent crop once the birds and chipmunks had picked off their share. They are some of the most tempting-looking fruits, but they are sour as all get out, so they require a decent amount of sugar to perk them up for the palate. But that taste, with or without sugar, is a pipeline to my childhood. *Johannisbeere*, as currants are called in Germany, were everywhere in our life. From concentrated black currant syrup that we'd stir into sparkling water in the summer, to red currant jam that we piped into doughnuts during Fasching, to Linzertorte fillings, this vitamin C–rich berry was everywhere in my mother's home country but in the US, nada. Why? Because, up until recently, planting currants, black currants specifically, was illegal. Black currant bushes were prolific until 1911, when it was discovered that they could carry white pine blister rust, a disease that was decimating white pines. Thousands of black currant bushes were ripped out and destroyed. Today, black currants are once again legal to grow in all US states as long as the cultivar is resistant to white pine blister rust. Despite the fact that black currant is no longer banned, it hasn't made a comeback as far as consumption is concerned. But perhaps that will change when you get a taste of this jam.

5 pounds ripe currants

1 cup water

7 cups granulated sugar

1 packet (1.75 ounces) powdered fruit pectin

½ teaspoon unsalted butter

Sterilize four pint-size mason jars (see page 227).

Remove the stems from the currants, placing the berries in a large stainless-steel saucepan, crushing the currants as you get a full layer. Add the water and bring to a boil. Lower the heat to low, cover, and simmer for 10 minutes, stirring occasionally. Line a sieve with a doubled cheesecloth and place over a stainless-steel bowl. Pour the currants into the cheesecloth. Draw the ends of the cheesecloth together and press gently to express all the juice from the berries.

Measure out exactly 5 cups of the juice (add water if needed to make up the full amount) and transfer to a stainless-steel stockpot. Stir in the sugar and the butter (this helps reduce foaming). Over high heat, bring the mixture to a full rolling boil, stirring constantly. Stir in the pectin and return to a full, rolling boil (you must see constant bubbling), stirring constantly. Remove from the heat and skim off foam from the top with a metal spoon.

Immediately ladle the jam into the prepared jars, filling to about ¼ inch from the top. Wipe the rims and cover with the lids. Screw on tightly. For complete canning and storage information, please refer to the USDA guidelines at https://nchfp.uga.edu/resources/category/usda-guide.

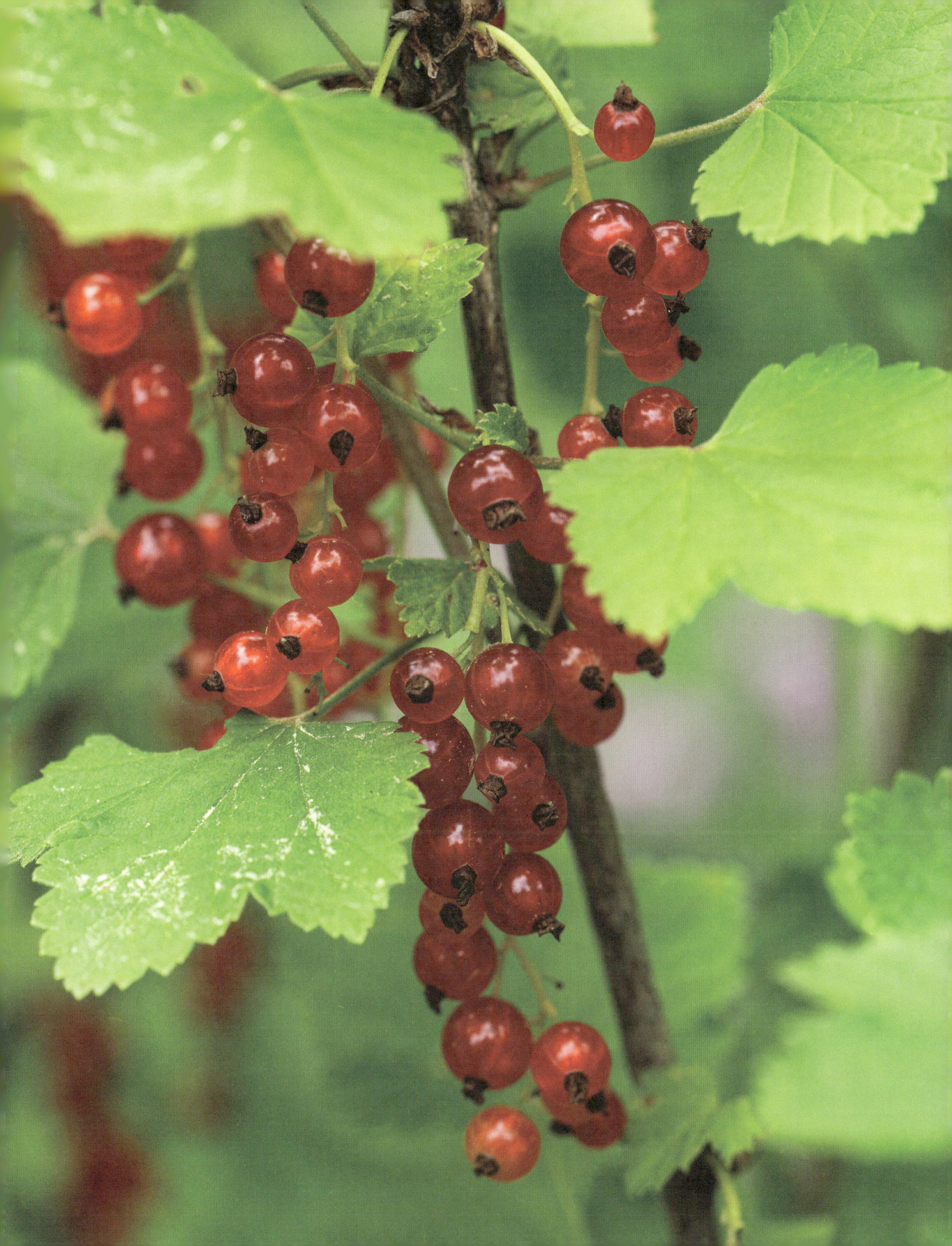

A NOTE FROM MY KITCHEN GARDEN

Name-Dropping and Deadheading

IN 1992, THE SUMMER AFTER GRADU- ating from college, my best friend Christine and I backpacked aimlessly through Europe, no concrete plans before us, except for a two-week internship scheduled at the Fondation Monet in Giverny. In June, we hopped on a train in Paris and made our way toward the Normandy region and to the home of the most famous water lilies in the world. When we arrived, we were given a bundle of keys to our temporary home: a garret apartment with two bedrooms, a kitchenette, and a little sitting area. We were thrilled not to sleep in a hostel dorm. Rooms of our own! We also had keys to a gate just across the narrow village road. The gate abutted the property's house and our new workplace, a sprawling pink manse with shockingly bright green shutters, and gave us access to the property's gardens. I think you've guessed which gardens, but if you haven't, we had unfettered access to Monet's gardens in Giverny. Including the ponds. After hours. Anytime we wanted. We were barely out of our teens, and grown people with authority gave us access to what is, arguably, the most famous garden on the planet. Yet, despite our tender years, both Christine and I understood our insane privilege and luck at that moment. We visited the garden every day after work, taking pictures at the lily pond, taking pictures on the Chinese bridge that spanned over the pond, dragging a Giverny bench to the edge of the pond and taking more pictures (we'd put the bench back). Taking pictures of the sign that pointed the way to the pond. It was extraordinary. And that was just during off hours. During our workdays, we either helped the French gift shop workers in what was once Monet's skylight-filled painting studio, ringing up purchases for silk scarves screen printed with water lilies, water lily post cards, water lily placemats. Once in a while, someone would purchase a set of official Haviland Monet dishes, a riotously Provençal blue, neon yellow, and white porcelain set that went for over $100 per plate. Those were very exciting transactions.

Other days, when it was sunny, we went to the garden and deadheaded roses. You'd think we'd have been under the watchful eye of the real gardeners, any gardener, but we weren't. We were given loppers, gloves, a bucket, a pantomime of cutting dead roses off the bush, and a shove out the shed door in the direction of pale creams, bright whites, soft yellows and pinks. Some were scented. Some weren't. We did meet the man who transformed the grounds (cue name drop), Gilbert Vahé, who in the 1970s took a tangled, overgrown mess that had been left fallow for a decade and transformed it back to Monet's vision. He was bespectacled and compact, with rough hands and quiet manner. Just an exemplar of a gardener if I've ever met one. And at the time, self-centered young person that I was, I knew I was in the presence of someone in possession of artistry and expertise unmatched in almost any profession. I was in awe. That's how amazing those gardens are and how beautifully he transformed them.

During those days, I was never told *why* we were deadheading. Monsieur Vahé wasn't the one who sent us off with loppers, and if he had, I'm sure he'd have told us not only what to do but why. But at the time I surmised our job was to keep the roses looking good for the masses of visitors (500,000 every year), lopping off the unsightly brown petals so that the beauties in bloom could get all the attention. Today I know that deadheading does, indeed, keep the plant looking good, but it also diverts the plant's energies to new growth and new blooms instead of setting seed. And it keeps the plant healthy, as rotting blooms invite fungal infections and rot.

I grow roses now. I have English climbing roses, shrub roses, and even wild roses. But I started with two rugosa roses in our courtyard just outside my kitchen. The things have grown wild and the abundance of blooms, a shocking magenta that gives the Giverny pink a run for its money, are so profuse that I can't keep up with all the deadheading. But, as it turns out, the rugosa rose is famous for its rose hips, the seed pod that comes from lack of deadheading. And from those seed pods, I make jam.

I searched online to see what had become of Monsieur Vahé. It seems he's still the steward of those magnificent gardens. Perhaps I'll send him a note and a jar of rose hip jam, thanking him for his service to and influence on the gardening world and my young burgeoning gardening soul. I think of him every time I deadhead a rose.

Rose Hip Jelly

MAKES ABOUT 6 CUPS

I might not like rose-flavored things, at all, but I sure love rose hip–flavored *anything.* From jelly to jam to tea, the slightly tart and aromatic flavor of rose hips is nothing like its floral and soapy petal. And they're full of vitamin C. And gathering rose hips is *free!* Just make sure the roses haven't been sprayed with pesticides, and keep clear of all those thorns. Usually, my English roses don't produce hips at all because I stay on top of pruning to prevent them from concentrating their energy on producing seed (a.k.a. rose hips). Instead I gather them from my rugosa climbing roses, which produce so many flowers that I can't keep up with the deadheading. I've also collected rose hips in Martha's Vineyard, where the beaches are absolutely resplendent with beach roses, and in the fall, when the summer people have left, the big, juicy rose hips remain for the taking. My wild roses produce ball bearing–size rose hips, making it impossible to ever get enough to produce a decent jelly. But my courtyard rugosas and my jaunts to the Vineyard have my buckets brimming with the most beautiful jelly to come.

- 2 pounds rose hips (about 8 cups)
- ½ cup freshly squeezed lemon juice
- 1 packet (1.75 ounces) powdered fruit pectin
- 3½ cups granulated sugar
- ½ teaspoon unsalted butter

Sterilize six half-pint mason jars (see page 227).

Rinse the rose hips and cut off the bud ends. Transfer the hips to a stainless-steel (nonreactive) stockpot. Add 6 cups of water and bring the mixture to a simmer. Cook for 45 minutes to 1 hour, until the hips are very soft and easily mashed with a fork.

Using a potato masher, smash the hips in the pot until you create a rough puree and the seeds are exposed. Line a sieve with doubled cheesecloth and place over a stainless-steel bowl. Drain the mixture and then gather the corners and squeeze out as much juice from the mixture as you can.

Measure out 3 cups of juice, adding water to make up any lack of juice. Transfer the juice to a stainless-steel stockpot. Add the lemon juice (this is required to help set up the jelly, as the hips don't have enough acid to interact with the pectin). Whisk in the pectin and bring the mixture to a boil, making sure all the pectin is dissolved. Add the sugar and then the butter. Bring the mixture to a rolling boil, making sure it is bubbling constantly without subsiding. At this point, boil for exactly 1 minute.

Immediately pour the jelly into the prepared jars, wipe the rims, seal, and process. For complete canning and storage information, please refer to the USDA guidelines at https://nchfp.uga.edu/resources/category/usda-guide.

A NOTE FROM MY KITCHEN GARDEN

Sterilizing Jars

THE USDA-APPROVED METHOD OF sterilizing jars is to boil glass jars for at least 10 minutes at altitudes under 1,000 feet. The higher the elevation, the more time you can add to ensure sterilization, adding 1 minute for every 1,000 feet of elevation.

First, wash the jars, lids, and bands in hot, soapy water.

Rinse well, but do not dry by hand. Place the jars, right side up, on a rack in a pot of water, making sure that they are submerged and filled, with the water 1 inch above the lip of the jars (these types of racks, and the tongs to remove the jars from the boiling water, are easily found at farm stores or online). Bring the water to a boil. Boil for 10 minutes. You can lower the heat and keep it simmering until you're ready to use the jars. As for the lids and rings, submerge them in a saucepan of water and bring to a simmer. Simmer for 10 minutes.

Immediately fill the jars with your hot mixture, leaving ¼ inch headspace at the top of each jar.

At this point, you can cover and refrigerate the jam or jelly for up to 3 weeks. If you'd like to preserve the jam or jelly for storage, once your jars are filled, cover with the lids and lightly screw on the bands. Place the jars on an elevated rack in a large pot or canner. Cover the jars with hot or boiling water; the water needs to reach 1 to 2 inches above the jars. Cover the pot and bring the water to a gentle boil. Allow the water to boil consistently for 5 minutes. Remove the jars from the canner using a jar lifter. Set the jars right side up on a towel to cool. Once fully cooled, press down on the middle of the lid. If the lid springs back, the jar is not properly sealed and should be refrigerated and used immediately. USDA guidelines recommend that properly sealed jars of jam or jelly be stored in a cool dry place and consumed within the year. For complete canning and storage information, please refer to the USDA guidelines at https://nchfp.uga.edu/resources/category/usda-guide.

MY HARVEST KITCHEN

Apple Butter

MAKES 4 CUPS

Apple butter is such a delight and we don't make and eat it enough. It's great on toast. It's a revelation on yogurt. It's a delight on ice cream. It's tart and sweet and lightly caramelly. And it's my number one way to process an overabundance of apples, too.

6 pounds apples, peeled, cored, and cut into large pieces
1 cup cider vinegar
1 cup dark brown sugar
1 cup granulated sugar
2 tablespoons freshly squeezed lemon juice
1 tablespoon ground cinnamon
Generous pinch of fine sea salt
1 teaspoon vanilla bean paste

Sterilize two pint jars (see page 227).

Place the chopped apples and cider vinegar in a Dutch oven and bring to a simmer over medium-high heat, stirring occasionally. Continue to cook until the apples are very tender, 20 to 25 minutes. Transfer the mixture in batches to a blender and puree until smooth. Return the puree to the Dutch oven, place a cast-iron heat diffuser over the burner if using a gas cooktop, and bring the mixture to a simmer over low heat. Add the brown sugar, granulated sugar, lemon juice, cinnamon, and salt. Continue to cook until it turns a deep golden brown and thickens, 1½ to 2 hours, making sure to occasionally stir and gently scrape the bottom of the pot with a rubber spatula to keep the mixture from burning.

Remove from the heat, stir in the vanilla bean paste, and allow to cool completely before transferring to the prepared jars. Apple butter can keep in the refrigerator for up to 2 weeks.

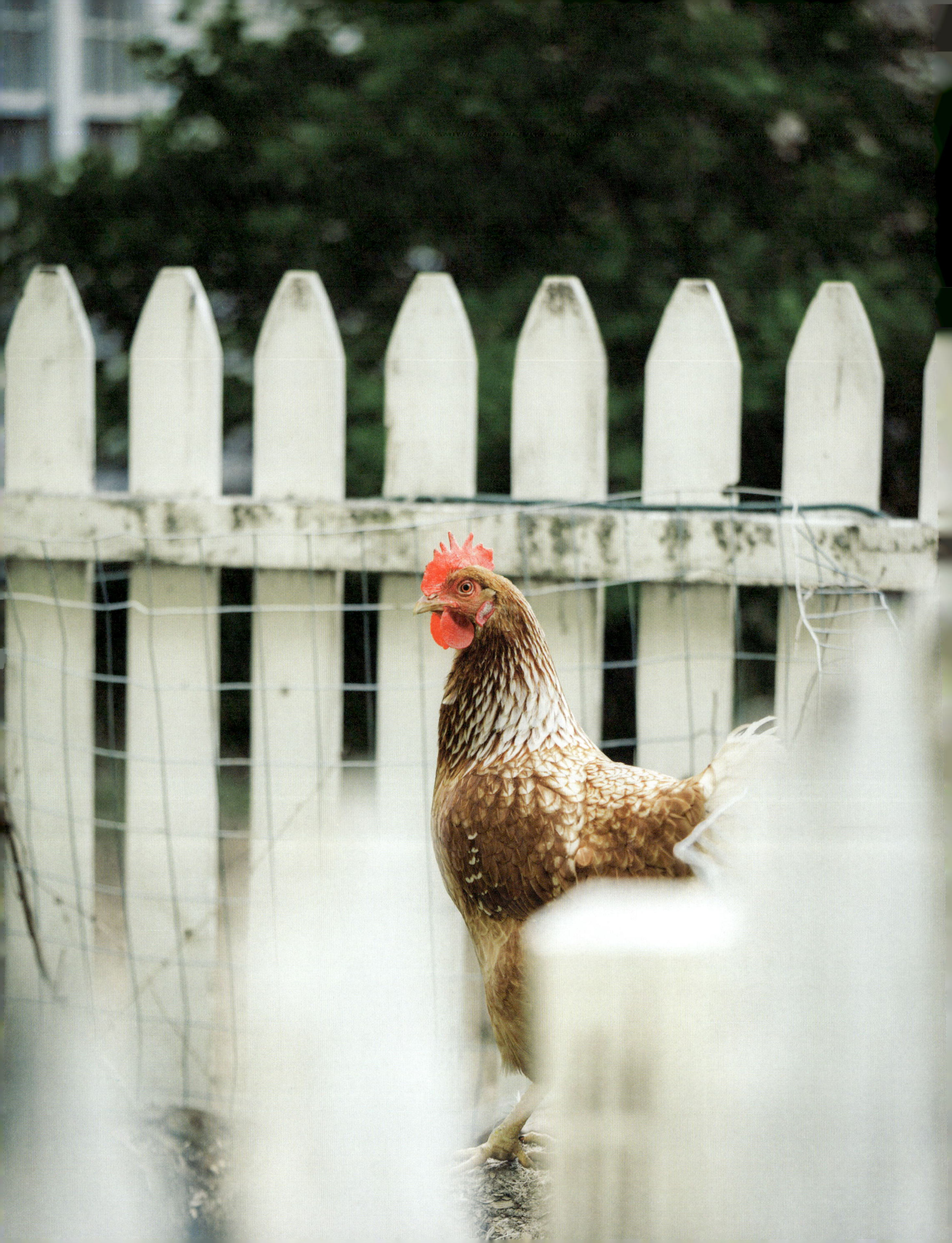

ACKNOWLEDGMENTS

Thank you, Laura Nolan, for being my partner from the very beginning.
Thank you, Raymo, for being so patient and talented. You are the best, Chicken Celeste.
Thank you, Ann T., for asking me to write and cook about the things and places I love.
Thank you, Schwester, for being the best Schwester that ever Schwestered.
And thank you, Mutti, for never being normal and for encouraging us to be brave (and to plant things).

INDEX

Note: Page references in *italics* indicate photographs.

Aioli, Garlic, 263
Ají Amarillo Verde Green Sauce, *160*, 161–62
almonds
    S'mores Schoko Crossies, 229, *232*
Apple(s)
    Butter, 279
    Crumble Tart, 215–16, *216*
    I Have Too Much Fruit Cake, 218–19, *219*
    Pudding, Caramel, *224*, 225
Arancini, Green Mountain, 118–19, *119*
arugula
    Salmon Panzanella Salad, 62–63, *63*
    Spring Risotto, 138–39, *139*
Asparagus
    growing, 122
    Spring Risotto, 138–39, *139*
    White, Butter and Wine-Poached, *86*, 87
Aunt Sis's Tomato Sandwich, 78, *79*
avocados
    Cali (Turkey) Meatballs, 168, *169*
    Fish Tacos, 158–59, *159*
    Savory Breakfast Toast, *26*, 27

Bacon. *See also* pancetta
    Dressing, Warm, 77
    The Wicked Wedge with Buttermilk Dressing, 58–59, *59*
baking ingredients, 13
Bao (Steamed Buns), 250–51, *251*
Barley, Sorrel, and Spinach Salad with Warm Bacon Dressing, *76*, 77
basil
    Fresh Tomato Pomodoro Sauce, 261
    Salmon Panzanella Salad, 62–63, *63*
Bean(s)
    Broad, and Peas, Creamy Mustard Potato Salad with, 74, *75*
    growing, 122
    Rancho Gordo, 16
    Salmon Panzanella Salad, 62–63, *63*
    Spring Risotto, 138–39, *139*
    Ugly Tomato Dip, Cheesy, 102, *103*
beef
    Korean BBQ Ssams (Lettuce Wraps), 148–49, *149*
    OK OK Burger, 152–53, *153*
    Ray's Bone-in Rib Eye with Scape Chimichurri, 150–51, *151*
    Saturday Night Meatballs, 154–55, *155*
    Stuffed Grape Leaves, 88–90, *89*
    White Wine–Braised Short Ribs, 156–57, *157*
bees and beekeeping, 214
beeswax wrap, 17
beets, growing, 123
Biscuits, Cheddar and Chive, 20–21, *21*
Blueberry-Lemon Bundt, 186, *187*
boiled cider, about, 16
braiser, 17
brassicas, growing, 123
Bread
    Brioche, 241–42, *242*
    Ciabatta Rolls, 246–47
    Corn Tortillas, 254–55, *255*
    Crusty, 248–49, *249*
    French Onion Soup (Soupe à l'Oignon), *48*, 49–50
    German Whole Grain (Vollkorn Brot), 243–45, *244*
    Salmon Panzanella Salad, 62–63, *63*
    Steamed Buns (Bao), 250–51, *251*
    Summer-to-Fall Focaccia, 108, *109*
Brined and Twice-Fried Fries, *124*, 125
Brioche, 241–42, *242*
broccoli, growing, 123
Brown Butter Butterscotch Ice Cream, *216*, 217
Brussels sprouts, growing, 123
Buns, Steamed (Bao), 250–51, *251*
Burger, OK OK, 152–53, *153*
Butter
    Chicken, 173–74, *175*
    high-fat, cultured, 15
    and Wine-Poached White Asparagus, *86*, 87
Buttermilk
    Dressing, 58–59, *59*
    powder, about, 15
Butterscotch Brown Butter Ice Cream, *216*, 217

Cabbage
    Cold Soba Noodle Salad with Peanut Dressing and Soy-Marinated Eggs, *64*, 65–67
    Fish Tacos, 158–59, *159*
    growing, 123
    Savoy, Creamed, 112, *113*
Cakes
    Blueberry-Lemon Bundt, 186, *187*
    Ellen's Sunshine, *188*, 189–90

Gâteau Concorde, 226–28, *227*
I Have Too Much Fruit, 218–19, *219*
Mandarin-Poppy Tea, 192, *193*
Rhubarb–Olive Oil, *200*, 201–2
Strawberry, German, *208*, 209–10
Cali (Turkey) Meatballs, 168, *169*
Caramel Apple Pudding, *224*, 225
carrots
    Cold Soba Noodle Salad with Peanut Dressing and Soy-Marinated Eggs, *64*, 65–67
    Giardiniera (Italian Garden Pickles), 267
    growing, 121
    Roasted Red Pepper Soup, 46–47, *47*
    Schweinebraten (German Pork Roast), 179–80, *180*
cauliflower
    Giardiniera (Italian Garden Pickles), 267
Chantilly Cream, 38, *39*
Cheese
    Cabot Creamery, 15
    Cheddar and Chive Biscuits, 20–21, *21*
    Cheesy Potatoes (Pommes Aligot), 130–31, *131*
    Creamed Spinach and Ramps, 96, *97*
    Creamy Roast Garlic Soup with Kale, 42–43, *43*
    Croque Madame, 28–29, *29*
    Farmer, Homemade Ramp-Infused, 95
    French Onion Soup (Soupe à l'Oignon), *48*, 49–50
    Goat, –Tomato Tart, French, *98*, 99
    "Goat Cheese Party" Pasta Salad, *60*, 61
    Green Mountain Arancini, 118–19, *119*
    Green Mountain Pradonara (A Nontraditional Carbonara), 140–41, *141*
    Jasper Hill, 15
    Mini Dumplings and (Käse Spätzle), *104*, 105–6
    OK OK Burger, 152–53, *153*
    Philadelphia brand cream cheese, 15
    Potato Gnocchi with Butternut Squash and Sage Bake, 181–83, *183*
    Poutine, 126, *127*
    Saturday Night Meatballs, 154–55, *155*
    Savory Breakfast Toast, 26, *27*
    Sorrel, Spinach, and Barley Salad with Warm Bacon Dressing, *76*, 77
    and Spring-Dug Parsnip Soufflé, 92–93, *93*
    Stinging Ravioli, *146*, 147
    Summer Sandwich, *80*, 81
    Ugly Tomato Cheesy Bean Dip, 102, *103*
    Upside-Down Leek Tart, *110*, 111
    Vermont Creamery, 15
    Zucchini Waffles, 30
Chermoula, 259
Cherry, Sour, Pie, 203–5, *204*
Chicken
    Butter, 173–74, *175*
    Cold Soba Noodle Salad with Peanut Dressing and Soy-Marinated Eggs, *64*, 65–67
    Leek, and Mushroom Pie, *176*, 177–78

Misty Knolls, buying, 22
    Roast, with Ají Amarillo Verde Green Sauce, *160*, 161–62
    Schnitzel, 163–64, *165*
    Spring Risotto, 138–39, *139*
    Tagine, Preserved Lemon and Saffron, *170*, 171
Chimichurri, Scape, 150, *151*
Chive and Cheddar Biscuits, 20–21, *21*
Chocolate
    bittersweet, buying, 13
    chips, buying, 13
    cocoa, buying, 13
    Gâteau Concorde, 226–28, *227*
    Oatmeal Squares, Tante Erika's Creamy, 231, *233*
    S'mores Schoko Crossies, 229, *232*
Choron, 260
Ciabatta Rolls, 246–47
cilantro
    Ají Amarillo Verde Green Sauce, *160*, 161–62
    Chermoula, 259
    Scape Chimichurri, 150, *151*
citrus. *See also* key lime; lemon(s); mandarin
    growing, in Vermont, 197
Clotted Cream, *35*, 36
Cobbler, Peach, 211–12, *212*
cocoa, buying, 13
Cookies
    S'mores Schoko Crossies, 229, *232*
    Spice, German (Pfeffernüsse), 230, *232*
    Tante Erika's Creamy Chocolate Oatmeal Squares, 231, *233*
Corn
    "Goat Cheese Party" Pasta Salad, *60*, 61
    growing, 122, 252–53
    Tortillas, 254–55, *255*
cornflakes
    S'mores Schoko Crossies, 229, *232*
couscous, types of, 258
Cream
    Chantilly, 38, *39*
    Clotted, *35*, 36
Creamed Savoy Cabbage, 112, *113*
Creamed Spinach and Ramps, 96, *97*
crème fraîche
    Creamed Spinach and Ramps, 96, *97*
    German Cucumber Salad, 56, *57*
Crepes, Lemon, with Chantilly Cream, 37–38, *39*
Croque Madame, 28–29, *29*
cucumbers
    Cheffy Quinoa and Tuna Salad with Preserved Lemon Vinaigrette, 70–71, *71*
    Cold Soba Noodle Salad with Peanut Dressing and Soy-Marinated Eggs, *64*, 65–67
    "Goat Cheese Party" Pasta Salad, *60*, 61
    Salmon Panzanella Salad, 62–63, *63*
    Tzatziki, 262, *262*
Currant Jam (Red or Black or Champagne), 272

dairy products, 15
desserts
　Apple Crumble Tart, 215–16, *216*
　Blueberry-Lemon Bundt, *186* 187
　Brown Butter Butterscotch Ice Cream, *216*, 217
　Caramel Apple Pudding, *224*, 225
　Ellen's Sunshine Cake, *188*, 189–90
　Gâteau Concorde, 226–28, *227*
　German Strawberry Cake, *208*, 209–10
　I Have Too Much Fruit Cake, 218–19, *219*
　Key Lime Ice Dream, 198, *199*
　Key Lime Tart, *194*, 195–96
　Mandarin-Poppy Tea Cake, 192, *193*
　Peach Cobbler, 211–12, *212*
　Pfeffernüsse (German Spice Cookies), 230, *232*
　Philadelphia-Style Vanilla and Honey Ice Cream, 213
　Pumpkin-Mandarin Tart, 221–22, *223*
　Rhubarb–Olive Oil Cake, *200*, 201–2
　S'mores Schoko Crossies, 229, *232*
　Sour Cherry Pie, 203–5, *204*
　Strawberry-Rhubarb Sherbet, 206, *207*
　Tante Erika's Creamy Chocolate Oatmeal Squares, 231, *233*
dill
　Cheffy Quinoa and Tuna Salad with Preserved Lemon Vinaigrette, 70–71, *71*
　Stuffed Grape Leaves, 88–90, *89*
　Tzatziki, 262, *262*
Dips
　Lemony Labneh, 84, *85*
　Tzatziki, 262, *262*
　Ugly Tomato Cheesy Bean, 102, *103*
doughnuts. *See* Krapfen
Dressings
　Buttermilk, 58–59, *59*
　Peanut, 66
　Preserved Lemon Vinaigrette, *70*, 70–71
　Tahini, *169*, 263
　Warm Bacon, 77
Dumplings
　Mini, and Cheese (Käse Spätzle), *104*, 105–6
　Sour Cream Spätzle, *114*, 115

Eggplant, Squash, Zucchini, and Tomato Casserole (Tian), 116, *117*
Egg(s)
　Croque Madame, 28–29, *29*
　Green Mountain Pradonara (A Nontraditional Carbonara), 140–41, *141*
　Hard-Boiled, 237
　Jammy, Perfect, 236
　Sando, 23, *24–25*
　Savory Breakfast Toast, *26*, 27
　Soy-Marinated, 238
　Soy-Marinated, and Peanut Dressing, Cold Soba Noodle Salad with, *64*, 65–67
　Tamago Don with Morels, *136*, 137
Ellen's Sunshine Cake, *188*, 189–90

Farmer Cheese, Homemade Ramp-Infused, 95
Fish
　Cheffy Quinoa and Tuna Salad with Preserved Lemon Vinaigrette, 70–71, *71*
　Salmon Panzanella Salad, 62–63, *63*
　Tacos, 158–59, *159*
　tinned tuna, buying, 16
flame tamer, 17
flours
　buckwheat, 13
　rye, 13
　spelt, 13
　unbleached, 13
Focaccia, Summer-to-Fall, 108, *109*
foraging, 134
French Onion Soup (Soupe à l'Oignon), *48*, 49–50
French Tomato–Goat Cheese Tart, *98*, 99
Fries, Brined and Twice-Fried, *124*, 125
Fruit. *See also specific fruits*
　I Have Too Much, Cake, 218–19, *219*

gardening, approaches to, 72
Garlic
　Aioli, 263
　Chermoula, 259
　flavor profiles, 44
　green germ, removing, 45
　growing, 121
　hardneck, 44
　Roast, Soup, Creamy, with Kale, 42–43, *43*
　softneck, 44
　Tzatziki, 262, *262*
garlic scapes. *See* scape(s)
Gâteau Concorde, 226–28, *227*
gelatin leaves, 13
German Cucumber Salad, 56, *57*
German Pork Roast (Schweinebraten), 179–80, *180*
German Spice Cookies (Pfeffernüsse), 230, *232*
German Strawberry Cake, *208*, 209–10
German Whole Grain Bread (Vollkorn Brot), 243–45, *244*
Giardiniera (Italian Garden Pickles), 267
Gnocchi, Potato, with Butternut Squash and Sage Bake, 181–83, *183*
"Goat Cheese Party" Pasta Salad, 60, 61
grain(s). *See also* quinoa; rice
　couscous, about, 258
　Sorrel, Spinach, and Barley Salad with Warm Bacon Dressing, *76*, 77
　Tante Erika's Creamy Chocolate Oatmeal Squares, 231, *233*
　Whole, Bread, German (Vollkorn Brot), 243–45, *244*
Grape Leaves, Stuffed, 88–90, *89*
grapes, wild, growing, 91
Green Mountain Arancini, 118–19, *119*
Green Mountain Pradonara (A Nontraditional Carbonara), 140–41, *141*
greens
　Cold Soba Noodle Salad with Peanut Dressing and Soy-Marinated Eggs, *64*, 65–67

Creamed Spinach and Ramps, 96, *97*
Creamy Roast Garlic Soup with Kale, 42–43, *43*
Homemade Ramp-Infused Farmer Cheese, 95
Korean BBQ Ssams (Lettuce Wraps), 148–49, *149*
Salmon Panzanella Salad, 62–63, *63*
Sorrel, Spinach, and Barley Salad with Warm Bacon Dressing, *76*, 77
Spring Risotto, 138–39, *139*
Ugly Tomato Cheesy Bean Dip, 102, *103*
The Wicked Wedge with Buttermilk Dressing, 58–59, *59*
G's Zippy, Flaky Pie Dough, 239–40
guanciale
    Creamy Roast Garlic Soup with Kale, 42–43, *43*
    Green Mountain Pradonara (A Nontraditional Carbonara), 140–41, *141*

ham. *See also* prosciutto
    Croque Madame, 28–29, *29*
    Summer Sandwich, *80*, 81
harvest time, 68
herbs. *See* basil; chive; cilantro; dill; oregano; parsley; sage
hibernation, ode to, 220
Honey and Vanilla Ice Cream, Philadelphia-Style, 213
hope, ode to, 31

Ice Cream
    Brown Butter Butterscotch, *216*, 217
    Vanilla and Honey, Philadelphia-Style, 213
Ice Dream, Key Lime, 198, *199*
Ida Mae's Red Salsa, 265
Italian Garden Pickles (Giardiniera), 267
Italian Sweet and Spicy Pickled Pepper Salad, 266

Jam
    Currant (Red or Black or Champagne), 272
    Krapfen, *32*, 33
    Strawberry, 270
Jammy Eggs, Perfect, 236
jars, sterilizing, 277
Jelly
    Peony, 271
    Rose Hip, 276

Kale, Creamy Roast Garlic Soup with, 42–43, *43*
Käse Spätzle (Mini Dumplings and Cheese), *104*, 105–6
Key Lime
    Ice Dream, 198, *199*
    Tart, *194*, 195–96
kitchen garden notes
    annual, biennial, and perennials, 191
    bees and beekeeping, 214
    citrus in Vermont, 197
    deadheading roses, 274–75
    flock of chickens, 22
    gardening, 72
    peppergate, 167

    saffron, 172
    sterilizing jars, 277
    vegetables to grow (and not grow), 121–23
    wild grapes, 91
kitchen scale, 17
kitchen tools, 17
Korean BBQ Ssams (Lettuce Wraps), 148–49, *149*
Krapfen, *32*, 33

Labneh, Lemony, 84, *85*
Lamb Chops, Sous Vide, *142*, 143
Leek(s)
    Chicken, and Mushroom Pie, *176*, 177–78
    Tart, Upside-Down, *110*, 111
    Vinaigrette, 107
Lemon(s)
    -Blueberry Bundt, 186, *187*
    Chermoula, 259
    Chicken Schnitzel, 163–64, *165*
    Crepes with Chantilly Cream, 37–38, *39*
    Ellen's Sunshine Cake, *188*, 189–90
    Lemony Labneh, 84, *85*
    Preserved, 269, *269*
    Preserved, and Saffron Chicken Tagine, *170*, 171
    Preserved, Vinaigrette, *70*, 70–71
Lettuce
    The Wicked Wedge with Buttermilk Dressing, 58–59, *59*
    Wraps (Korean BBQ Ssams), 148–49, *149*
lime. *See* key lime

Mandarin
    -Poppy Tea Cake, 192, *193*
    -Pumpkin Tart, 221–22, *223*
mandoline, 17
marshmallows
    S'mores Schoko Crossies, 229, *232*
mayonnaise, 16
    Ají Amarillo Verde Green Sauce, *160*, 161–62
    Buttermilk Dressing, 58–59, *59*
    Garlic Aioli, 263
Meatballs
    Cali (Turkey), 168, *169*
    Saturday Night, 154–55, *155*
microplane grater, 17
Monet's gardens, 274
Morels, Tamago Don with, *136*, 137
Mushroom(s)
    Chicken, and Leek Pie, *176*, 177–78
    Tamago Don with Morels, *136*, 137
Mustard Potato Salad, Creamy, with Broad Beans and Peas, 74, *75*

Noodle, Cold Soba, Salad with Peanut Dressing and Soy-Marinated Eggs, *64*, 65–67
nuts
    Peanut Dressing, 66
    S'mores Schoko Crossies, 229, *232*

Oatmeal Chocolate Squares, Tante Erika's Creamy, 231, *233*
OK OK Burger, 152–53, *153*
olives
    Giardiniera (Italian Garden Pickles), 267
    Preserved Lemon and Saffron Chicken Tagine, *170*, 171
Onion(s)
    caramelizing, 49
    growing, 53–54, 121
    Käse Spätzle (Mini Dumplings and Cheese), *104*, 105–6
    OK OK Burger, 152–53, *153*
    Rose de Roscoff, about, 53
    Schweinebraten (German Pork Roast), 179–80, *180*
    Soup, French (Soupe à l'Oignon), *48*, 49–50
    Tamago Don with Morels, *136*, 137
oranges. *See* mandarin
oregano
    Saturday Night Meatballs, 154–55, *155*
    Scape Chimichurri, 150, *151*

pancetta
    Creamy Roast Garlic Soup with Kale, 42–43, *43*
    Green Mountain Pradonara (A Nontraditional Carbonara), 140–41, *141*
Panzanella Salad, Salmon, 62–63, *63*
parsley
    Chermoula, 259
    Scape Chimichurri, 150, *151*
    Spring Risotto, 138–39, *139*
    Stuffed Grape Leaves, 88–90, *89*
Parsnip, Spring-Dug, and Cheese Soufflé, 92–93, *93*
pasta
    Barilla, 16
    couscous, about, 258
    Green Mountain Pradonara (A Nontraditional Carbonara), 140–41, *141*
    Stinging Ravioli, *146*, 147
Peach(es)
    Cobbler, 211–12, *212*
    I Have Too Much Fruit Cake, 218–19, *219*
    Pickled, 268
Peanut Dressing, 66
Peas
    and Broad Beans, Creamy Mustard Potato Salad with, 74, *75*
    Cheffy Quinoa and Tuna Salad with Preserved Lemon Vinaigrette, 70–71, *71*
    Green Mountain Pradonara (A Nontraditional Carbonara), 140–41, *141*
    growing, 122
    Spring Risotto, 138–39, *139*
pectin, 16
Peony Jelly, 271
Pepper(s)
    Ají Amarillo Verde Green Sauce, *160*, 161–62
    growing, 167
    Ida Mae's Red Salsa, 265
    Pickled, Salad, Italian Sweet and Spicy, 266
    Roasted Red, Soup, 16 17, *47*
perilla leaves
    Korean BBQ Ssams (Lettuce Wraps), 148–49, *149*
Pfeffernüsse (German Spice Cookies), 230, *232*
Philadelphia-Style Vanilla and Honey Ice Cream, 213
Pickled Peaches, 268
Pickled Pepper Salad, Italian Sweet and Spicy, 266
Pickles
    "Goat Cheese Party" Pasta Salad, *60*, 61
    Italian Garden (Giardiniera), 267
    Quick! Let's Pickle!, 264
Pie Dough, G's Zippy, Flaky, 239–40
Pies
    Chicken, Leek, and Mushroom, *176*, 177–78
    Sour Cherry, 203–5, *204*
Pommes Aligot (Cheesy Potatoes), 130–31, *131*
Poppy-Mandarin Tea Cake, *192*, 193
Pork. *See also* bacon; guanciale; ham; prosciutto
    OK OK Burger, 152–53, *153*
    Potato Gnocchi with Butternut Squash and Sage Bake, 181–83, *183*
    Roast, German (Schweinebraten), 179–80, *180*
    Saturday Night Meatballs, 154–55, *155*
    Summer Sandwich, *80*, 81
Potato(es)
    Brined and Twice-Fried Fries, *124*, 125
    Cheesy (Pommes Aligot), 130–31, *131*
    Creamy Roast Garlic Soup with Kale, 42–43, *43*
    Gnocchi with Butternut Squash and Sage Bake, 181–83, *183*
    growing, 121
    Mustard Salad, Creamy, with Broad Beans and Peas, 74, *75*
    Pavé, 128–29, *129*
    Poutine, 126, *127*
    Roast Chicken with Ají Amarillo Verde Green Sauce, *160*, 161–62
    Roasted Red Pepper Soup, 46–47, *47*
    Schweinebraten (German Pork Roast), 179–80, *180*
Poutine, 126, *127*
Pradonara, Green Mountain (A Nontraditional Carbonara), 140–41, *141*
Preserved Lemon(s), 269, *269*
    and Saffron Chicken Tagine, *170*, 171
    Vinaigrette, *70*, 70–71
prosciutto
    Del Duca brand, 16
    Summer Sandwich, *80*, 81
    Upside-Down Leek Tart, *110*, 111
Pudding, Caramel Apple, *224*, 225
Pumpkin-Mandarin Tart, 221–22, *223*

Quinoa
    Cali (Turkey) Meatballs, 168, *169*
    Perfect, 257
    and Tuna Salad, Cheffy, with Preserved Lemon Vinaigrette, 70–71, *71*

radishes
    Cheffy Quinoa and Tuna Salad with Preserved Lemon Vinaigrette, 70–71, *71*
    growing, 121
    Schweinebraten (German Pork Roast), 179–80, *180*
Ramp(s)
    -Infused Farmer Cheese, Homemade, 95
    and Spinach, Creamed, 96, *97*
    Spring Risotto, 138–39, *139*
Ravioli, Stinging, *146*, 147
Ray's Bone-in Rib Eye with Scape Chimichurri, 150–51, *151*
Red Salsa, Ida Mae's, 265
Rhubarb
    -Olive Oil Cake, *200*, 201–2
    -Strawberry Sherbet, 206, *207*
Rice
    Green Mountain Arancini, 118–19, *119*
    Japanese Short-Grain, Perfect, 256
    Jasmine, 258
    Korean BBQ Ssams (Lettuce Wraps), 148–49, *149*
    Spring Risotto, 138–39, *139*
    Stuffed Grape Leaves, 88–90, *89*
    Tamago Don with Morels, *136*, 137
Risotto, Spring, 138–39, *139*
Rolls, Ciabatta, 246–47
rondeau, 17
Rose Hip Jelly, 276

Saffron
    about, 172
    growing, 172
    and Preserved Lemon Chicken Tagine, *170*, 171
Sage and Butternut Squash Bake, Potato Gnocchi with, 181–83, *183*
Salads
    Cold Soba Noodle, with Peanut Dressing and Soy-Marinated Eggs, *64*, 65–67
    Cucumber, German, 56, *57*
    Mustard Potato, Creamy, with Broad Beans and Peas, 74, *75*
    Pasta, "Goat Cheese Party," *60*, 61
    Pickled Pepper, Italian Sweet and Spicy, 266
    Quinoa and Tuna, Cheffy, with Preserved Lemon Vinaigrette, 70–71, *71*
    Salmon Panzanella, 62–63, *63*
    Sorrel, Spinach, and Barley, with Warm Bacon Dressing, *76*, 77
    The Wicked Wedge with Buttermilk Dressing, 58–59, *59*
Salmon Panzanella Salad, 62–63, *63*
Salsa, Ida Mae's Red, 265
salt, kosher, 16
Sandwiches
    Croque Madame, 28–29, *29*
    Egg Sando, 23, *24–25*
    Savory Breakfast Toast, *26*, 27
    Summer, *80*, 81
    Tomato, Aunt Sis's, 78, *79*

Sauces
    Ají Amarillo Verde Green, *160*, 161–62
    Chermoula, 259
    Choron, 260
    Fresh Tomato Pomodoro, 261
    Garlic Aioli, 263
    Scape Chimichurri, 150, *151*
    Tahini Dressing, *169*, 263
    Tzatziki, 262, *262*
sausage
    Potato Gnocchi with Butternut Squash and Sage Bake, 181–83, *183*
    Summer Sandwich, *80*, 81
scale, 17
Scape(s)
    about, 44–45
    Chimichurri, 150, *151*
    harvesting, 44
    preparing powder from, 45
    Stuffed Grape Leaves, 88–90, *89*
Schoko Crossies, S'mores, 229, *232*
Schweinebraten (German Pork Roast), 179–80, *180*
Scones with Clotted Cream, 34–36, *35*
seeds, buying, 16
Sherbet, Strawberry-Rhubarb, 206, *207*
S'mores Schoko Crossies, 229, *232*
Sorrel, Spinach, and Barley Salad with Warm Bacon Dressing, *76*, 77
Soufflé, Spring-Dug Parsnip and Cheese, 92–93, *93*
Soups
    Creamy Roast Garlic, with Kale, 42–43, *43*
    French Onion (Soupe à l'Oignon), *48*, 49–50
    Roasted Red Pepper, 46–47, *47*
Sour Cherry Pie, 203–5, *204*
Sour Cream
    Buttermilk Dressing, 58–59, *59*
    Creamed Spinach and Ramps, 96, *97*
    German Cucumber Salad, 56, *57*
    Spätzle, *114*, 115
Sous Vide Lamb Chops, *142*, 143
Soy
    -Marinated Eggs, 238
    -Marinated Eggs and Peanut Dressing, Cold Soba Noodle Salad with, *64*, 65–67
Spätzle
    Käse (Mini Dumplings and Cheese), *104*, 105–6
    Sour Cream, *114*, 115
Spice Cookies, German (Pfeffernüsse), 230, *232*
spices, buying, 16
Spinach
    and Ramps, Creamed, 96, *97*
    Sorrel, and Barley Salad with Warm Bacon Dressing, *76*, 77
    Ugly Tomato Cheesy Bean Dip, 102, *103*
Squash
    Butternut, and Sage Bake, Potato Gnocchi with, 181–83, *183*

Squash (*continued*)
    Eggplant, Zucchini, and Tomato Casserole (Tian), 116, *117*
    growing, 122
    Pumpkin-Mandarin Tart, 221–22, *223*
    Zucchini Waffles, 30
Ssams, Korean BBQ (Lettuce Wraps), 148–49, *149*
stinging nettles
    about, 144
    blanching, 144
    Stinging Ravioli, *146*, 147
    using as fertilizer, 144
Strawberry
    Cake, German, *208*, 209–10
    Jam, 270
    -Rhubarb Sherbet, 206, *207*
Stuffed Grape Leaves, 88–90, *89*
Summer Sandwich, *80*, 81
Summer-to-Fall Focaccia, 108, *109*
sunflower seeds
    Vollkorn Brot (German Whole Grain Bread), 243–45, *244*

Tacos, Fish, 158–59, *159*
Tagine, Preserved Lemon and Saffron Chicken, *170*, 171
Tahini Dressing, *169*, 263
Tamago Don with Morels, *136*, 137
Tante Erika's Creamy Chocolate Oatmeal Squares, 231, *233*
Tarts
    Apple Crumble, 215–16, *216*
    Key Lime, *194*, 195–96
    Leek, Upside-Down, *110*, 111
    Pumpkin-Mandarin, 221–22, *223*
    Tomato–Goat Cheese, French, *98*, 99
Tian (Eggplant, Squash, Zucchini, and Tomato Casserole), 116, *117*
Toast, Savory Breakfast, *26*, 27
Tomato(es)
    Butter Chicken, 173–74, *175*
    Cheffy Quinoa and Tuna Salad with Preserved Lemon Vinaigrette, 70–71, *71*
    Choron, 260
    determinate, about, 100
    Eggplant, Squash, and Zucchini Casserole (Tian), 116, *117*
    Fresh, Pomodoro Sauce, 261
    "Goat Cheese Party" Pasta Salad, *60*, 61
    –Goat Cheese Tart, French, *98*, 99
    growing, 100–101, 121
    Ida Mae's Red Salsa, 265
    indeterminate, about, 100–101
    Roasted Red Pepper Soup, 46–47, *47*
    Salmon Panzanella Salad, 62–63, *63*
    Sandwich, Aunt Sis's, 78, *79*
    Ugly, Cheesy Bean Dip, 102, *103*
    The Wicked Wedge with Buttermilk Dressing, 58–59, *59*
Tortillas
    Corn, 254–55, *255*
    Fish Tacos, 158–59, *159*
Tuna
    and Quinoa Salad, Cheffy, with Preserved Lemon Vinaigrette, 70–71, *71*
    tinned, buying, 16
Turkey Meatballs (Cali), 168, *169*
tweezers, culinary, 17
Tzatziki, 262, *262*
Upside-Down Leek Tart, *110*, 111

Vahé, Gilbert, 274
Vanilla and Honey Ice Cream, Philadelphia-Style, 213
vegetables. *See also specific vegetables*
    annual, biennial, and perennials, 191
    to grow (and not grow), 121–23
    harvesting, 68
    Quick! Let's Pickle!, 264
    Summer-to-Fall Focaccia, 108, *109*
Vinaigrette, Preserved Lemon, *70*, 70–71
Vollkorn Brot (German Whole Grain Bread), 243–45, *244*

Waffles, Zucchini, 30
White Asparagus, Butter and Wine–Poached, *86*, 87
Whole Grain Bread, German (Vollkorn Brot), 243–45, *244*
Wine
    and Butter–Poached White Asparagus, *86*, 87
    White, –Braised Short Ribs, 156–57, *157*
The Wicked Wedge with Buttermilk Dressing, 58–59, *59*
Wraps, Lettuce (Korean BBQ Ssams), 148–49, *149*

yeast, 13
yogurt
    Cabot Creamery, buying, 15
    German Cucumber Salad, 56, *57*
    Lemony Labneh, 84, *85*
    Tzatziki, 262, *262*

Zucchini
    Eggplant, Squash, and Tomato Casserole (Tian), 116, *117*
    Waffles, 30